The British Kitchen

Housewifery since Roman Times

The British Kitchen

Housewifery since Roman Times

Doreen Yarwood

B.T. Batsford Ltd · London

First published 1981
© Doreen Yarwood 1981

Filmset in Monophoto Apollo 10 on 12pt by
Servis Filmsetting Ltd, Manchester

Printed and bound in Great Britain by
Morrison & Gibb Ltd, London and Edinburgh

ISBN 0 7134 1430 8

Contents

Preface

During the 1970s interest has accelerated, in Britain no less than in the rest of Europe and in North America, in the social history of domestic life.

This is evidenced partly in the increasing stress and importance laid upon the subject in secondary education and, even more notably, in the space allocated to it in museums all over the country. In larger museums displays of appliances and aids of all kinds include completely equipped hearths, stoves and whole kitchens, all presented in an imaginative manner accompanied by clearly detailed information. Smaller museums are following suit and, even during the last five years, many new folk museums (both indoor and open air) have been established to display local features and artefacts.

Kitchens and domestic equipment have traditionally been thought of as unimportant and uninteresting subjects in the study canvas of social history. This is no longer so. The surge of public interest, both in education and museums, has helped to establish housewifery as a vital part of this study in its own right.

A testimony of this interest has been in the number of books published in the 1970s which deal with one or more aspects of the life and work of the housewife over the centuries. In this book I have attempted to cover the complete canvas in Britain from Roman times until the present day and have tried to trace the reasons and form of how this has developed during the last 2000 years.

In research for this work I have visited, during the last two years, 71 museums in all parts of the British Isles. All the illustrations are based upon first-hand study, the drawings being taken from my own sketches and photographs made on the spot; and the photographs being supplied by manufacturers and museums or being taken by my husband Professor John Yarwood.

The superscript numerals in the text refer to the Notes at the end of the book.

Acknowledgment

The source of all the photographs printed in this book and almost all the drawings is given in the appropriate caption: only a very few have been omitted from small drawings due to lack of space. I would like, in addition, to express my appreciation of the help, courtesy and encouragement which I have received from museum staffs everywhere, many of whom have devoted a considerable amount of their time to displaying items from their reserve collections for my visit. I am equally grateful to the many institutions and manufacturers who have given me similar assistance. A list of the chief of these is given here.

Museums and Houses
Abergavenny Museum
Aylesbury: Buckinghamshire County Museum
Banbury Museum
Bangor: Museum of Welsh Antiquities
Barnard Castle: The Bowes Museum
Beamish, Stanley: North of England Open Air Museum, Beamish Hall
Brechin: Glenesk Trust Museum
Bristol: Georgian House, Blaise Castle House Museum
Carlisle Museum and Art Gallery
Cheltenham: Central Museum and Art Gallery, Holst Birthplace Museum
Chepstow Museum
Chester: Grosvenor Museum
Cirencester: Corinium Museum
Cogges: Manor Farm Museum
Colchester and Essex Museum
Dawlish Museum Society
Dumfries Museum
Exeter: St Nicholas Priory, Rougemont House
Fort William: The West Highland Museum
Glencoe and North Lorn Folk Museum
Great Yarmouth: Elizabethan House Museum
Hereford: Old House, Churchill Gardens Museum, City Museum
Hollingbourne: Eyhorne Manor
Ironbridge, Telford: Ironbridge Gorge Museum Trust
Kendal: Abbot Hall Museum of Lakeland Life and Industry
Kilbarchan: The Weaver's Cottage
King's Lynn: Lynn Museum, Museum of Social History
Kingussie: Highland Folk Museum
Leeds: Abbey House Museum, City Museum
London: British Museum, Geffrye Museum, Museum of London, Science Museum, Victoria and Albert Museum

Lullingstone Roman Villa
Marshfield: Castle Farm Folk Museum
Millom Folk Museum Society
Newcastle-upon-Tyne: Museum of Antiquities
Northampton: Abington Museum
Norwich: Stranger's Hall Museum of Domestic Life
Oxford: Museum of Oxford
Paisley Museum and Art Gallery
Plymouth: City Museum and Art Gallery, The Elizabethan House, Buckland Abbey
St Albans: Verulamium Museum
St Fagans: National Museum of Wales, Welsh Folk Museum
Salisbury and South Wiltshire Museum
Shaftesbury Museum
Snowshill Manor
Stowmarket: Museum of East Anglian Life
Tiverton Museum
Torquay Museum
Totnes Museum
Woodstock: Oxfordshire County Museum
Wrexham: Erdigg House
York: The Castle Museum

Manufacturers and Institutions
Agaheat Appliances
Bissell Appliances Ltd
The British Brush Manufacturer's Association
British Gas
Brooke Marine Ltd
B.V.C. Ltd, Goblin Works
Carron Company
Crompton Parkinson Ltd
Electrolux Ltd
The Electricity Council
Formica Ltd
General Motors Ltd
Hygena Ltd
The Institution of Gas Engineers
Lord Chamberlain on behalf of H.M. The Queen
The National Trust
The Royal Institution
The Royal Society
The Royal Society of Arts
Thorn Domestic Appliances (Electrical) Ltd (Bendix, Kenwood, Moffat, Tricity)
Tube Investments (Creda Ltd, Radiation Ltd, Russell Hobbs Ltd, Tower Housewares Ltd)

CHAPTER ONE

The Kitchen

For 2000 years the kitchen has been the heart of the British home. It has remained so whether it constituted the sole living room of a cottage, a building adjacent to its castle or palace or in a bourgeois Victorian basement. It is not the place or the time or its size which has determined its importance but its function. This working centre of the home has existed to provide hot food, a warm fire, comfort and cleanliness, relaxation to mind and body for all the members of a family, many of whom over the centuries laboured hard for long hours in inclement conditions. The kitchen fire especially – open hearth or iron range – was vital to the well-being of the home. It kept the structure, utensils and garments dry, provided hot water for washing and heat for cooking the food. It was not allowed to go out.

In structure and architectural style houses have changed more slowly than other buildings and the kitchen even more slowly than the rest of the house. Despite its functional importance, the kitchen (until recently), rarely aroused the interest of the architect, builder or designer; it was the cinderella of rooms in a home. Largely because of this disinterest, it is not easy to find pictorial evidence of what kitchens looked like in past ages. Kitchens were less often painted or drawn by artists than other rooms and, before the later eighteenth century, most of the examples which we can find are of great houses or palaces. However, the structures of many kitchens have survived for us to visit and study and these can be found in houses of varied size and type, palaces and monastic buildings. Hearths, equipment and utensils have survived in greater numbers and can be seen *in situ* as well as displayed in many museums all over Britain.[1]

Over the centuries since the Roman occupation the work carried out in a British kitchen has remained much the same: boiling, baking, broiling or roasting of food, scrubbing and polishing of the home and its utensils, careful storage, preservation and preparation of food. Only infinitesimally slowly has the means of carrying out these duties changed. Alterations over the years in the mode of living have influenced the design and layout of the kitchen but for centuries the working processes were almost unaltered. In the Middle Ages many people lived in the great monasteries, mass-fed from the enormous monastic kitchens or, in contrast, ate rudely in their primitive cottages. From the seventeenth century on, in large houses, the kitchen was not one room but a group of rooms with varied vital functions; for self-sufficiency these might well include a scullery, still-room, pantry, buttery, dairy, bakehouse and brewery.

Until the late nineteenth century the improvements and advances in kitchen design, equipment and utensils took a long time to percolate through the strata of society; indeed, many such improvements never reached the poorer homes at all. The variation in comfort and means of cooking was very great between the large house and the small cottage. There were also large regional differences between a kitchen of a similar home in one part of Britain compared to that in another. This could be due to climate, to the wealth of the respective communities, to terrain or available communications by land and water but, most importantly, it derived from the availability of raw materials. For example, in the Highlands of Scotland, china clay for making ceramic vessels was not readily available so, before communications permitted an established trade with England and the Continent of Europe in the seventeenth century, the Highlander had to rely on the materials locally to hand – metal, horn, wood. Because of this the region developed a high standard of craftsmanship in utensils and vessels made from horn and feathered staving (see page 37).

The major change in kitchen design and means of cooking only came with the development of technology and, thus, of new sources of power. Fuel was the vital factor. Over the centuries cooking had progressed via the use of wood as a fuel, followed by charcoal then coal. The widespread use of coal brought the kitchen range to replace the open hearth, but it was the research and discoveries of the nineteenth and twentieth centuries leading to the supply of gas and electricity in the home which made possible the development of powered labour-saving devices such as washing machines and spin driers, refrigerators and cookers and all the gadgets which a modern housewife takes for granted.

While it was the benefit of technological advance which made such machinery possible, the present-day kitchen is also the product of a different revolution, that of human society. Before the First World War there was no need for labour-saving devices because there was an adequacy of labour. It did not matter if washday for the home took three days or a week or if the kitchen range had to be black-leaded daily. There was a human servant to do this work.

After 1918 this sociological pattern had changed for ever. It was no longer easy to get servants. Many women found work outside the house. Those who did so, as well as housewives who stayed at home, demanded a pleasant, airy kitchen to work in and were not satisfied with a dark basement with windows high up in the wall to avoid distracting the servants' attention from their work by looking out. After the Second World War the process had accelerated. More women worked outside the home. Kitchens became planned units, designed on 'organisation and method' lines to avoid wasted energy and effort. Colour was introduced, easy-care surfaces and equipment which functioned at the touch of a switch. The trend towards comfort and ease of living and efficiency of performance, which had been speeding up since 1900, had almost reached its apogee.

The Roman kitchen

Archaeological remains from Romano-British houses are fragmentary, chiefly confined to artefacts such as the gridiron found at Silchester and cooking vessels and smaller utensils from various sites. Apart from pictorial evidence in sculptural reliefs and wall paintings, our knowledge of what a Roman kitchen must have been like is gained from what has been excavated

in Italy at Pompeii and Herculaneum. At Pompeii the shallower layer of ash has uniquely preserved the lifestyle of the people, fossilised at that moment on 24 August in AD 79 when the rain of cinders and small stones from Vesuvius descended on the town. In addition to the streets and buildings, this covering of ash has preserved many of the humble, ordinary articles used in daily life, from loaves being baked in the oven to utensils in daily use.

The Roman kitchen was small and simple. Under the earlier years of the Republic it was to be found in the *atrium*, the central part of the house which was open above to the sky (*compluvium*). This opening let out the smoke and it also supplied the rainwater collected from the roofs around it which drained into a cistern below (*impluvium*). Under the later Republic and during the Empire, especially in larger houses, the *atrium* became the main living area of the home and the kitchen was relegated to a separate room at the back of the house. In such homes most of the work was carried out by slaves who included stokers to gather and prepare the fuel and tend the fires, bakers and pastrycooks, storekeepers, general cooks and cleaners. The lady of the house supervised and planned their work and made up the daily menus. In farmhouses and smaller homes the kitchen also served as the main living room.

The kitchen contained a simple hearth on which food was grilled. This was raised on a masonry platform faced on top with bricks. The preferred fuel in general use was charcoal, though in smaller, poorer homes wood had to be burnt; this was less satisfactory as, since there were no adequate ventilating flues, smoke tended to fill the kitchen. The hearth was often centrally placed or it might be set against a wall, which was usually protected by a reinforcement of stone or flint. An opening at floor level in front of the hearth was used for storing the fuel. Nearby would be

1 Roman kitchen c. 100 AD. Reconstruction displayed in the Museum of London incorporating original cooking pots and implements. Note: on the floor, amphorae (including, on the left, a carrot amphora) and storage jar. Working tables of wood. Hearth with gridiron and cooking pot over charcoal fire. Utensils, containers and mortaria (chapters 2, 3 and 5)

2 The Roman kitchen based upon a reconstruction of a kitchen in a Romano-British house of about 200 AD displayed in the Corinium Museum, Cirencester. Note: hearth on the right with bricks supporting gridiron over charcoal fire

3 Roman water heater from Pompeii (replica). Science Museum London

an oven of rubble and clay or one of a portable type. The cistern (*impluvium*) supplied piped water for washing up to a sink made of mortar-covered stone and a drain would carry away the water (3). A stone or wood table stood near for the preparation of food.

An excellent reconstruction of a Romano-British kitchen may be seen in the Museum of London (1) and in the Corinium Museum in Cirencester (2) as well as a Roman hearth, utensils and vessels at Verulamium Museum, St Albans and Colchester and Essex Museum at Colchester (chapters 2, 3 and 5).

The Medieval kitchen

The Roman cuisine was sophisticated and varied. The kitchen layout and methods of cooking were simple, but the tastes of Roman society demanded and obtained a high culinary standard. With the departure of the Roman garrisons this standard quickly deteriorated to a much more primitive level. A millenium had to pass before even the ruling class could once again enjoy a varied diet and an adequate skill in the cooking and presentation of food.

During the Middle Ages cooking for many was communal, carried out in the great kitchens of abbey or castle. Particularly in the earlier centuries monastic centres would cater for 800–900 persons for each meal. The kitchens were large structures; that at Canterbury, for instance, was 45 feet square, at Gloucester over 36 feet in length. They were equipped with several immense wall fireplaces in which could be roasted an entire ox, or the rows of spits could accommodate a multitude of small animals or birds for roasting. Adjacent were great ovens for baking. The heat for cooking was provided by heavy logs, supported only on iron firedogs, burning continuously on these immense hearths, so fire was a constant hazard. Because of this, especially in earlier years when many of even the larger structures were still built from timber, the kitchen was housed in a separate, nearby building, generally connected to the main refectory or dining hall in the main part of the abbey by a covered way.

The kitchen itself was generally a one-storeyed building with a louvre in the roof through which smoke, steam and cooking smells found their exit. Many great abbey kitchens were of stone, and were frequently octagonal in shape with narrow windows in the walls. A stone-vaulted roof supported a lantern with its louvre. The structures of some examples of such kitchens survive, for example, the abbot's kitchen in the conventual buildings of Durham Cathedral and the interesting separate structure of the abbot's kitchen at Glastonbury (4).

In the castle and large manor house feeding was also communal, though for rather smaller numbers (200–400 persons) than in the monastic establishments (5). Cooking was carried out in similar large kitchens with great fireplaces; these fires in most cases being sited at a prudent distance from the living quarters in the main building but with easy access to the dining area in the great hall. Raby Castle, County Durham is a

4 *Abbot's Kitchen, Glastonbury Abbey, fourteenth century*

surviving fourteenth-century example, while Compton Castle, Devon, derives from the late fifteenth century. At Orford Castle, Suffolk, a royal castle built by Henry II in 1165–73, the kitchen is situated in the south-west tower of the keep (6). This first-floor chamber, which is furnished with two flues extending to the top of the tower and a sink with drainage to the exterior, leads off the two-storeyed main hall which occupied the central part of the keep. Adjacent to the kitchen is a narrow chamber with chutes giving on to the moat below. Water was stored in a cistern on the battlemented roof of the tower.

By the later Middle Ages the kitchens of large manor houses and castles, many of which were now being built of brick or stone, were situated within the house. Adjoining such kitchens were several ancillary chambers designed for storage of food, cutlery, dishes, utensils and napery and for carrying out the work vital to maintaining a self-supporting community of a hundred people or more. Such chambers included a buttery, pantry and larder, one or more sculleries, a chamber for making spices and one for conserves, a bakehouse, brewhouse and dairy.

The kitchens, which generally had access to the great hall via the 'screens' passage, were of stone or brick at least for the floor and lower part of the construction, though the upper part and roof might be of timber. From the beams would be hanging sides of bacon and salt beef, hams, dried fish and herbs. Bread was kept in boxes or baskets well above floor level to protect it from the depredations of rats and mice. The working conditions were still simple and limited. Racks were fastened to the walls from which implements were hung. Logs were stacked on the floor. Working surfaces were provided by heavy wood tables, often of trestle type. An example of such a fifteenth-century kitchen belonging to a great house or palace is shown in 7. In this the roof, walls and floor are of stone; there is an open, slatted louvre in the vaulted roof. Three large fireplaces are shown, one for roasting meat on a spit, a second for boiling water and cooking food, the third for further cooking and adjacent to the ovens which are built into the thickness of the walling on each side and heated by flues from the fire. Each oven is fitted with an iron door.

The kitchens of large houses in the sixteenth, seventeenth and eighteenth centuries

During the next 300 years kitchens became more comfortable. They were increasingly better furnished and the utensils and equipment for preparing and storing food were of improved and more varied design, but the basic methods of cooking and preparing food were little altered.

The Tudor kitchen of a great house was constructed of stone or brick with flagged floor and timber or stone-vaulted roof. It was a hive of industry, staffed by about 80 servants and retainers. Characteristic was Hampton Court Palace, where the structure of one of the three kitchens, that of Henry VIII's Great Kitchen, can be seen in almost unaltered condition. In the walls of this immense room, which measures 37 feet by 27 feet, are constructed two massive four-centred arched fireplaces, containing fires for roasting whole animals and for boiling and stewing food. A third fireplace contains a row of later brick ovens. A reconstruction of the interior is shown in 8.

By the seventeenth century arrangements for feeding, even in larger houses, were less communal and the

5 *Fifteenth-century kitchen at Stanton Harcourt,*
Oxfordshire (as it was c. 1850). This kitchen is built
separately from the house. The walls and floor are of stone,
the octagonal vault of wood with louvred air vents. Ovens
are set in the walls

6 *Kitchen sink in the keep of Orford Castle, Suffolk,*
1165–73

7 *A palace kitchen of the late Middle Ages based upon that*
at Windsor Castle. The Windsor Castle Great Kitchen was
largely built in the fourteenth and fifteenth centuries. Later
alterations include structural changes to the roof and
fenestration by Wyatville in the early nineteenth century
and afterwards the installation of gas ranges. The Great
Kitchen is still in use; the stone-flagged floor is now covered
with vinyl tiling and the stone walls have been painted
over. Drawing and caption reproduced by gracious
permission of H.M. The Queen

8 Tudor kitchen. A reconstruction based upon Henry VIII's Great Kitchen at Hampton Court Palace, c. 1530–40

kitchens were smaller and less lofty and draughty. Stone walls were plaster covered and the flat ceiling was of timber beams or was also plastered. The floor was still stone flagged. The kitchen was generally situated on the ground floor and within the large house where, adjacent to it and as far as possible from the general living quarters of the home, were the still-room (used for the making and storing of jams, marmalades, pickles and wines as well as medicines and lotions), also the scullery, pantry, larder and china closet. Most large houses, especially in country areas, were still self-sufficient, so a bakehouse, laundry, dairy and brewery were needed too.

The seventeenth-century kitchen was well lit and warm. Round the walls were cupboards and shelves for storing utensils and equipment for preparing food. The dresser began to make its appearance during this century. At first it consisted only of a flat board or a table fixed to the wall on which the food was prepared or 'dressed' to make it ready for cooking. Shelves were fixed to the wall above the board. In later Stuart times this board, the shelves and some cupboards were united to become one piece of furniture – the dresser – which often extended the full height of the room. The back part was boarded and, in the upper part, shelves of different widths were graded to suit crockery of different sizes while, below the flat worktop, were capacious cupboards for storage of linen. Working surfaces were still provided by wooden tables and servants took their meals at one of these set at one end of the kitchen where they sat on wooden forms.

An illustration of how slowly kitchen design changed over the centuries, the equipment being made to the same pattern again and again over two or three hundred years, is shown in the photograph of the kitchen at St Fagans Castle (9). Here, the room dates from the sixteenth century and the dog turnspit cage at the left-hand fireplace, the spit and utensil racks as well as the wooden bread car hanging from

9 *Kitchen at St Fagans Castle, Cardiff, 1540–80. This belonged to a house built within the walls of the twelfth-century castle. Note: seventeenth-century dog turnspit (fireplace on left), while fireplace on right has a spit powered by an eighteenth-century smoke jack. Bread car of slatted oak hangs from ceiling of type in use from sixteenth century. See also settle, spit rack, dripping tins, firebacks and dresser. National Museum of Wales (Welsh Folk Museum)*

the ceiling (in order to keep the contents safe from predators) are all of sixteenth-century design but these examples date from the seventeenth and even eighteenth centuries, as do the dresser, settle and table.

During the later seventeenth century and the eighteenth advances were very slowly taking place (10, 11, 12, 13). The larger, sash windows let more light into the kitchen. The long, stone or earthenware sink, resembling a trough, was fitted with short pipes from which water (cold) gushed, but this had to be pumped from outside and there was no control of the flow. Coal was replacing wood as a fuel and the design of grates, spits and utensils altered accordingly (chapter 3), but the methods remained the same and the labour of cooking, preparing and cleaning had been little eased. This was not considered to be of great importance as there was no shortage of servants. The coal fire, which like its timber predecessor, was always kept burning, provided warmth in winter, but the kitchen became stiflingly hot in summer. More

cupboarding and shelving was now provided, separately and in dressers. From the rafters of the ceiling still hung large hams sewn into linen bags and bunches of herbs for cooking and to make the kitchen smell sweet. Bread was still stored in a hanging car or crate. The spacious kitchen in the country house of Erddig, near Wrexham, is a fine, modern example of the 1780s. For fear of fire it was built separate from the house. It is lit by a large Venetian window (13).

The nineteenth-century kitchen
More care and thought was given to the planning of kitchens in middle and upper class homes than in the

10 Stuart kitchen, 1660–1710. Note: fireplace on left has chimney crane supporting cauldron for boiling. On right, basket spit is turned by weight jack. Earthenware trough sink with water supply pipes

eighteenth century and they were not situated so far away from the dining rooms as they had been previously. The families in these homes were prosperous and lived in comfort for, despite the immense labour of keeping clean and bright a great quantity of cast iron, copper and brass, and scrubbing and polishing large areas of wooden floor and furniture, this posed no problem as there was more than a sufficiency of low-cost servant labour. Early rising by the staff was regarded as a cardinal virtue and, in a well-run house, the mistress set an example. Cleanliness and diligence were believed to be of no less importance (chapter 6). Mrs Beeton[2] mentions these points, stressing that if the cook, for example, does not rise early she will not catch up with her work that day. She says 'an hour lost in the morning, will keep her (the cook) toiling, absolutely toiling, all day, to overtake that which might otherwise have been achieved with ease. In large establishments, six is a good hour to rise in the summer, and seven in the winter'. Further advice on not wasting time is given: 'a place for everything and everything in its place, must be her rule [the cook], in order that time may not be wasted in looking for things when they are wanted'.

Mrs Beeton also advises upon the qualities to be found in the situation and layout of an ideal kitchen. In paragraph 62 she says 'A good kitchen, therefore, should be erected with a view to the following particulars:

1   Convenience of distribution in its parts, with largeness of dimension.
2   Excellence of light, height of ceiling, and good ventilation.
3   Easiness of access, without passing through the house.
4   Sufficiently remote from the principal apartments of the house, that the members, visitors or guests

of the family, may not perceive the odour incident to cooking, or hear the noise of culinary operations.

5 Plenty of fuel and water, which, with the scullery, pantry, and storeroom, should be so near it, as to offer the smallest possible trouble in reaching them.[3]

Alas, some of these conditions of Mrs Beeton's ideal kitchen were, more often than not, destined to remain unfulfilled, at least in middle-class town houses. The rapidly increasing population of the time, which was causing acute overcrowding in towns, engendered a boom in house building, with a consequent steep rise in the cost of land. The Victorian town house, therefore, began to expand upwards rather than laterally and the kitchen, with its attendant scullery, pantry, wine-store, laundry and servants' rooms were usually to be found in the basement or, at least, a semi-basement. This group of rooms then had direct access to an outside area where coal and other tradesmen's goods could be delivered. Such basement kitchens were often ill-lit, from windows high up in the wall, and were also frequently ill-ventilated.

The kitchen was, however, usually warm (in summer, stiflingly so), for the cooking facilities were revolutionised in the nineteenth century by the advent of the kitchen range. These cast-iron monsters had been installed in the majority of homes by the second half of the century and, while consuming large quantities of coal and pumping smoke into an already heavily polluted atmosphere, were a remarkable advance on the open fire in providing cooking and water-heating facilities (chapter 4). Apart from the range, which occupied much of one wall of the kitchen, there would be a large dresser extending from floor to ceiling, wooden tables providing working surfaces, wooden chairs and further shelving to accommodate utensils of all kinds. Such basement kitchens relied heavily on artificial light (chapter 8). In the first half of the century this was furnished by candles and oil lamps. By the 1860s gas lighting was general in middle class homes and, from the 1880s, electric lighting was slowly being introduced.

Servants often had their own room next to the kitchen, where they could take their meals, sew and sit when they had free time, though their sleeping quarters would be at the top of the house in the attics. Nearby, in the basement, would be a wash-house or laundry, containing a mangle, wash-boiler, ironing

equipment and tables (chapter 7). The pantry or larder was a walk-in room which was an essential part of the basement area. This contained fresh foods and utensils, generally stored on stone or marble shelves to keep the food cool (chapter 5). The scullery was next to the kitchen, usually opening out of it. This would contain the sink, draining boards, plate racks and shelving for storage of pans and other cooking utensils.

In country areas the kitchen of a well-to-do home was a larger room, well lit and probably situated on the ground floor. In addition to the other rooms already mentioned, there would also be a dairy, built on the shady, sheltered side of the house. To keep the milk as cool as possible, walls were generally tiled, the floor stone flagged and tables and shelves were of

11 Wooden plate rack. Kitchen of Georgian House, Bristol, late eighteenth century

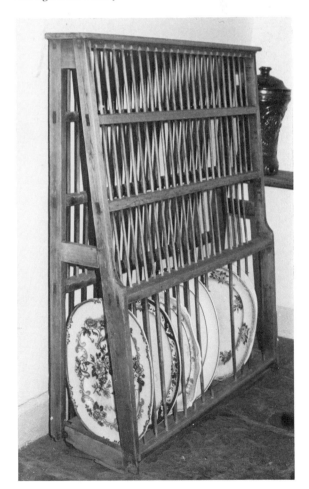

12 Georgian kitchen, 1780–1805. Note: dresser, stone sink, wooden draining board. Dog turnspit, spit rack. Coal-burning hob grate. Hot cupboard at side with iron door. Used for keeping plates or food hot or mulling wine

stone, marble or slate. The windows were covered by wire gauze to keep out flying insects (chapter 2, page 49, fig. 113).

A description of the utensils to be found in nineteenth-century kitchens is given in chapters 2 and 4 and cooking methods and facilities in chapter 4. Illustration 14 shows a Regency palace kitchen and 15 a ground floor kitchen in a well-to-do country house. Fig. 16 illustrates a middle class kitchen in the mid-Victorian period and 17 and 18 one of the end of the century, where can be seen the door opening into the scullery. The box fixed to the wall over the kitchen door contains the bells which would sound in the kitchen when a servant was required elsewhere in the house. The numbers indicate the room where service was needed and each bell would usually make a slightly different sound.

The cottage kitchen

Traditionally, over the centuries, one room served in country cottages as combined kitchen, dining and living room. There was one hearth with its open fire burning, well into the nineteenth century, when it was slowly replaced by an iron kitchen range. The fire provided warmth, means of cooking, of heating water and of drying wet clothes and damp linen. This was the centre of life in the home, where everyone relaxed in their free time and ate at a table near the fire. The floor was of beaten earth strewn with rushes or, in areas where materials were readily available, paved with stone or brick. Before the fire was a high-backed wood settle to keep out the draughts and a wooden or basketwork chair for the master of the house (19). By the nineteenth century some cottages had a scullery or back kitchen where washing, washing up and preparing of food was done. Some cottages also boasted a parlour, but this was 'special'. In the north of England it was called 't' room' and only used for the great occasions of life – and death.

13 *The new kitchen, Erddig, Clwyd, late eighteenth to later nineteenth century. Large room, about 25 ft × 15 ft and 20 ft high. Note: steel range and utensils with hastener. Dressers and shelves on three sides of room. Ceiling racks for hanging game and herbs. Wooden work-tables with implements. By courtesy of* Country Life

In the more remote areas of Wales, northern England and Scotland these cottages were smaller and life was more primitive and hard. In the Highlands of Scotland in the early centuries a central hearth burned peat which provided both warmth and light. The smoke escaped as best it could through a hole in the roof or a small wooden chimney but, on windy days, much of it came back into the room again through the heather or thatch. A little later, the hearth was built against the wooden partition which divided the living room from the bedroom but this then developed into a chimney built into one of the gable ends of the cottage with the hearth set below it. This was a great improvement as the fire hazard was greatly reduced.

In the crofter's[4] home all kinds of equipment and utensils had to be stored in the living room/kitchen for the family needed to be completely self-sufficient. Apart from the cooking utensils, bellows and creel for peats kept round the fire, there would be a gun held,

to keep it dry, in a rack over the fireplace, a box bed for sleeping and storing linen, a barrel for oatmeal, a spinning wheel, carders and all kinds of possessions stored on shelves round the room. Such incongruous companions as a pony saddle, a fetter for tying cow's legs while milking, bagpipes, a baby's cradle, a barrel for salt herring, a Gaelic Bible and a butter churn would be found places in such a room. Lighting was provided by home-made candles and/or cruisie lamps burning fish oil (chapter 8).

In the West Highland Museum at Fort William is a display of a living room interior of such a nineteenth-century croft house. The photograph (20) shows a part

14 *A Regency palace kitchen, 1820. Drawing based upon the kitchen in the Royal Pavilion at Brighton. Plastered stone walls, lower part tiled. Stone flagged floor. Gas lighting in glass and metal lanterns. Bronze smoke canopies over ovens and fireplace. Cast-iron oven doors. Wood tables. Iron and copper (later) utensils*

15 *Kitchen at Aynho House, Northamptonshire. A drawing made by Mrs Cartwright (née Countess von Sandizell) in 1847 of her kitchen. Note: dressers displaying tea-pots, jelly moulds, silver salvers and herbs. Food mincer attached to wall. Hanging oil chandelier. Open fireplace with spit. In front is (temporarily) a drying cupboard for crockery. Large square holes in wall were for access to chimney for cleaning*

16 *Victorian kitchen, 1850–60. Dark painted walls and woodwork. Stone flagged floor. Gas lifghting. Note: iron chimneypiece, range and boiler, stone hearth. Dark painted wood dresser. Scrubbed wood shelves and table. Stone sink, wood cupboards below*

of the display, which includes the figure of a grand-mother sitting by the hearth where she minds the baby and tends the peat fire while the younger members of the family work on the land. In the background can be seen the spinning wheel and wooden dresser.

During the nineteenth century large numbers of simple dwellings were built in the towns of Britain to house workers who were flocking from the country to the urban areas to find work in the developing industries. Many of these, such as the artisan's cottage

of the 1830s displayed in the Abbey House Museum at Kirkstall, Leeds, catered for a somewhat primitive living standard unaccompanied, certainly according to modern thinking, by many aids to comfort. Commonly of two-room design, the living-room/kitchen on the ground floor opened directly in from the street, while a staircase led to a bedroom above. As in the Leeds example, the living room was fitted with a coal-fired kitchen range and a sink, but there was no lighting other than candles and oil lamps and there was no piped water supply or indoor sanitation (21).

Not very different were the rows of stone colliery pit cottages at Hetton-le-Hole, near Sunderland, which were built by the Hetton Coal Company in 1860–5 to house their miners. These cottages were occupied by pitmen until 1976, after which a short

17 Late Victorian kitchen and scullery, 1880–95. Dark green painted walls. Dark brown oilcloth covers the floor. Coconut mat in front of brass fender. Woodwork of dresser and cupboards painted in brown graining. Gas lighting. Note: coal-burning kitchener of iron and steel. Wooden table, chairs and clothes horse. Scullery: Floor of red quarry tiles. Walls and woodwork to match kitchen. Enamelled fireclay sink. Wood plate-rack and draining board. Iron washing copper to burn coal or coke

18 Stone kitchen sink on brick supports. Brass tap. Displayed in the basement kitchen of the Gustav Holst Birthplace Museum, Cheltenham. Late nineteenth century

19 Beehive Chair. National Museum of Welsh Antiquities, Bangor. A coiled basketry (lip work) chair typical of old Welsh kitchens. Lip work is a straw rope construction lashed and bound with bramble strips. A peasant craft

20 Reconstruction of the interior of a nineteenth-century croft house displayed in the West Highlands Museum, Fort William. Note: cooking pots hanging over peat fire from the chain (slabraidh), fish grilling on gridiron, tea-pot keeping warm, iron girdle. On the window sill, candle moulds, carding comb, wicker plate for oatcakes, goffering iron. On dresser, jug, bottle, whisky jar. Grandmother seated on wooden chair tends the fire and minds the baby in cradle. By courtesy of the British Tourist Authority

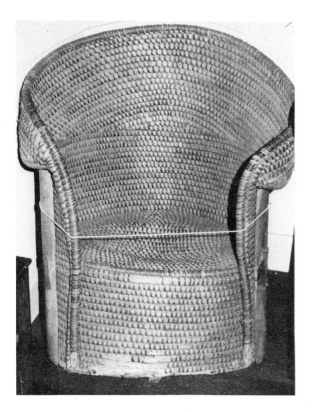

row of them was presented by the National Coal Board to the Beamish North of England Open Air Museum, where they were re-erected and are now suitably furnished to show how pitmen and their families lived in the area over a period of some 70–80 years. The photograph (22) shows how the living room/kitchen of such a cottage would have looked in the 1890s, with its iron kitchen range and round oven characteristic of the area, fired by free coal supplies. The 'dess' bed would be let down at night. At this date the cottage had no indoor piped water or sanitation. The miner would take his bath in a galvanised tin bath in front of the fire. For this the cold water had to be fetched from a stand pipe in the street and heated in kettles or cauldrons on the kitchen range. Lighting was by oil lamp and candles.

Only slowly did modern conveniences come to cottages like these in many industrial areas of Britain. In Hetton, for example, piped water supplied a cold tap in the pantry by 1900 and gas was introduced in 1931. The kitchen ranges were replaced by Triplex ones in 1938 and the cottages were wired for electricity in 1952.

The twentieth-century kitchen

For a thousand years kitchen design had been developing, infinitesimally slowly, advancing inch by inch from the most primitive way of organising the preparation, cooking and preservation of food and the care and well-being of a family towards the stage reached in 1900 when, providing a limitless supply of helping hands was available, a condition of reasonable comfort and efficiency had been reached. In the twentieth century the pace of change accelerated so greatly that the whole manner of domestic life was totally transformed. It was altered so much that, in the space of one lifetime, every aspect of housewifery has been revolutionised. The reasons for this have been

21 Stone sink on brick pillars. Living room of an artisan's cottage displayed in the Abbey House Museum, Kirkstall, Leeds, c. 1830–5. Note: no water supply in the room. Laundry tray, bowl and pegs

22 Colliery pit cottage interior. Re-erected in the Beamish North of England Open Air Museum from Hetton-le-Hole, near Sunderland (see page 25). Note: cast-iron kitchen range and round oven and, on the left, a 'dess' bed. This resembles a sideboard but was folded out to provide a bed at night

two-fold: fundamental changes in society consequent upon the upheavals of two world wars linked with the emancipation of women and the rapid pace of scientific invention and resulting technological progress and achievement.

The first wave of social change was brought about as a result of the First World War. Before 1914 there was still more than adequate labour to run efficiently and well the intensively labour-demanding Edwardian kitchen. Gas cookers had been available for several decades (and gas lighting since early in the nineteenth century), but the iron and steel, coal-fired kitchen range still dominated the majority of kitchens. It was a brute to clean and countless hours of work were needed to tend and care for it but, no matter, there were plenty of servants. China and utensils were still displayed on an immense open-fronted dresser and, with gas and oil lighting and coal-burning kitchener, the china became dirty and needed frequent washing. The stone-flagged or quarry-tiled floor needed daily washing, the working surfaces of tables daily scrubbing, menus were complex and meals had many courses. But, so far, it all worked well. Some concessions to the eternal labour were being made. Linoleum was laid on many kitchen floors, making them easier to wash. Piped water was brought into more homes and water heating devices were being installed. A few kitchens were being fitted with closed cupboards and dressers. Innumerable gadgets were flooding the market for cutting, mincing, mixing food, for preparing coffee and tea, for toasting, for grilling, for washing clothes and cleaning the home. But, until the development of electric power and its availability in the home, many of these were status symbols rather than labour-saving devices. Certainly the early washing machines and vacuum cleaners were harder work to operate than cleaning in the old-fashioned way (chapters 2, 6 and 7).

It was during the war that the immense army of servants began to melt away. Job opportunities for the intelligent, well-educated girl had existed for some time and a number had worked in shops and offices, but the war brought openings in factories, canteens, the army, the medical services, the post office and many other organisations. And this was no temporary phase. After 1918 only a modest proportion of women returned to the hard, restrictive life of domestic service.

During the 1920s and 1930s both the kitchen itself and the way of using it were altered effectively. Within a few years after the war had ended it became apparent that the servant army had vanished for good. By 1930 staff in domestic residence had become a tiny fraction of the numbers in such service before 1914. Only well-to-do homes could afford to employ this new class of servant. Middle-class housewives found themselves for the first time for centuries with only daily help or just an hour or two a week to give a hand with the cleaning. Being articulate, also being in some demand for work outside the home, such women made clear to their husbands and the department stores that they expected a vast improvement in the working conditions which their servants had had to put up with in the kitchen for decades. With the new building of smaller houses for smaller families, the basement kitchen and scullery became a thing of the past. The new kitchen was on the ground floor, it was smaller and brighter than its nineteenth-century predecessor and it contained an increasing quantity of labour-saving equipment. Indeed, the term 'labour-saving' was one barely heard in Victorian England, but in the inter-war years it became a fashion, a movement. Designers and manufacturers grasped this opportunity and took advantage of a seller's market in gadgets and equipment of all kinds designed to reduce the tedium and save the time of the housewife running her own home and bringing up her family almost single-handed.

In Britain the era of the unit-designed kitchen had not yet arrived: that was, for most women, an occurrence of the 1950s. Still, the new-style kitchen was very different from the pre-war one. The window was larger. Gas and electric-powered equipment was installed – cookers, water heaters, irons, toasters and, for a fortunate few, refrigerators and washing machines. The interior decorative scheme was lighter in colour, the dark brown grained paint was replaced by white or cream, the floor covered by gaily designed patterned linoleum. The biggest single change in kitchen furniture design was in the replacement of the open dresser by the kitchen cabinet. In the early years after the war many dressers had been converted by fitting doors to the upper shelves, so enclosing the china and glass. What the 1920s' housewife needed was a further step towards giving her a convenient storage place for all her utensils and necessary items for cooking and preparing food which was close to hand and easy of access. Food was at this time still mainly stored in a walk-in or cupboard larder, but a new piece of furniture designed especially for kitchen use was sorely needed.

The Americans had led the field in the design of labour-saving equipment in the home and kitchen furniture since the later nineteenth century. America had never possessed the ready availability of an ample supply of servant labour that upper and middle class Europeans had enjoyed for so long, so housewives there had always been more conscious of the need for as much mechanical help in the home as possible. The kitchen cabinet had been in use in America for some time before its introduction to England in the 1920s. One of the early designs introduced then was by a Canadian, Wilson Crowe. His cabinet contained a vitreous enamel-covered working surface which let down as a flap and had storage space above and below as well as drawers to hold cutlery.

In 1925 a British firm, Hygena Cabinets Ltd was set up which made craftsmen-built wood cabinets. These had been the idea of the furniture manufacturer Len Cooklin, who saw a need for a purpose-built kitchen cabinet. By the late 1920s and the 1930s the firm was turning out some beautifully made cabinets, many of large dimensions and containing a complex arrangement of fittings and equipment which provided all that a housewife could need. The cabinets were divided into compartments of cupboards and shelves (all enclosed) to house cleaning equipment, storage jars, shopping lists and bills, spice racks and cooking utensils, as well as being fitted with a pull-out ironing board, a flour sifter, egg racks and a pull-down work top. One design even included seats and a kitchen table (23).

The kitchen cabinet was a utilitarian, flexible, free-standing unit but, before the 1950s in Britain, it was one item of an unrelated scheme. Much of the preparation work was still done on a separate kitchen table. There was a sink and draining board and, probably, an old-fashioned dresser or cupboards as well. The introduction of hire purchase in the 1930s enabled many couples to buy these items to furnish their kitchens, and manufacturers brought out more and varied designs for kitchen needs, but, as yet, these were unrelated to one another in shape, size and materials used.

The idea of kitchen planning in relation to the work to be done by the then available labour force had been thought out in America in the 1920s. Efficiency experts had considered the co-ordination of the work

with the time and facilities available on a time and motion study basis and discovered what millions of housewives had known for centuries, that a tremendous amount of time and energy had been used up unnecessarily in kitchens where utilisation of the space had not been carefully planned to eliminate such wastage. By the later 1930s the concept of planning worktops at one level in easy proximity and suitable order of arrangement to the sink, the cooker and the storage units had been accepted in America by architects, kitchen furniture designers and manufacturers and standardised units began to be made which could be co-ordinated into kitchens of different sizes and shapes. In order to make these streamlined fitted kitchens available at a price suitable to the majority of families it had to be possible to pre-fabricate the units to completely standardised sizes and shapes.

Apart from the convenient spacing and arrangement of these units, the efficiency experts decided that the housewife would work better and more happily if the kitchen were a pleasanter, more cheerful place. It was recommended that there should, if possible, be windows on two sides of the room, facing east and south respectively so that sunlight would enter during most of the working day[5]. Artificial lighting should be carefully designed so that the housewife did not stand in her own light as, in past ages, she so often had when one centrally placed gas or electric fitting was suspended from the ceiling. It was also recommended that an electric fan should be inserted into the wall or window frame to expel steam and cooking odours.

These ideas were all put into practice in America in much of the new housing erected before the Second World War and, in the 1950s, began to be accepted in Britain also. It is only strange that this process of acceptance and installation should have taken so long. After all, Mrs Beeton had considered the 'convenience of distribution of parts' of a kitchen and the desirability of not having too far to walk between one part of the domestic quarters and another (see page 20). The disappearance of the kitchen helpers had been foreseen in 1869 by Catherine Beecher, the American domestic reformer and sister of Harriet Beecher Stowe,

23 This craftsman-made cabinet was the latest design in the 1920s. Made of solid oak, incorporating pull-out enamelled work top, cupboards with ventilating grilles, storage jars, flour sifter and shopping list reminder. Photograph supplied by Condor Public Relations Ltd. by courtesy of the manufacturers, Hygena Ltd.

24 Modern easy-to-assemble kitchen units by Hygena Ltd. Note: storage cupboards, sink and drainer, split-level electric hob, ovens and storage capacity. By courtesy of Hygena Ltd.

author of *Uncle Tom's Cabin*. Miss Beecher wrote a book entitled *The American Woman's Home* in which she put forward ideas on kitchen planning which were startling to her contemporaries and were certainly more than 50 years ahead of their time. She proposed that a kitchen be planned so that only a few steps need be taken between work-table and sink, work-table to cooker, work-table to storage cupboards. She envisaged a streamlined kitchen where everything needed was accessible and easy to handle.

In Britain, after the Second World War the coordinated kitchen began to be built into new houses and by the 1960s many older kitchens were being redesigned and modernised. Kitchen units were standardised in manufacture so that work-tops could be fitted at one level round the room, leaving spaces to accommodate equally standardised refrigerators, cookers, sink units, washing machines, etc.

At this time also small houses were being built for couples who expected to move into their own home at or soon after marriage and no longer share part of a larger home with their parents. Eating in the kitchen, once regarded as only suitable for servants, became acceptable for everyone. The idea of a dining recess in the kitchen had been adopted in a number of houses, especially in the USA, in the 1920s, but it was after the Second World War that the concept of a dining area as part of a large kitchen space became popular, especially for families with younger children.

In these dining areas as, indeed, in the kitchen as a whole, decorative schemes became gayer and more colourful. Washable vinyl wallpapers or coloured tiles were easy to apply to walls and ceiling. New flooring materials were also attractive and easy to clean. Picture windows were inserted screened by brightly-patterned curtains or blinds. New materials of all kinds, plastics and vitreous enamels, made easy-care kitchens a reality. They were utilised for, among other things, worktop and cupboard surface cladding, self-clean ovens and non-stick utensils with gay, bright

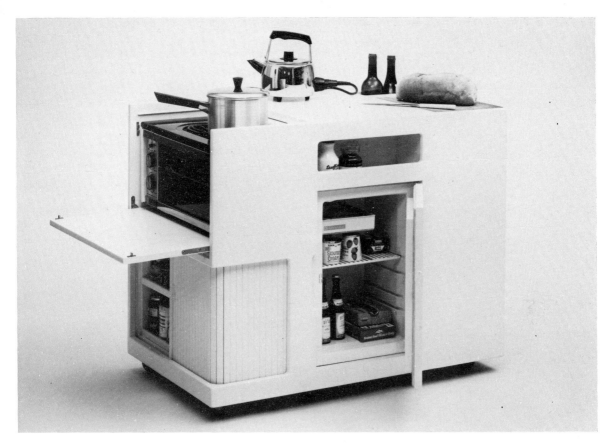

25 Capsule kitchen, 1971–2. A mobile, self-contained electric kitchen. Incorporates oven, hot plate, refrigerator, storage unit and worktop. By courtesy of Brooke Marine Ltd., manufacturers, and Council of Industrial Design

finishes.

The working surfaces of the kitchen which, for centuries, had been scrubbed wood, were revolutionised by the development of plastic laminates which could be applied to units made of wood or chipboard and provided an easy care, hard, resistant surface for all kitchen needs. The household name in this field is the Formica laminate which is now produced in a wide range of colours and patterns as well as impressive quality imitations of many forms of wood surfacing. It was in 1913 that a method was evolved in America of producing a laminated, plastic sheet and decorative laminated plastics were being manufactured in the 1930s, but it has been since 1945 that the development has accelerated so that nearly all kitchen surfaces are finished with these materials.

Apart from a gayer, more cheerful kitchen, the modern housewife also works in a warmer (often centrally heated), but much better ventilated and evenly heated one. She has at her disposal more efficient easy-to-use equipment and gadgetry. The modern sink unit, with one bowl or two, may be fitted

with a waste disposal unit and have single or double drainers. The whole unit is pressed out from one sheet of steel which might then be finished with coloured vitreous enamelling. Mixer taps were introduced for these units about 1950. Hot water may be provided by the central heating system or by a sink water heater powered by gas or electricity.

This availability of power has led to an impressive array of electrical aids which chop, mince, liquidise and beat, freeze, cook, wash and dry all at the touch of a switch. If the housewife is a working wife she may prefer to take advantage of buying pre-packaged convenience foods at the supermarket or cook and lay in supplies in her own freezer (24,25).

What of the future and what are the latest trends? Is it possible and desirable to take the push-button kitchen further? In the 1970s there have been designed kitchens where the housewife sits at a control panel and simply presses buttons to set in motion freezer and refrigerator, oven and grill and then dishwasher. Such 'preparation centres', as they are called, are usually built into (some of the equipment under floor level) a revolving carousel so that the housewife sits in front of the panel keeping an eye on everything at once. Some operations still need to be done by hand, such as getting out utensils and putting them away again but, no doubt, time will deal with that problem too.

But although nearly all housewives like to have the chores done for them they do not all, or one suspects, not even a majority of them, want to have a factory production line in their kitchen nor live solely on convenience foods. Many women like cooking and take a pride in creating a home of which the kitchen is the living centre. Many also, in days of steeply rising prices, prefer to cook and bake, especially if there are hungry, energy-consuming children to feed, then fill the freezer so that the contents will last the family for a week or a month. The future kitchen will probably, therefore, include more and more labour-saving machines to do the dull chores but leave the housewife free to experiment and use her time as she personally prefers.

CHAPTER TWO

The Preparation of Food

Over the centuries the form and appearance of utensils used in preparing food for cooking changed barely at all. The needs of the housewife were constant: she required containers to hold powders, solids and liquids and equipment to cut, grate, sieve, pound and grind, mash, squeeze and press, mix and beat. Because her requirements did not alter and the needs of all human beings are similar, equipment to carry out these processes bore a close resemblance wherever it was to be found in the civilised world. A competent housewife would certainly find herself familiar with the utensils of any kitchen at any time between the days of Ancient Rome and the early nineteenth century in Britain or Western Europe.

In the earlier centuries utensils were made chiefly from wood, horn, earthenware and metals such as iron, brass, copper and pewter. From the late eighteenth century onwards development in materials made kitchen-work easier and more pleasant. Advances in the ceramics industry brought inexpensive and attractive earthenware and china into everyone's home and, later, the production of aluminium and stainless steel removed much of the drudgery of cleaning from everyday tasks.

By the eighteenth century equipment had also become more varied and complex in design. In the nineteenth, especially from about 1850 onwards, labour-saving gadgets began to proliferate. Many of these originated in America where there was frequently an insufficiency of servant labour to carry out the boring tasks of preparing food in the kitchen by the use of knife or chopper. Mechanical appliances were put on the market, each claiming to reduce magically such chores as peeling and coring apples, stoning raisins or cherries, slicing bread, cleaning knives or making sausages.

The breakthrough came with the development of the electric motor to drive the gadgets which had been designed for kitchen use. Much of the impetus for creating a small electric motor which would drive domestic equipment came again from America. Joseph Henry (1797–1878), the American physicist, had devised and constructed the first electromagnetic motor in 1829, but despite research contributions by a number of famous scientists, including Faraday, Siemens and Wheatstone, it was not until after 1873 that transmission of power by electricity became practical, and it was made possible by Edison and others in the 1880s. Even then commercial motors were far too large and heavy to be suitable for general domestic use and it was not until after the First World War that designs could be adapted for use in small items of kitchen equipment such as mixers, beaters and choppers.

Containers

Most of the types of vessels common to twentieth-century kitchen use were known to the mistress of a Romano-British home in the first and second centuries AD. These were made from earthenware, glass, pewter and, occasionally, silver. Bowls of various sizes were used for mixing and containing food, jars with lids for storing, platters and dishes for handling food and small bowls, beakers and cups for drinking (29). There were jugs of differing sizes and shapes and ewers[1] or pitchers which were designed primarily for water; these had a wide mouth for ease of pouring and a handle for carrying (28, 32). Flagons were in general use. These were large bottles with carrying handles and were intended for holding wine. The bottle narrowed at the top towards the neck, which was stoppered (30).

Pottery was made in quantity in Britain during the Roman occupation. It was plain or enriched by incised, piped, painted, moulded or relief ornamen-

26 Beaker of Castor ware, Roman, fourth century AD. Museum of Antiquities, Newcastle-upon-Tyne

27 Bog oak quaich. Scottish Highlands. West Highland Museum, Fort William

28 Bronze ewer, c.1400. Museum of London

29 Romano-British earthenware mug, second century AD. Cheltenham City Museum

30 Romano-British flagon, first century AD. Cheltenham City Museum

31 Staved wood vessel, cane bound exterior. Scottish Highlands. Highland Folk Museum, Kingussie

32 Medieval bronze ewer. Carlisle Museum

34 Bowl of Samian ware, Roman. British Museum, London

33 Roman dimpled pots. Salisbury Museum

tation. Notable was the black burnished ware of south-west England, also the pottery from the Castor kilns in Northamptonshire which was coloured grey or of a reddish tint and enriched by a piped decoration (26). Most valued was the rich red glazed pottery, *terra sigillata*, commonly known as Samian ware. This term is a misnomer which stems from the fact that the rich red colour led English antiquaries many years ago to confuse its origin with the Greek ware from the Island of Samos. Actually the pottery derives from that developed at Arretium (Arezzo) in Italy but later made in quantity in Gaul where the clay was most suited to its production. Samian ware was imported into Roman Britain (34). Glass, for domestic use, likewise was mainly imported from Gaul and the Rhineland.

The same categories of vessels for kitchen use continued to be made during the succeeding centuries, simple in design and decoration during the Middle Ages and becoming more varied in form and function from the seventeenth century onwards. Leather was used to make jugs and tankards from the Medieval period. The large leather jugs were often referred to as black jacks because they were made from jack leather. This was a hard leather coated with tar or pitch (chapter 5, page 113).

In many remote areas the material from which vessels were made was determined by local availability. In the Highlands of Scotland, for instance, lack of suitable clay for making pottery led to the development of the skilled feathered staved vessels. These were made in all sizes from the larger wash tubs, milk cogs and butter churns, mixing bowls and porringers down to the tiny quaich[2]. Some staved vessels were bound with canes or withies and many were made in alternating staves of dark and light wood (of varying hardness and water absorption) which were then feathered into one another[3](31).

Highland vessels were also made from turned wood and wood continued to be used widely for all kinds of vessels until at least 1800, though earthenware was being imported in some quantity from the late seventeenth century. Another material generally in use for making vessels here, as well as in the north of England and in some other areas, was horn which came from cattle. Drinking tumblers and bowls were made from this material as were also spoons and ladles. Working the horn was a skilled craft, largely carried out by tinkers who were careful to keep secret their methods of heating and manipulation of the horn.

Cutting implements

Until the later nineteenth century all cutting and chopping was done by hand using a knife or chopping blade attached to a wooden handle or pair of kitchen scissors or shears (39, 40, 41, 46). The blades of such cutting instruments were made of steel which had to be sharpened regularly and kept very clean for fear of rusting (page 127, chapter 6). In the nineteenth century various patent sharpeners were introduced wherein the blade was drawn across a V of hardened steel segments (48). In the 1890s a serrated bread knife which did not need such regular sharpening was put on the market. In the 1920s stainless steel made its appearance and, though for a long time knives made from it were not very sharp, it was a great boon for keeping cutlery clean.

A characteristic cutting agent was developed over the years for handling sugar. During the Middle Ages sugar was a rare commodity and very expensive as it had to be imported from Syria or North Africa. People used honey and must[4] as sweetening agents. Consumption of sugar increased in Western Europe when sugar cane was introduced and grown in Spain and Sicily. A new demand arose in Britain for a sweetening agent with the seventeenth-century advent of tea and coffee. At the same time plantations were established in the West Indies, Madeira and Central and South America so both supply and demand increased, though the poor still used honey as the cost of sugar was high. By 1800 demand had risen astronomically and the price had fallen greatly as supplies had markedly increased.

In the refining process the liquid substance was poured into moulds in which the sugar set in a conical shape of between one and three feet in height and weighing up to 14 lb (47). These sugar loaves were stored in cord cradles suspended from the kitchen ceiling. For table use the sugar was cut up into lumps and for cooking it was pounded into crystalline powder. Metal sugar cutters were used, hand ones of moderate size (37) or larger designs mounted on wood blocks (47). Grippers were available for holding the sugar loaf while the cutter was operated (38).

Another traditional cutting and marking utensil was the pastry jigger and crimper, which were usually made from brass. The jigger (35) comprised a handle attached to a wheel which was marked with flutes and

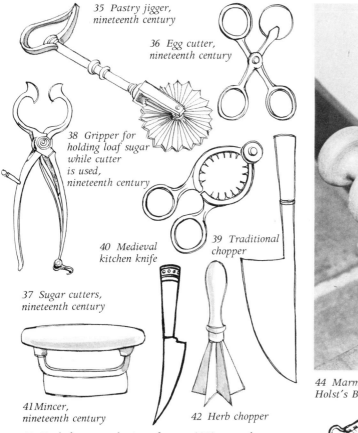

35 *Pastry jigger,
nineteenth century*

36 *Egg cutter,
nineteenth century*

38 *Gripper for
holding loaf sugar
while cutter
is used,
nineteenth century*

40 *Medieval
kitchen knife*

39 *Traditional
chopper*

37 *Sugar cutters,
nineteenth century*

41 *Mincer,
nineteenth century*

42 *Herb chopper*

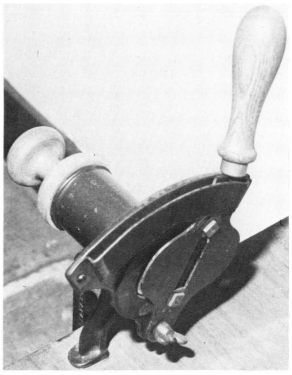

44 *Marmalade cutter, late nineteenth century. Gustav
Holst's Birthplace Museum, Cheltenham*

43 *Food chopper and mixer, from c. 1850 onwards.
Gustav Holst's Birthplace Museum, Cheltenham*

46 *Medieval iron
shears*

45 *Aluminium egg slicer,
Price 6½d. (2½p) in Harrods'
1929 catalogue*

47 *Sugar cutters and loaf*

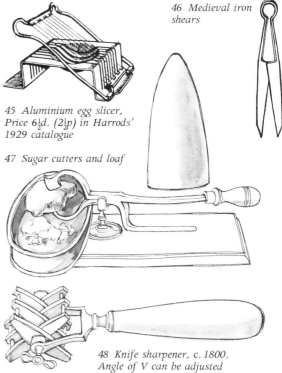

48 *Knife sharpener, c. 1800.
Angle of V can be adjusted*

ridges radiating from its centre. When run round the edge of a pie crust or rolled out pastry the jigger made a deckled wavy edge. Pastry crimpers trimmed and pressed pie crust edges.

In the second half of the nineteenth century several designs of mechanical cutting agents appeared. The marmalade cutter was one of these. It was clamped to a table and the fruit was fed into a hopper, pressed down with a wooden spatula then cut by a blade which was operated by a handle (44). Egg toppers resembled a pair of scissors, but instead of the usual blades, one side terminated in a metal ring which gripped the egg while the other was a circular blade (36). Bread slicers appeared in the 1880s and bean slicers soon afterwards. Hand-operated food choppers and mixers became available after 1850. These were made of metal and were mounted on a wooden board. When the handle was turned a two-bladed chopper rose and fell while simultaneously the cylindrical vessel was rotated by a ratchet mechanism (43).

Ladles, spoons, scoops

Traditional utensils were in use from very early times which varied in size from the long-handled designs intended for the open fire, for stirring and ladling out food, to small spoons and ladles for mixing and measuring ingredients at the kitchen table (50, 51, 52, 53, 54, 58). The long handles protected the cook from being burnt at the fire. At the other end of the scale were the small toddy[5] ladles (55) which were intended for transferring the hot liquid into a drinking vessel. Spoons and ladles were made from a variety of materials: wood, horn, bone, iron, brass, pewter.

The apple scoop or corer is of ancient origin. This was a primitive but effective design used to scoop out the flesh from an apple and leave aside the core and skin, so making it easy for people who had lost their teeth to enjoy the fruit. It could also be used only as a corer. Such scoops were made from wood or ivory, but the majority were carved out from the metacarpal bones of sheep; the knuckle which formed a handle was decoratively carved (56, 57).

Scales and balances

Most weighing equipment for domestic use has for centuries been made on the equal-arm balance principle invented in the early days of Ancient Egypt and improved on by the Romans about the time of Christ by the insertion of a pin through the centre of the beam. In this type of weighing mechanism, (of which large numbers of nineteenth-century scales survive), the beam supports a dish on one side to hold the food to be weighed and a plate on the other on which the weights are piled (60).

Self-indicating weighing machines in which the weight is shown on a graduated dial have also been used for a long time: an early example was invented by Leonardo da Vinci (1452–1519) and is described and drawn in one of his notebooks. The spring balance type of such mechanism was most commonly used in the home. This may have been designed to stand on a table or be suspended from the ceiling (49, 59).

Pounding and grinding, mashing, squeezing, pressing

Many types of food needed pounding and grinding, the most basic being the treatment of grain to make bread. The pestle and mortar is of most ancient origin, used in some form by almost all peoples from primitive times onwards. By the classical period the preparation of grain was carried out in two stages; first, it was pounded to remove the husks, then ground, or milled, to make flour.

Public bakehouses were established in Rome by the second century BC, but for several hundred years many housewives, especially in colonies such as Britain, far from the centre of the empire, still baked their own bread. In early times the milling equipment consisted of the saddle quern (called a thrusting mill by the Romans). It was a large, slightly concave stone on which the grain was placed and was then ground by rubbing a smaller stone across it by hand (61). From this developed the pushing mill in which both stones were flat and grooved. The upper stone was shaped like a hopper into which the grain was poured and it escaped to the lower stone through a slit in its base. Work could be made easier by fitting a wooden handle across the upper stone.

An important advance was the introduction by the second century AD into Western Europe of the rotary quern, a handmill worked with a circular motion. The lower stone of this quern was cone-shaped and the upper, formed as a hollow cone, fitted neatly over the lower one. Grain was poured in through a hole in the upper stone and a handle was fitted to the side of it for grinding. This classical handmill was portable and was carried by Roman soldiers to grind their own supply of corn (62).

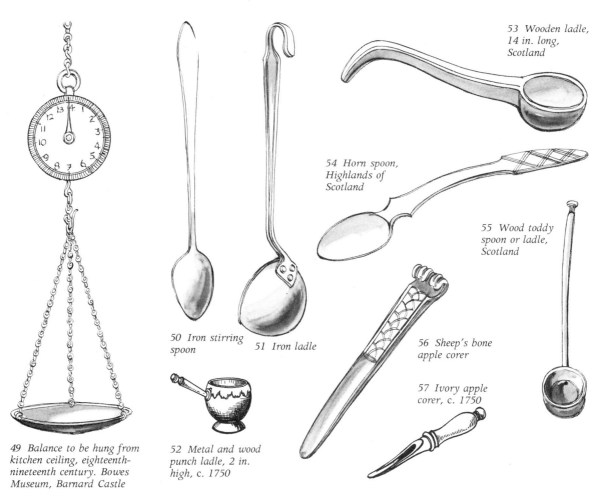

53 Wooden ladle, 14 in. long, Scotland

54 Horn spoon, Highlands of Scotland

55 Wood toddy spoon or ladle, Scotland

50 Iron stirring spoon

51 Iron ladle

56 Sheep's bone apple corer

57 Ivory apple corer, c. 1750

49 Balance to be hung from kitchen ceiling, eighteenth-nineteenth century. Bowes Museum, Barnard Castle

52 Metal and wood punch ladle, 2 in. high, c. 1750

58 Medieval pewter spoon

59 Hughes family balance, 9s 3d. (46p) in Harrods' Catalogue of 1929

60 Metal scales and weights. Late nineteenth century. Gustav Holst's Birthplace Museum, Cheltenham

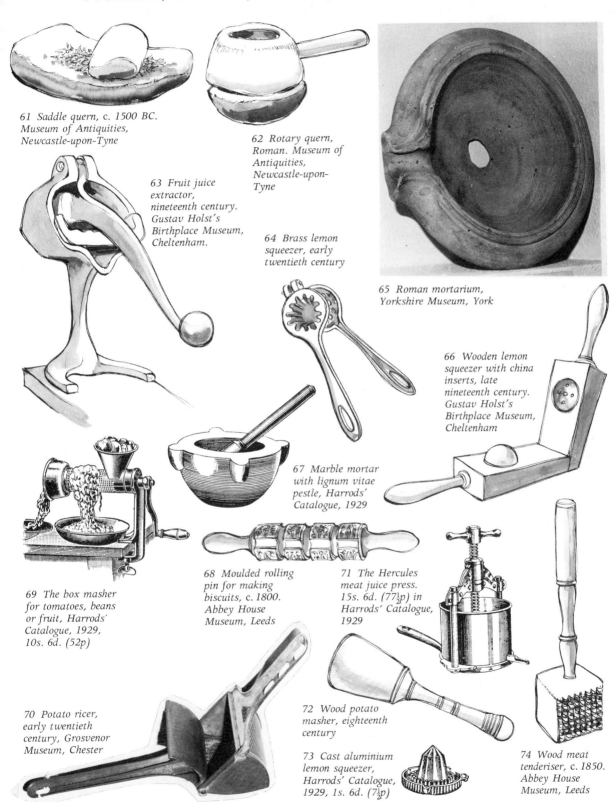

61 Saddle quern, c. 1500 BC. Museum of Antiquities, Newcastle-upon-Tyne

62 Rotary quern, Roman. Museum of Antiquities, Newcastle-upon-Tyne

63 Fruit juice extractor, nineteenth century. Gustav Holst's Birthplace Museum, Cheltenham.

64 Brass lemon squeezer, early twentieth century

65 Roman mortarium, Yorkshire Museum, York

66 Wooden lemon squeezer with china inserts, late nineteenth century. Gustav Holst's Birthplace Museum, Cheltenham

67 Marble mortar with lignum vitae pestle, Harrods' Catalogue, 1929

69 The box masher for tomatoes, beans or fruit, Harrods' Catalogue, 1929, 10s. 6d. (52p)

68 Moulded rolling pin for making biscuits, c. 1800. Abbey House Museum, Leeds

71 The Hercules meat juice press. 15s. 6d. (77½p) in Harrods' Catalogue, 1929

70 Potato ricer, early twentieth century, Grosvenor Museum, Chester

72 Wood potato masher, eighteenth century

73 Cast aluminium lemon squeezer, Harrods' Catalogue, 1929, 1s. 6d. (7½p)

74 Wood meat tenderiser, c. 1850. Abbey House Museum, Leeds

The Roman army also introduced the *mortarium* into the British home. It was a large, shallow general-purpose mixing bowl which had a moulded rim round the exterior edge and a pouring spout on one side. Grit was worked into the clay surface of the bowl before the mortarium was fired and this roughened it for grinding purposes (65). Although this type of bowl disappeared with the departure of the Romans some type of rotary quern and mortar and pestle have continued in use in the home until modern times (67).

Mashers and crushers have also been used for centuries. The traditional design of potato masher was in the form of a gavel or club as was also that of the sugar crusher (72). More complex designs appeared in the nineteenth century (70). Meat tenderisers were also club-shaped but with a diamond-cut surface on the pounding side (74).

There has always been a need for equipment to press and squeeze the juice from fruit and vegetables, as well as meat and fowl. The Romans crushed olives to make oil with the aid of a mill which consisted of two cylindrical stones rolled back and forth over the fruit contained in a circular trough. They then pressed the crushed fruit, having first removed the stones. Different designs of lemon squeezer have been used over the centuries. Most of these were made of hard wood fashioned with a depression to receive the fruit. The most usual nineteenth-century design was formed from two flat pieces of wood hinged together. Inset into one piece was a glazed pottery cone and into the other a perforated dish. These were then closed to squeeze the fruit (66). By the later nineteenth century various mechanical devices had become available for extracting juice, operated by a handle or lever (63, 64, 69, 71).

Grating, straining and sieving, mincing, peeling, coring, stoning

Utensils for straining and sieving, as also for grating food are traditional. Funnels, sieves, colanders and strainers of different kinds have been found at Pompeii and other archaeological sites of Ancient Rome. These were made of pottery or bronze and, where needed, with fine metal mesh (82, 84, 85, 86). Graters have also been used from earliest times for various foods. They varied in size from large ones for breadcrumbs to tiny graters complete with lid to form a fitted box which could be slipped into a person's pocket so that a little spice, nutmeg for example, could be grated into a hot drink (77, 80, 83).

Until the second half of the nineteenth century the other processes in this group had to be carried out by knife or chopper. It was in the late 1850s that the earliest machines for peeling and coring fruit and vegetables began to be designed, first in the USA. From then onwards a number of hand-operated mechanical appliances were produced from America, Britain and Europe. Many, especially in the 1880s and 1890s, were of complex design, comprising numerous wheels, cogs and levers. There were machines to core, peel and slice apples, peel potatoes, stone raisins or cherries (79, 81, 87). There were also the invaluable mincing machines, to be found in all well-run kitchens. These altered little from the original cast-iron models, changing only to cast aluminium from the 1890s (76).

Mixing and beating

These again are operations which cooks have been required to carry out since earliest days. There was no relief from the hard work involved until hand-operated mixers appeared on the market in the last quarter of the nineteenth century and, even then, turning the handle for a long period, though easier than beating with fork or spoon, was still tiring (89, 90). It was the provision of electric power which made all the difference to such equipment and this became a possibility for various designs of blending and beating machines, mixing bowls attached, by 1918. In Britain electric food mixers did not become generally available until after the Second World War. The Kenwood design appeared in 1947 as a free-standing table model which developed over the years to become, in the words of the manufacturer, 'a complete food preparation appliance'. The latest Kenwood Chef is equipped with an impressive array of attachments which, among other activities, extract juice, shred and slice, beat, blend and liquidise, make cream and grind coffee. Moreover, modern technology has also helped to reduce the cost of operating the appliance by the fitting of a new electronic (thyristor) device which enables the electric power from the mains to be employed more efficiently (88). The latest labour-saver in this field is the food processor which carries out all the different tasks done by the food mixer, including its attachments but using only one bowl and one of the four blades provided.

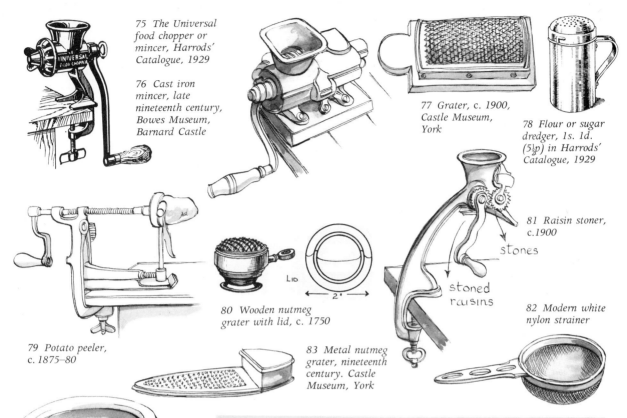

75 The Universal food chopper or mincer, Harrods' Catalogue, 1929

76 Cast iron mincer, late nineteenth century, Bowes Museum, Barnard Castle

77 Grater, c. 1900, Castle Museum, York

78 Flour or sugar dredger, 1s. 1d. (5½p) in Harrods' Catalogue, 1929

81 Raisin stoner, c.1900

stones

stoned raisins

82 Modern white nylon strainer

80 Wooden nutmeg grater with lid, c. 1750

LID

2″

79 Potato peeler, c. 1875–80

83 Metal nutmeg grater, nineteenth century. Castle Museum, York

84 Earthenware colander, Roman. Corinium Museum, Cirencester

85 Cast aluminium colander, 30s. (£1.50p) in Harrods' Catalogue, 1929

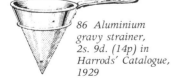

86 Aluminium gravy strainer, 2s. 9d. (14p) in Harrods' Catalogue, 1929

87 'Dandy' apple peeler, slicer and corer, c. 1900. Metal, 18–20 in. high. Science Museum, London

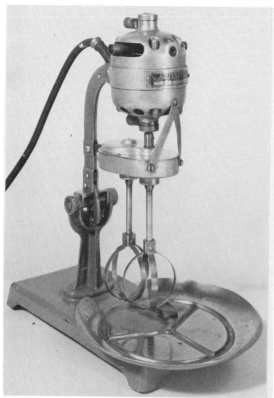

88 *'Universal' electric mixer-beater, 1918, made by Landers, Frary and Clark, USA. Double rotary mixer with many attachments. Science Museum, London*

89 *Home cake mixer, 1896. Hand-operated. Twin plates rotate in opposite directions when handle is turned. Science Museum, London*

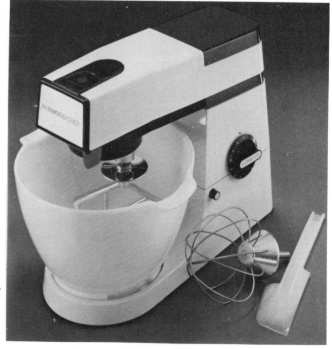

90 *Tin egg beater made in two parts. Cheltenham City Museum*

91 *The electronic Kenwood Chef, 1978. By courtesy of Thorn Domestic Appliances (Electrical) Ltd*

Moulds and cutters

Jelly was made from Medieval times from calves' feet and bone-stock. With the addition of flavouring and colouring it was used as a base for sweet and savoury dishes. From the sixteenth century isinglass[6] was being produced commercially for sale as a base for jellies; aspic was an eighteenth century creation. Shaped moulds were used more widely as time passed for jellies of all kinds, brawn, puddings, butter, cakes – especially gingerbread – soft cheese and biscuits. Such moulds were made in an infinite variety of forms based on animal, floral and geometrical shapes (94, 95, 96). Metal cutters were made in fancy designs to shape the edges of pastry, cakes and biscuits (93).

Tea and coffee making

The first shipment of tea from the East was brought to Europe by the Dutch East India Company in 1609. It was very expensive, selling in London at £3 10s. (£3.50p) per pound. Despite its cost the new beverage soon became a fashionable drink and by 1689 the price had fallen to £1 per pound and 20,000 pounds were imported that year. By the eighteenth century tea had become cheap enough to be a popular drink though it was carefully hoarded in the home, kept under lock and key in a caddy[7] by the mistress of the house or the housekeeper who doled it out when required.

This vogue for tea-drinking brought about the design of utensils needed for the new beverage: teapots, hot-water jugs, milk and cream jugs, tea-caddies and sugar bowls.[8] This vogue also brought the kettle into greater prominence. Originally a kettle was a vessel for boiling water or cooking food immersed in liquid over the open fire. There were fish kettles[9], ham kettles, etc. and these were metal, lidded containers (see page 65). Gradually the kettle developed into a lidded vessel with handle and spout, in which water was boiled (153, 154, 155, 230). With the advent of tea-drinking, elegant tea-kettles were made in silver, brass and copper which could be heated by a spirit stove below and were supported on a stand; these were for drawing-room use (97). The traditional design of kettle, made of iron or copper, was still boiled over the fire or on the range hot-plate (99).

The first electric kettle was shown at the Chicago World Fair in 1893 and this was quickly followed by other designs, but all the early electric kettles were very slow to boil, (indeed, it was quicker to boil one's kettle on a gas cooker) because the element was fixed to the base of the kettle so a great deal of energy was lost in warming up the base as well as the water. With the introduction of a heating element enclosed in a

MOULDS AND CUTTERS

92 China blancmange mould, nineteenth century. Paisley Museum

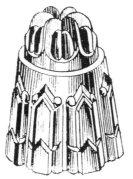

94 Tin jelly mould, 1 pint size, 1s. 10d. (9p) in Harrods' Catalogue, 1929

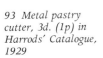

93 Metal pastry cutter, 3d. (1p) in Harrods' Catalogue, 1929

95 Balmoral fluted copper cake mould, 1 pint, 11d (5p) in Harrods' Catalogue, 1929

96 Copper jelly mould (standing on bone apple corer), Cheltenham City Museum

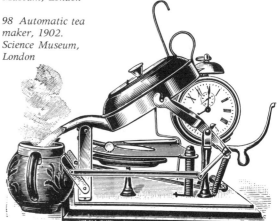

97 Silver tea-kettle and stand, 1730–1. Victoria and Albert Museum, London

98 Automatic tea maker, 1902. Science Museum, London

99 Iron kettle with brass tap hanging over open fire, eighteenth century. Manor Farm Museum, Cogges

100 Goblin teasmade, 1937. Drawn from Goblin booklet 'The Teasmade Story starts here'. By courtesy of BSR (Housewares) Ltd.

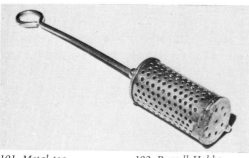

101 Metal tea infuser, 2 in. long. Grosvenor Museum, Chester

102 Russell Hobbs K2 automatic electric kettle, 1970s. Drawn from photograph supplied by manufacturers

103 Polished aluminium whistling kettle, 1949. Tower Brand. By courtesy of TI Housewares Ltd

tube and immersed in the water a great improvement in efficiency was achieved. The Swan kettle was the first to have this new element incorporated and appeared on the market in the early 1920s. Early designs of electric kettle were, like other early utensils powered by electricity, not very safe or reliable. Gradually improvements and safety factors were introduced; these were mainly aimed at breaking the contact by plugs which melted or were self-ejecting if the apparatus overheated. Modern electric kettles are automatically controlled to switch off when the water reaches boiling point (102).

The luxury of being able to enjoy one's early morning tea in bed inspired the early designers of mechanical gadgets to produce a tea-making appliance. Some of these were extremely hazardous with a more-than-even chance of being woken up with an explosion rather than a friendly cuppa. Mr Rowbottom patented a complex device in 1891 which comprised an alarm clock, a gas burner, kettle, teapot and a complicated arrangement of levers, valves and tubes, including a lighted gas jet. In 1902 Frank Smith, a Birmingham gunsmith, produced a tea-making machine which was heated by methylated spirits ignited by the automatic striking of a match. The action of the apparatus was initiated by the ringing of an alarm clock which would ring a second time when the tea was ready for drinking. One suspects that the repeated sounding might have been superfluous (98). The household name in tea-making machines is Goblin. The Teasmade was invented in 1936 by Brenner Thornton and put on the market the following year. Powered by electricity, this comprised an alarm clock, tea-pot, water-boiling container or kettle, two cups and saucers, cream jug and sugar-basin, all for £5 15s. 6d. (£5.77½p) (100).

Coffee first appeared in Britain at much the same time as tea. First harvested in Ethiopia in 1450, it became a popular drink with the Moslem peoples by the sixteenth century and the custom soon spread to the Venetian sphere of influence. The first coffee house in England opened in Oxford in 1650.

Whereas tea has in general been made in Britain in a traditional manner with only small variations in the method, coffee-making has inspired a variety of procedures which have been employed from the eighteenth century onwards. Tea is purchased in the form in which it is required for making the infusion. Coffee beans need roasting and grinding and the ground coffee may then be heated in a pan or pot with water, percolated, filtered or infused by steam under pressure.

A variety of appliances were introduced in the nineteenth century for grinding coffee in the home. Many people preferred to do this themselves, although ground coffee could be purchased from about 1850. The small domestic models were set on a table; the coffee was ground by turning a handle and a drawer was generally provided to receive it (106, 108). Hand-operated roasters were also put on the market in the nineteenth century (107). Some models could be attached to the fire-bars of the grate and were operated mechanically by clockwork (112).

In the early years of the nineteenth century Count Rumford[10] designed a coffee-maker which worked on the drip method. As a result of his research into the roasting of coffee beans, he believed this system to be the most suitable for retaining the flavour of the coffee since the water would not be over-agitated. He illustrated and described his appliance in a paper entitled 'Of the Excellent Qualities of Coffee'. This was not the earliest example of the drip method but almost certainly would have worked more satisfactorily than previous ones. Rumford's coffee-maker was heated by a spirit stove and was encased in a water jacket which was filled with boiling water to keep the coffee hot. The ground coffee was held in a container with a filter beneath. The heated water trickled through the ground coffee to be retained in the main vessel beneath(104).

From the early years of the twentieth century a variety of designs of coffee-makers became available. There were percolators heated by attached spirit-stove or suitable to be placed on the gas cooker (105), simple, two-part metal containers to be heated on the stove and French-style filter coffee pots (109). The Cona system was marketed, consisting of two glass bowls one placed above the other and fitting into it with a central glass pipe held by a rubber seal. This apparatus, which retains its popularity today, contains water in the lower vessel and ground coffee in the upper. When heated beneath, the water boils, then is forced up the pipe into the upper vessel by the steam. The heat is removed, the coffee is infused and, as the lower bowl cools and the steam condenses, a partial vacuum is created. The higher pressure in the upper vessel then forces the liquid coffee down into the emptied lower vessel (110).

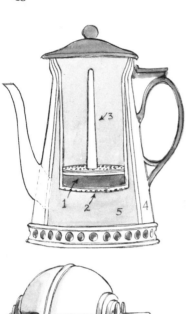

104 Rumford's design for a coffee-maker on the drip method. (Drawn from illustration in original paper).
1 Coffee grounds in container
2 Filter through which coffee drips
3 Rammer holding container lid in place
4 Jacket containing hot water
5 Coffee vessel
6 Perforated copper base which stands on spirit lamp

105 Aluminium coffee percolater. Tower Brand, 1949. By courtesy of Tower Housewares Ltd

106 Coffee grinder, nineteenth century. St Nicholas' Priory Museum, Exeter

107 Hand-operated metal coffee roaster, mid-nineteenth century. Torquay Museum

108 Wooden coffee mill. Salisbury Museum

109 Tin cafetière on French pattern. 5s. 6d. (27½p) in Harrods' Catalogue, 1929

110 Cona coffee machine, 21s. (£1.05p) in Harrods' Catalogue, 1929

111 Bialetti Moka Express coffee maker, 1974 (author)

112 Mechanical, metal coffee roaster designed to hang on fire bars. Torquay Museum

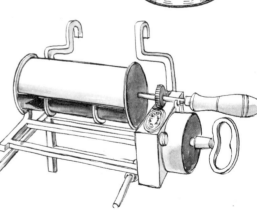

Typical of the modern coffee-maker are the Italian metal espresso designs of which Bialetti's Moka Express is very popular. Heated on the gas or electric cooker, the water in the lower vessel is forced by steam pressure upwards through the ground coffee contained in a metal filter compartment through a metal tube to the upper vessel. This method has a high extraction rate though the water only passes once through the coffee (111). The first fully automatic electrically powered coffee percolator with a keep-hot device was invented in the early 1950s by Bill Russell and Peter Hobbs and is now a classic of its kind.

Cream, butter, cheese

Dairy-work was an important factor in enabling households to remain self-sufficient. Until comparatively modern times large country homes and farmhouses still produced their own cream, butter and cheese and sold produce to the towns. The dairy (113) (see chapter 1 page 21) had to be kept spotlessly clean and the utensils, which were mostly of wood,[11] even more so or the milk would not keep. In early times, and later in remote areas, there was no hot water available for this purpose so the vessels were filled with cold water and pebbles made hot in the fire were put in to them.

The milk from the cow was collected in wooden milk cogs;[12] in Scotland this was a luggie[13] (116). The milk was then poured into a lead tray or wide, shallow bowls made of wood, earthenware or enamelled metal to cool it from the 90°F, which was its temperature when taken from the cow, to about 50°F (124). The cream, which had then risen to the surface, was skimmed off with a flat skimmer which had holes in it for the milk to drain through (120), and agitated in a churn to separate the butter from the buttermilk.

There were many types of butter churn. The oldest designs were very simple. One was a wooden tub which was tilted up and down. Another was a lidded wooden bowl which was suspended by cords from the handles fitted to its sides and swung to and fro. In both these models the butter forming process took many hours. The most common type was the plunger churn (129) which consisted of a tall, slender, wooden staved barrel bound with wooden hoops or metal bands. The churn was fitted with a lid through the centre of which ran a long wooden handle which had a perforated plunger attachment at its foot. The

113 *Mid-eighteenth century dairy. Setting milk and making butter*

dairymaid had to push this handle up and down to make the butter form (113). Also often used was the rocker churn (128) which was made in a number of forms which could either be rocked like a cradle or swung suspended from a stand.

In the nineteenth century most butter churns were of the box or barrel type where wooden paddles inside were turned by a handle outside. The paddles were fitted into a square-shaped structure on legs or a barrel on a stand (126, 127). This developed into the more advanced end-over-end barrel churn where the external shape and construction was unaltered but usually there were no internal paddles. When the handle was operated the whole barrel was turned over and over (131).

The butter then had to be salted. It was soaked in brine for an hour or two, then removed by scoop (123) into a sieve. It then had to be worked to expel all excess moisture. In earlier times this was done by kneading it against the sides of a wooden bowl or squeezing it with a rigid wooden roller (118). In the

114 Roman cheese press. Yorkshire Museum, York

115 Metal cream scalder. Bowl would be filled with burning charcoal and cream pan placed on top. Torquay Museum

116 Wooden milk luggie with iron bands. Highland Folk Museum, Kingussie

117 Wooden mungle used for stirring cream. City Museum, Hereford

118 Wooden butter roller. Christchurch Mansion, Ipswich

119 Butter patters (Scotch hands). City Museum, Hereford

120 Wooden cream skimmer. Highland Folk Museum, Kingussie

121 Wooden cheesart and lid. Highland Folk Museum, Kingussie

122 Wooden butter stamp. Museum for Social History, Kings Lynn

123 Butter scoop, late nineteenth century. City Museum, Hereford

124 Milk setting lead on wooden stand, late nineteenth century. Manor Farm, Cogges

125 Butter-maker, mid-nineteenth century. City Museum, Hereford

126 Wooden box churn nineteenth century. Manor Farm Museum, Cogges

130 Wooden butter worker on wooden stand, nineteenth century. Buckinghamshire County Museum, Aylesbury

127 Wooden box churn in barrel shape, metal bands, nineteenth century. Carlisle Museum

131 End-over-end barrel butter churn. Manor Farm Museum, Cogges. Late nineteenth century

128 Wooden rocker churn, late nineteenth century

129 Wooden plunger churn, iron bands, nineteenth century. Highland Folk Museum, Kingussie

nineteenth century the butter worker was made which provided an easier and more efficient way of carrying out the task. This was a wooden tray mounted on a stand which was fitted with a ridged wooden rolling pin. The operating handle was turned to move the roller over the butter so expelling the liquid which drained away through a hole in the tray (130).

The butter was finally weighed and stored in casks. To prepare it for sale it was shaped into pats by a pair of butter patters, also known as butter hands or Scotch hands (119). These were wooden bats with grooved blades. Pats were often finished by imprinting the house or farm symbol with a carved butter stamp (122).

Cheese-making was a longer process. First the milk was heated in a large vessel (cheese kettle) and rennet[14] was added to curdle the milk, after which it was poured into covered wooden tubs. When the curds had formed various methods, according to the locality or the size of house or farm, were used to make the cheese. For soft cheeses, fresh buttermilk and a little milk were mixed with the curds and this was then poured into a cheese mould and pressed to extract the whey. These moulds were made of pottery or metal and were designed with holes through which the whey could drain out.

For hard cheeses made at home the usual method was to wrap the curds in a muslin cloth and place this in a cheeser or cheesart, which was a wooden vessel with a shelf with holes bored in it, set part-way down inside to allow the whey to drain into the bottom of the vessel when pressure was put on the curds; a heavy stone generally acted as a weight for this. In larger establishments a cheese press would be used (114, 121).

When the cheese had been sufficiently pressed it was stamped in the same way as butter and stored in a cheese cupboard or room. The cheese then had to be turned regularly until ripe.

The preserving and preparing of food stocks in the home

Before the development of the fertiliser industry and the days of refrigerators the maintaining of stocks of food and drink for the survival of the household through the winter months constituted a serious problem. Until the seventeenth century the greater part of the cattle, sheep and goats, apart from breeding

stock, had to be slaughtered in autumn as there was no winter feed available for them. This meat was then salted and cured for winter consumption (see chapter 5 page 111). Even as late as the mid-eighteenth century animal winter feed was not adequate to avoid extensive slaughtering. The problem was a dual one. Because the feed was inadequate the cattle had to be killed. Because the animals were killed, the fields had no natural manure to grow winter feed. It was only in the eighteenth century that improvements in agriculture – better transport and communications, more effective equipment and increased knowledge – led to the growing of winter crops of clover, rye-grass, buckwheat and root vegetables for winter fodder. At the same time a system of summer stall feeding of cattle and housing of sheep produced accumulations of organic manure and arrangements were made for town sewage waste to be collected and supplied to farms. In the nineteenth century came the development of the artificial fertiliser industry to supplement the organic material and help to feed the rapidly growing population.

The preserved meat used throughout the winter required strong flavouring to disguise its doubtful taste. From Roman times onwards cooks used a quantity of herbs and spices for this purpose. Most households grew and dried their own herbs. The costly spices were imported and so were carefully kept under lock and key in boxes and cabinets in which they were stored whole and ground as needed (132, 138). Great quantities of salt were needed for the preservation of meat and fish. It came from coastal areas where it was produced by evaporation processes, and also from salt mines. In some coastal districts meat was soaked in the sea because the salt was too expensive – it bore a tax – for poorer families. The salt box in the home was hung on the wall near the fire to keep the contents dry. The box was made of wood usually with a leather hinge to avoid rusting. Salt was also kept by the fire in an earthenware jar (133, 136).

Other tasks to prepare the household for the winter were smoking and curing bacon and ham, pickling vegetables, making conserves of flowers and fruit, bottling fruit and vegetables, making lard and other cooking fats. All kinds of drinks were made at home. Ale was brewed and cider, perry and mead were also made regularly. Fruit wines and cordials were produced in quantity. The Romans made wine from

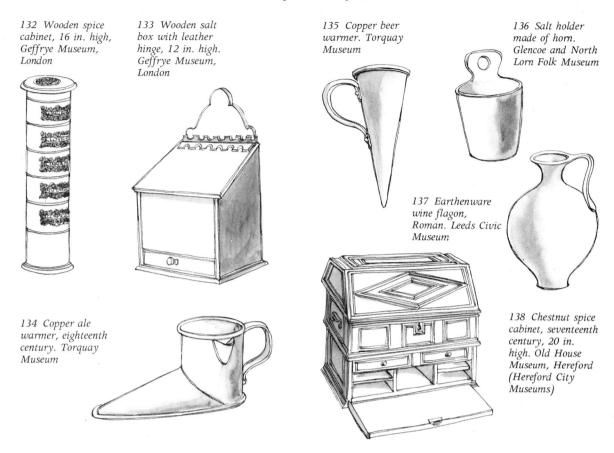

132 *Wooden spice cabinet, 16 in. high, Geffrye Museum, London*

133 *Wooden salt box with leather hinge, 12 in. high. Geffrye Museum, London*

135 *Copper beer warmer. Torquay Museum*

136 *Salt holder made of horn. Glencoe and North Lorn Folk Museum*

137 *Earthenware wine flagon, Roman. Leeds Civic Museum*

134 *Copper ale warmer, eighteenth century. Torquay Museum*

138 *Chestnut spice cabinet, seventeenth century, 20 in. high. Old House Museum, Hereford (Hereford City Museums)*

grapes which they grew in terraces, mainly in the West Country. The custom largely died out in the Middle Ages and wine was imported from the Continent thereafter. Ale and wine were usually taken mulled in cold weather. The liquid was mixed with sugar, spices and, sometimes, yolk of egg and heated at the fire in special warmers or mullers. These were made of copper or iron in a slipper or conical shape with an attached handle. The slipper design was preferred as it would stand in the hearth without need of attention (134, 135).

CHAPTER THREE

The Cooking of Food 1

The Open Hearth: Roman Times to *c.* 1800

Fuel, hearth and chimney

In Roman Britain most of the cooking was done on the raised hearth (see chapter 1, page 12). Although coal was known to the Romans, it was not mined but was dug from outcrops and used chiefly for heating. Charcoal was the preferred fuel for cooking; it is thought that the fumes, which would have been injurious to health, would have been directed into a wall flue by a hood erected over the hearth. Holes, about one foot in diameter and six inches deep, were set into the hearth and charcoal fires were lit in them. The cooking vessels – metal (generally bronze) skillets and frying pans, also earthenware pots – were supported over these fires on iron tripods or stood on an iron gridiron (1, 2, 139, 140). Such a hearth with charcoal in the cavities and gridiron with cooking vessels in place was found at Pompeii, just as it had been in use when the volcano erupted.

Slow cooking could be carried out in a large metal, lidded cauldron or earthenware casserole which stood on legs over a hearth fire. Cooking in this way, gently over a low heat for a long period of time, was the commonest method because it was difficult to judge the time and control the fire at higher temperatures. However, roasting was done over an open wood fire; larger animals were turned on a spit, smaller ones, such as sucking pig or fowl, were cooked in cauldrons which were suspended over the fire by chains from an iron tripod. Baking was done in an oven (see page 14).

For several centuries after the departure of the Romans cooking in Britain was conducted in a primitive manner over or in front of an open wood fire. For a long time this was stacked up in the open and the control of temperature and timing was a hit-and-miss affair with the food being charred on the exterior and undercooked within.

During the early Middle Ages slowly the hearth was brought indoors and the fire burned on a flat stone slab set in the centre of the room. Logs were piled up against a pair of andirons[1] which supported them while burning. An andiron was a horizontal iron bar which had a foot at one end and, at the other, a pillar extending upwards; the lower end of this pillar divided into a pair of feet (149, 152). This central fire supplied both warmth for the living room and heat for cooking. The smoke escaped through the rafters above. In larger buildings a slatted louvre was built into the roof to allow for exit of smoke (144).

Until the development of the kitchen range in the later eighteenth century (chapter 4) all cooking of food, with the exception of baking (see ovens, page 78) continued to be done above or in front of the open fire, although over the centuries methods advanced to become more sophisticated and labour-saving. The food was roasted in front of the fire on a turning spit or broiled or grilled on a gridiron over or in front of the fire. Alternatively, and most often, it was stewed or boiled in a vessel which was suspended over the fire or which stood on short legs in or at the edge of the fire. Sometimes pans were held over the fire by means of long handles. In the early Middle Ages vessels were suspended over the fire by the simple arrangement of a horizontal iron bar, which held one or two pots, attached to a vertical post set in the hearth. All water had to be boiled in large metal cauldrons suspended in this way or in a cauldron standing on legs and set in the fire (7, 141, 151).

The medieval hearth was gradually moved from the centre of the room to stand against a wall where the fire was built on a slab of stone or metal raised slightly above the general floor level. Such a wall hearth, generally referred to as a down hearth, was set in a deep recess, usually arched, under a wide flue up which the smoke could escape to the exterior (7, 8, 9,

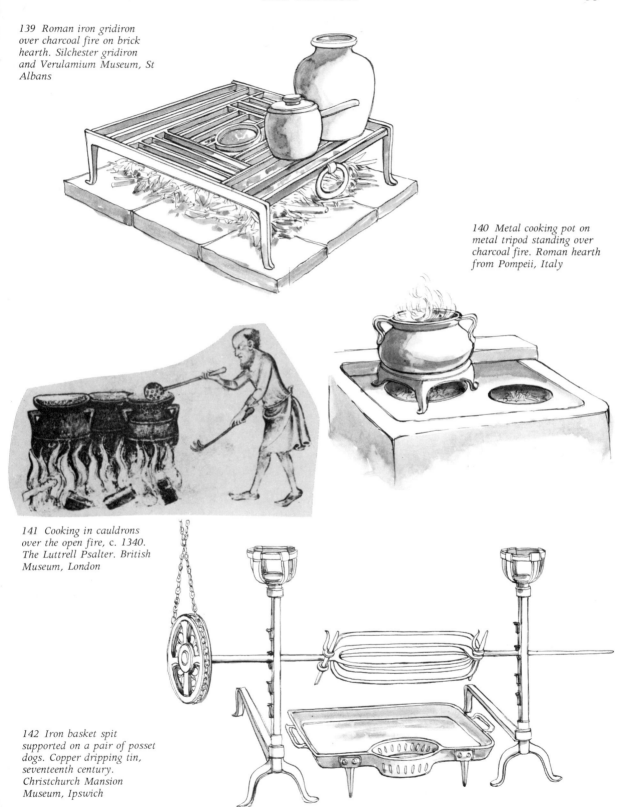

139 Roman iron gridiron over charcoal fire on brick hearth. Silchester gridiron and Verulamium Museum, St Albans

140 Metal cooking pot on metal tripod standing over charcoal fire. Roman hearth from Pompeii, Italy

141 Cooking in cauldrons over the open fire, c. 1340. The Luttrell Psalter. British Museum, London

142 Iron basket spit supported on a pair of posset dogs. Copper dripping tin, seventeenth century. Christchurch Mansion Museum, Ipswich

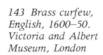

143 *Brass curfew, English, 1600–50. Victoria and Albert Museum, London*

144 *Brick central hearth. Iron fire-dogs, c. 1200. Penshurst Place, Kent*

145 *Steel and brass basket grate, c. 1760*

146 *Mechanical bellows. A steady draught was obtained by turning the handle. Torquay Museum*

147 *Hand bellows, nineteenth century. Tiverton Museum*

148 *Wood fan bellows, operated by turning the handle on the disc. Torquay Museum*

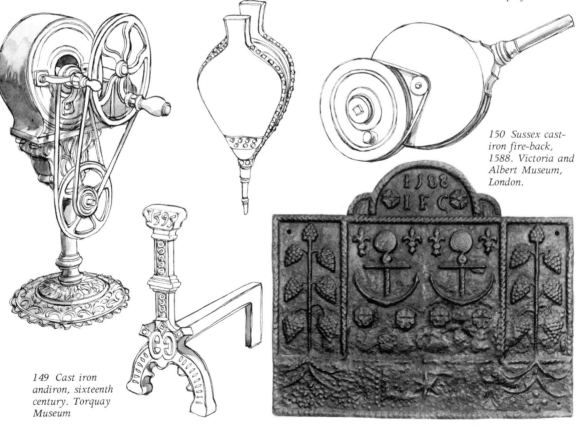

150 *Sussex cast-iron fire-back, 1588. Victoria and Albert Museum, London.*

149 *Cast iron andiron, sixteenth century. Torquay Museum*

151 St Fagans castle kitchen hearth, Welsh Folk Museum, National Museum of Wales, Cardiff, sixteenth century. Spit turned by smoke jack set in chimney, eighteenth century. Note eighteenth- and nineteenth-century equipment. Left to right: spit rack, salamanders, wafering iron, standing toaster, chimney crane, kettle with tilter, iron fire-back, dripping pan, pronged spit, cauldron, cob-irons, camp type of oven

10, 151). In large wall fireplaces, in particular, the heat was so fierce that it would damage the wall at the back of the flue, so cast-iron firebacks were placed in front of the wall behind the fire. These performed a dual function: to protect the wall and to reflect the heat of the fire. Early examples were plain but, by the sixteenth and seventeenth centuries, many were very decorative. Such ornamented firebacks came chiefly from the iron foundries of Kent and Sussex (9, 10, 150, 151, 152).

Andirons also became ornamented from the fifteenth century onwards, particularly the front pillar and feet. This pillar became taller and was often finished at the top in a saucer or cup form to hold a mug or small vessel and keep the contents hot. Because these cups were generally in use for hot drinks, this type of andiron was referred to as a posset-dog (10, 142). As time passed more complex means of suspen-sion of pots over the fire were evolved, using chimney hooks, chains, bars and cranes. This development is described on page 75 under chimney crane. In the Highlands of Scotland the cooking pot or girdle was often suspended from an iron chain (*slabhraidh*), which was itself attached by means of an iron bar or rope to a wooden crossbar high up in the chimney flue, or, if a central hearth was still in use, from the roof. These chains could be looped up or let down to adjust the suitable position for the pot over the fire (153).

Until the second half of the seventeenth century the

usual fuel for the kitchen fire was wood, though peat was widely used in more remote country districts. The burning of one type of wood produced much the same heat as the burning of another, but certain woods were preferred for fuel because of other attributes. For instance, the wood from the ash-tree burns with a hot, clear flame, beech gives an even heat, cherry wood is particularly suited to oven cooking. On the other hand, conifer and other resinous woods were avoided

because of the dark smoke which they produce when burning and poplar because it gives out an unpleasant smell.

Coal had been in use for burning in domestic grates since the thirteenth century, but was only readily available in colliery districts and in coastal towns which were accessible to the sea-coal supplies brought

152 *Stone hooded kitchen fireplace, based upon that in the Old House, Hereford, fifteenth century. Note: spit rack above fireplace also later chimney crane, cast iron fireback, andirons and cauldron. Hereford City Museums*

153 *Scottish Highland cottage hearth, based on that in Glenesk Trust Museum, Brechin. Note: wood canopy, peat fire, iron fender and cauldron hanging from pot chain*

in by small boats plying from the collieries. Transport of coal was costly over long distances and people did not waste it by using it on kitchen fires unless they lived in an area readily accessible so that they could collect it themselves. Also, coal was unsuitable for burning on the open fire so it was only in colliery and coastal areas that hearths were developed to burn it (see page 61).

Every endeavour was made to keep the fire burning in the kitchen open hearth because re-lighting it was so difficult (see chapter 8). At night the ashes were drawn over the embers to bank the fire down and a curfew placed over the top because it was dangerous to leave a fire uncovered when untended, especially in a wooden building. The curfew[2] (also known as a nightcap) was an oval- or bell-shaped cover with a handle on top and was usually made of iron or brass. Some designs were elaborately decorated (143). An alternative pattern was more conical in shape and had a handle at the side. This design could also serve,

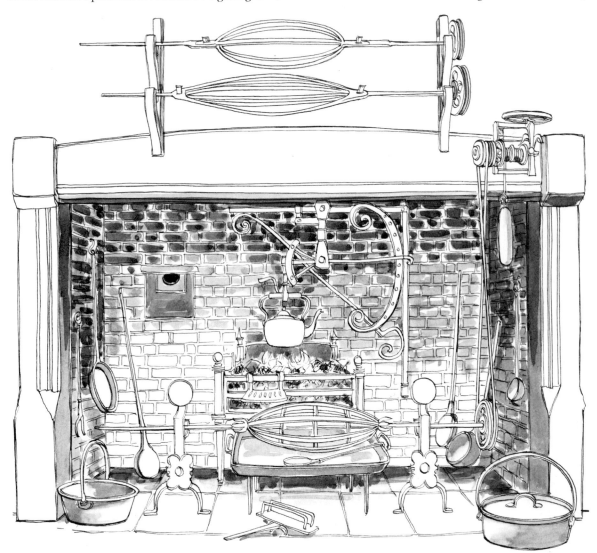

154 *Brick fireplace with wood surround, c. 1680–1720. Based upon that displayed in the Hearth Gallery in Castle Museum, York. Note: basket spit rack on chimney breast then, left to right, frying pan, salamander, brass cauldron, iron and steel grate, cob-irons, basket spit, dripping tray and down-hearth toaster. Spit driven by mechanical weight jack. Chimney crane fixed to back of hearth carries copper kettle with tilter. Wafering iron, ladles, iron cauldron. Note especially salt container built into wall of chimney (left) to keep salt dry, with hole for hand to extract salt*

when inverted, for carrying some embers away to light a fire elsewhere in the house.

Although in country areas poorer people continued to burn wood or peat until well into the nineteenth century[3], coal was steadily replacing wood as the general domestic fuel in the later seventeenth century. The great forests which had covered so much of the country when William of Normandy conquered Britain in 1066 had been steadily depleted by clearance for cultivation and felling for the use of the

wood. In the sixteenth century shortage of timber was beginning to become apparent and this was aggravated by the development of the iron trade, centred at that time in the heavily wooded areas of Kent, Sussex and the Forest of Dean where extensive felling was carried out to make charcoal for smelting, without any replanting schemes to replace the timber. From this time onwards various forms of legislation were passed in order to restrict the indiscriminate felling of certain types of timber, so that gradually coal began to take

155 *Eighteenth-century stone fireplace. Based upon that in Bowes Museum, Barnard Castle. Spit powered by smoke jack in chimney. Fire basket, cob-irons, dripping tray,* chimney crane, spits with wheels and implements of iron, steel or brass. Note also: standing toaster, copper kettle, brass cauldron, hanging spit wheels

the place of wood as a domestic fuel. But this was a slow process and many households continued to burn permitted and dead woods in an open kitchen hearth until nearly the end of the eighteenth century, while in the remote areas the practice continued long after this.

The change-over to the use of coal posed a problem in that the open hearth, which had been traditional for centuries, had to be adapted in order to light and burn coal satisfactorily. It was difficult to kindle coal on a flat hearth as a draught was needed underneath the fire[4]. Also, the andirons which had been suitable to support logs were of no use in containing lumps of coal, or 'sea-coles' as they were then termed. It was found helpful to put the coal in an iron firebasket which had bars in front and a slatted floor beneath. By the late seventeenth century this basket was attached to the andirons which stood, as before, flanking the basket which was then raised above the level of the hearth. This type of design was known as a dog grate (10, 155). It was fairly quickly followed by the next stage, where the fireback became attached to the andirons so making a robust basket standing on legs well above hearth level and a self-contained unit

156 Cast-iron hob grate, late eighteenth century. Drawn from a combination of museum sources. Brick hearth and chimney. Iron chimney crane and griddle. Steel and brass fender and fire irons. Brass bottle jack. Copper kettle. Note also: salamander, rushlight container attached to brick walling and marram grass besom

within the fireplace. This was the basket grate which was in use for much of the eighteenth century and could be seen in its plain form suited to the kitchen and in various beautifully decorated designs in polished steel of which the Robert Adam grates of the 1760s and 1770s were superb examples (10, 145).

The final stage of open grate came about mid-eighteenth century. In this design, the hob grate (12, 156), the firebox was flanked by iron plates which fitted into the fireplace instead of standing free as before. Kettles and pans could then be placed on the flat horizontal surfaces on each side of the fire: these were the hobs. In order to increase the draught to make the fire burn hotter and better, the fireplace aperture had now been considerably decreased. The hob grate was popular despite its tendency to smoke and various means were experimented with to deal with the problem, such as designing different forms of flue and incorporating blowing mechanisms. Despite these efforts the smoke nuisance was not noticeably abated until the development in the late eighteenth century of the kitchen range. Though they were difficult to clean and they overheated the kitchen in summer, these appliances represented an advance on the hob grate in efficiency and economy of fuel consumption. Designs are fully discussed in chapter 4.

Most eighteenth-century hearths were equipped with a cavity or cupboard inserted into the wall at one side of the fireplace and this was closed by an iron door. These spaces were used for keeping dishes hot and for mulling wines. If the fire was large and hot enough, pies could be baked there (12).

With the contraction of the fireplace opening, the chimney flues became narrower also. Before the eighteenth century it had been a relatively simple matter to set up ladders inside the great chimney flues so that the opening could be brushed and scraped to clean it. With the narrower eighteenth-century flues, the dangerous practice was often followed of lighting a fire in the chimney to burn off the soot. The alternative was to send for the chimney sweep, most of whom were employing small boys who were able to get inside the restricted flues to clean them. This iniquitous practice continued until 1875.

Cooking vessels

The form of these changed hardly at all over the centuries from those used in Romano-British kitchens until the development of the hob grate in the eighteenth century. They were heavy and strongly made in order to stand up to being set by or over a hot open fire and were simple in design. The vessels which came near or into contact with the fire were made of metal: iron, copper, brass, bronze. Those which were supported near the fire or were put inside within a metal container were often of earthenware.

Boiling, stewing and simmering were widely employed methods of cooking, so vessels of varied size had to be available. Since they did not need to be set down on a flat surface until the availability of the eighteenth-century hob grate, they were made with rounded bottoms in order to achieve an even distribution of heat. They could be suspended over the fire by a handle which was hooked on to a ratchet mechanism or chain or, as developed later, a chimney crane (page 75). Alternatively, the vessel stood at the edge of the fire supported on its three sturdy legs. Bar-lip vessels were widely used in the Middle Ages. Instead of a central handle or side handles, these were fitted with two bars across each side of the interior at the top of the pot and were suspended by chains or ropes, so avoiding overheating of the handles.

A cauldron was the oldest of these kitchen vessels. Made of iron or bronze, it was often very large. It could be suspended over the fire (7, 9, 10, 151, 152, 153, 155, 158, 167, 223, 226, 227, 228), or set on a brandreth, a long-handled iron tripod which was placed in or near the fire. The brandreth (164) was of especial importance before the ratchet and crane came into use to adjust and accommodate the suspension of various cauldrons because it enabled the position of the cauldron to be varied according to the heat of the fire. Some cauldrons stood upon their own short legs (7, 8, 162). The vessel was used for a variety of purposes. It was essential for boiling all the water needed for washing up and for personal bathing. Stews and soups were cooked in the cauldron and it also served a vital need in cooking complete meals for a large number of persons. Many different foods were cooked at one time, immersed in boiling water in such cauldrons. The food was contained in linen bags or earthenware jars and a board pierced with holes was inserted part way down so that the jars could be accommodated safely and easily. Many cauldrons were made with metal lids which had centrally placed handles (151, 153, 154). The kail-pot (or kilp-pan)[5] was one of these. It was used especially for making porridge in northern England and Scotland, the

157 Game pie dish, c. 1810–15. Wedgwood biscuit ware.
Museum of Lakeland Life and Industry, Abbots Hall,
Kendal

158 Bronze cauldron, Roman.
Colchester and Essex Museum

159 Brass skillet, eighteenth
century. Castle Museum,
York

160 Iron skillet, Medieval.
Carlisle Museum

161 Biscuit ware char pot,
c. 1880. Museum of Lakeland
Life and Industry, Abbots
Hall, Kendal. The char is a
prized fish, not unlike
salmon, to be found in
mountain lakes particularly;
in Britain, in Cumbrian lakes

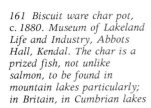

162 *Bronze cooking vessel, fourteenth century. Museum of London*

163 *Glazed brown earthenware cockle pot, 1802. Fitted with attachment to pipe for steaming cockles. Museum of Lakeland Life and Industry, Abbots Hall, Kendal*

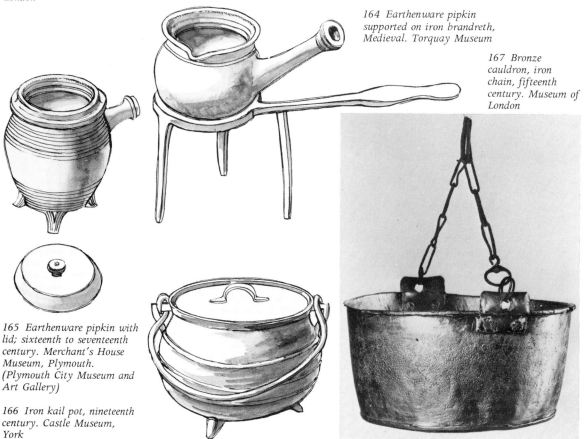

164 *Earthenware pipkin supported on iron brandreth, Medieval. Torquay Museum*

167 *Bronze cauldron, iron chain, fifteenth century. Museum of London*

165 *Earthenware pipkin with lid; sixteenth to seventeenth century. Merchant's House Museum, Plymouth. (Plymouth City Museum and Art Gallery)*

166 *Iron kail pot, nineteenth century. Castle Museum, York*

oatmeal being sprinkled into boiling water and stirred until cooked (166). In remote rural areas where poor people could not afford a cauldron, food was often cooked enclosed in the skin of an animal suspended over the cottage fire on sticks.

The skillet (or posnet), which was the ancestor of the saucepan, was used for cooking a smaller quantity of food. Having a similar, rounded shape and bottom, it was smaller, had a long handle and stood on three legs. It was either made of iron, the handle being cast in with the pot or was of brass with a long, iron handle attached (152, 159, 160). The pipkin was a vessel of similar shape but was generally of earthenware. It was often supported by the fire on a brandreth (164, 165).

The saucepan was any size or design of handled pan which had a flat base; it was originally produced for making sauces. Early saucepans resembled the Roman small pan referred to by Apicius[6] as a *patella* or *patina*. These were usually made of bronze (168). The more modern saucepan came into use as the trivet was evolved to support it. In the same way that the brandreth had enabled the earthenware pipkin to be set near the fire on its leg supports, so the flat-bottomed saucepan could be placed on a trivet or hob in a similar position (page 69). The sauces being made in the pan were often milk-based, so needed a gentle heat. With the development of the hob grate the saucepan could be set on the side hobs (169, 170). The double saucepan was also introduced for gentler cooking; in this, the lower vessel contained boiling water (171, 174). The idea had also been adopted by the Romans.

Frying pans have been in use since Roman times, when they were made of bronze; they were round or oval in shape and had a pouring lip. The Medieval frying pan, intended for use with an open hearth, was of heavy iron and had a long handle so that the cook could keep her distance from the hot fat (154, 177). Many frying pans stood on three stubby legs by the side of the fire (175). Other designs hung from a pot hook or ratchet by a metal half-hoop handle (176). The deeper sauté and omelette pans appeared much later (178).

With the introduction of the hob grate, which enclosed the firegrate in the fireplace and subsequent development of the kitchen range, all vessels were made with flat bases and without legs.

The kettle (see page 45) was, in the Middle Ages, a large pan with a lid used for boiling water or food. The name survived in this context for similar vessels each adapted to the shape of the type of food to be cooked in it. For example, Mrs Beeton[7] describes a glaze-kettle (172) as one 'used for keeping the strong stock boiled down to a jelly, which is known by the name of glaze. It is composed of two tin vessels, one of which, the upper – containing the glaze, is inserted into one of larger diameter and containing boiling water. A brush is put in the small hole at the top of the lid, and is employed for putting the glaze on anything that may require it'. Other kettles were in use for ham or fish.

The fish-kettle (173) was oblong with a handle at each end and another in the centre of the lid. Mrs Beeton describes it as having 'a movable bottom, pierced full of holes, on which the fish is laid, and on which it may be lifted from the water, by means of two long handles attached to each side of the movable bottom. This is to prevent the liability of breaking the fish, as it would necessarily be if it were cooked in a common saucepan.' A turbot-kettle is wider and less deep to reflect the shape of the fish.

Various means were evolved over the years for keeping the food hot until required, without drying it up or spoiling its flavour. A cupboard or cavity beside the fireplace was used for this or a chafing-dish was set beside the fire. This consisted of one vessel placed over another, the latter containing burning charcoal or hot water (180, 181). A traditional method used from Roman times was the *bain-marie*.[8] This was an open vessel filled with almost boiling water in which were stood pans and jars of the food which was required to be kept hot. By this means the flavour of the food was best retained (179).

Grilling, toasting and baking at the open fire

There gradually evolved, especially from the sixteenth century onwards, a great variety of implements and appliances which stood in front of the fire, were hung on the fire-bars or were suspended over the heat to cook all kinds of small items of food. These were grillers or gridirons which were used to broil (grill) cuts of meat, fish and small birds. The simplest form of gridiron was a long-handled framework of iron bars on which the food was placed (187); more sophisticated examples included a container into which the juices and fat would drip (188). Some gridirons were designed to hang on the fire bars; others were supported over the fire or stood in front of it (154, 184, 189).

168 Bronze saucepan (patera), Roman. Museum of Antiquities, Newcastle-upon-Tyne

169 Iron pan, nineteenth century. Abbey House Museum, Leeds

170 Iron pan, lid with separate handle, nineteenth century. Gustav Holst's Birthplace Museum, Cheltenham

171 Iron saucepan with steamer, nineteenth century. Mrs Beeton

172 Glaze kettle, nineteenth century. Mrs Beeton

173 Metal fish kettle, nineteenth century. Mrs Beeton

174 Metal braising pan, nineteenth century. Mrs Beeton

175 Iron frying pan on legs, sixteenth century

176 Iron hanging frying pan, Medieval. Tiverton Museum

177 Iron frying pan, eighteenth century

178 Copper sauté pan, nineteenth century. Tiverton Museum

179 Metal bain-marie, nineteenth century. Mrs Beeton

180 China chafing dish. Hot charcoal is placed in perforated bowl and plate or dish of food is set on top to warm. Merchant's House Museum, Plymouth (Plymouth City Museum and Art Gallery)

181 Pewter chafing dish with double bottom, the lower part being filled with very hot water to warm food in top dish, nineteenth century. Abbey House Museum, Leeds

183 Copper plate warmer, about 2 ft high, nineteenth century. Stands beside open range. National Museum of Welsh Antiquities, Bangor

182 Metal food warmer (Tala), early twentieth century. Four pans each about 5 in. deep, set in a hot water filled tin container. Grosvenor Museum, Chester

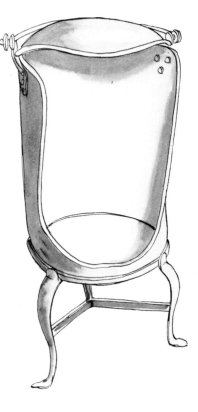

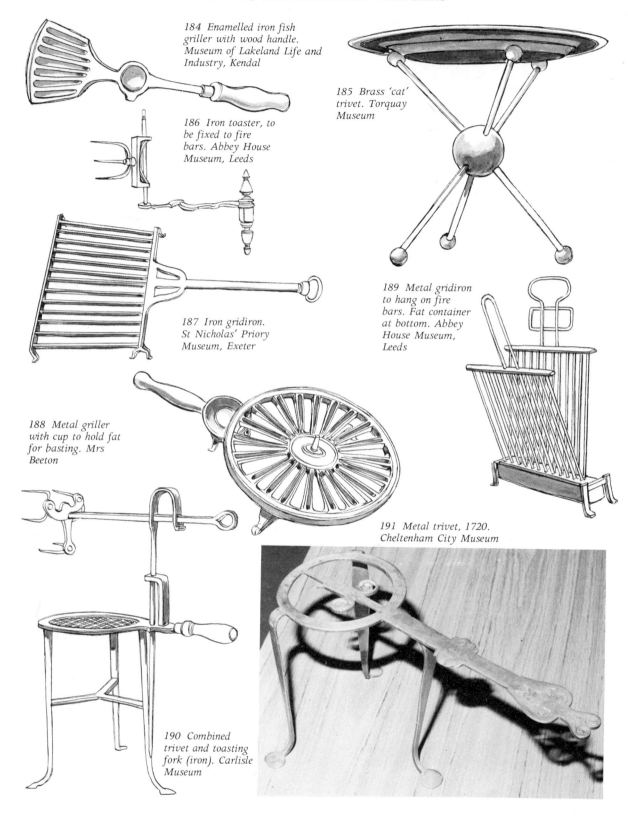

184 *Enamelled iron fish griller with wood handle. Museum of Lakeland Life and Industry, Kendal*

185 *Brass 'cat' trivet. Torquay Museum*

186 *Iron toaster, to be fixed to fire bars. Abbey House Museum, Leeds*

187 *Iron gridiron. St Nicholas' Priory Museum, Exeter*

189 *Metal gridiron to hang on fire bars. Fat container at bottom. Abbey House Museum, Leeds*

188 *Metal griller with cup to hold fat for basting. Mrs Beeton*

191 *Metal trivet, 1720. Cheltenham City Museum*

190 *Combined trivet and toasting fork (iron). Carlisle Museum*

There was also a variety of toasters used for bread, cheese and slices of meat. The simplest of these was the traditional toasting fork held in the hand in front of the fire (192). There were a number of designs of standing toaster set in front of the fire, which comprised a stand with pronged attachments fixed at different levels and holders for dishes to contain food. The attachments could be adjusted to raise or lower the prongs (151, 155, 193, 194). Some trivet designs also included a toasting unit (190). Some toasting attachments were designed to be clipped or screwed on to the fire bars and these could be of most decorative ironwork (186, 196, 201). A popular model was the small toaster set on the floor of the hearth known as a down-hearth toaster. Used for bread and slices of meat, this pattern consisted of a narrow metal platform fitted with two or four semi-circular hoops an inch or two apart which supported the slices of food. A long handle was fitted which could be turned when desired to adjust the angle of the toaster to the fire in order to toast the food evenly (154, 195, 198).

The circular baking sheet of iron suspended by a metal half hoop over the fire was used in all parts of the country for a variety of baking needs. This was usually known as a griddle in the southern half of Britain and a girdle in the north; in many dialects it was also termed a bakstone or bakestone, words which relate to early times when the baking was done on slate or stone. A Scottish version which was sometimes used was bannock-stone. The common design of girdle was a plain flat sheet of iron forming a complete circle in shape (204). More ornate versions consisted of narrow iron bars, some straight and some twisted; these were often called branders (205).

The girdle was used chiefly for baking flat loaves of bread, oatcakes and pies, which, when partly or wholly cooked, were turned or removed by means of an iron or wooden spade-shaped instrument called, according to the purpose and the area of the country, a scone lifter, oatcake turner, spurtle or bannock spade[9] (202, 203). Bannock was a term used in Scotland and the north of England for home-baked bread which was made in a round or oval flattish form. It was usually baked from barley- or pease-meal or, sometimes, wheatmeal, and was generally unleavened. A fruit bun of similar shape was called a currant-bannock.

In the hilly areas of northern England and Scotland oats were the most suitable cereal to be grown and oatcakes and porridge became a staple food over extensive mountain and moorland areas of Britain. Oatmeal had to be baked in thin cakes on a girdle as the material would not make a highly risen dough. The oatmeal was mixed with water, buttermilk and yeast and, after standing a little to rise as far as it was able, was shaped on a riddleboard[10] (199) and rolled by a ridged rolling pin[11] (200) then was quickly cooked on a heated girdle. Similar flat breads or cakes of oatmeal in the north of England were known as clapbread, riddlebread and haverbread.

Wafering irons had been used since the Middle Ages to cook sweet, crisp, patterned biscuits. The implement was made of iron or steel. It consisted of two blades hinged together and attached to very long handles. The inside of the blades was cut into a decorative pattern which was stamped on to the biscuits. The wafering iron – ancestor of the waffle iron – resembled a pair of tongs or long handled scissors. A batter of cream, eggs, flour and sugar was poured into the pan blades, which had been pre-heated and greased, the tongs were closed and the mixture quickly cooked over the fire (154, 206).

Another long-handled implement was the salamander which also had a long history. In this case the long handle was attached to a block of metal which was made red hot in the fire and was then held over pastry, cheese or other dishes to brown the food (151, 154, 207). Employed since Medieval times, the salamander only ceased to be in use when gas and electric cookers were fitted with a grilling mechanism.

A most important adjunct to cooking at the open fire was the trivet. This was a three-legged pot stand. Its use enabled the cook to control the heat of the fire for the particular food or stage of cooking which she was dealing with. The trivet, which was made in various sizes, of different heights and of many designs, could be set at whatever distance or height from the fire was required at a given moment and moved when needed.

Trivets were made of iron, steel or brass and had handles of wood or metal. Many, used for keeping food hot, were only five or six inches high; others could be three or four feet tall and might incorporate a toasting device (190, 191, 192, 197). One design, which had six spokes radiating from the centre (three at the top and three at the bottom) was called a 'cat'. This was in reference to the fact that it could be used either way up and so 'always fell on its feet' (185).

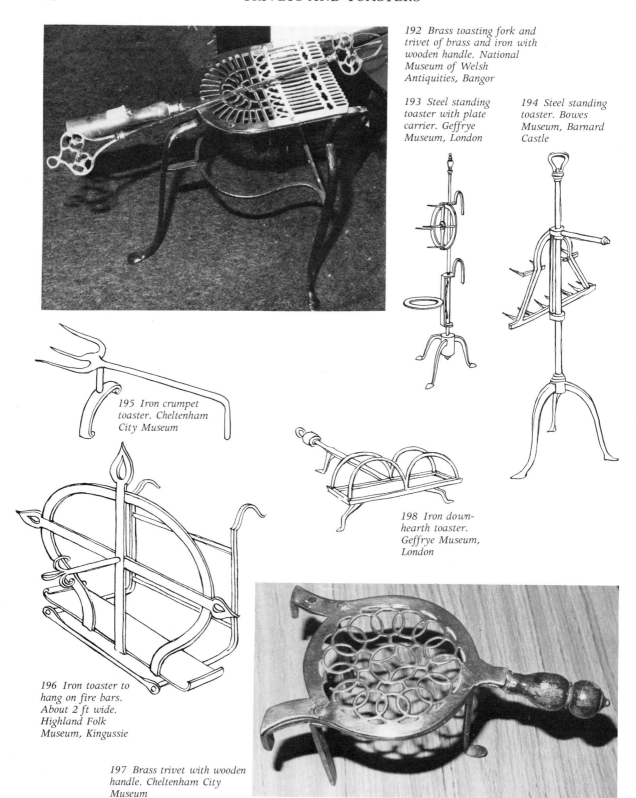

192 Brass toasting fork and trivet of brass and iron with wooden handle. National Museum of Welsh Antiquities, Bangor

193 Steel standing toaster with plate carrier. Geffrye Museum, London

194 Steel standing toaster. Bowes Museum, Barnard Castle

195 Iron crumpet toaster. Cheltenham City Museum

198 Iron down-hearth toaster. Geffrye Museum, London

196 Iron toaster to hang on fire bars. About 2 ft wide. Highland Folk Museum, Kingussie

197 Brass trivet with wooden handle. Cheltenham City Museum

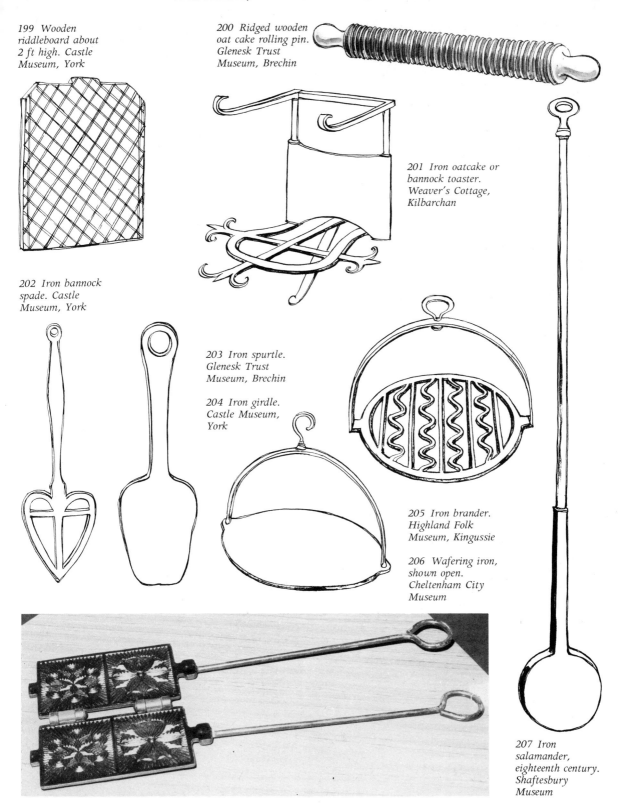

199 Wooden riddleboard about 2 ft high. Castle Museum, York

200 Ridged wooden oat cake rolling pin. Glenesk Trust Museum, Brechin

201 Iron oatcake or bannock toaster. Weaver's Cottage, Kilbarchan

202 Iron bannock spade. Castle Museum, York

203 Iron spurtle. Glenesk Trust Museum, Brechin

204 Iron girdle. Castle Museum, York

205 Iron brander. Highland Folk Museum, Kingussie

206 Wafering iron, shown open. Cheltenham City Museum

207 Iron salamander, eighteenth century. Shaftesbury Museum

*208 Boy turnspit, Medieval.
Wet straw target to protect
boy from the heat of the fire*

*209 Brass bottle
jack, early
nineteenth century*

*210 Steel and brass
adjustable hook for
holding joint of the
meat. Attached at
the top to a bottle
jack. Castle
Museum, York*

*211 Steel basket
spit, eighteenth
century. Castle
Museum, York*

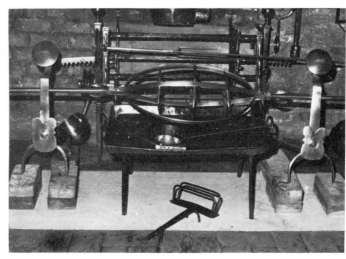

*212 The roasting of
a baron of beef.
North of England,
c. 1775–80. A
screen protects the
woman from the
heat of the fire.
British Museum*

The spit

Roasting food by means of spearing it with a rod and turning this in front of a bright fire was one of the earliest ways of cooking meat and fish. Primitive man used a sharpened stake of hard wood to spear the animal and supported this on Y-shaped wooden posts one fixed on each side of the fire. Carcases required cooking in this manner for a long time, an hour or more according to size, and it was important that they should be continuously and steadily rotated so that cooking was effected evenly. For centuries this turning of the spit was done by hand and, to make this easier, the blunt end of the spit was made into a handle.

By Roman times the spit was made of iron and was supported on iron fire-dogs which flanked the hearth. This method was in use throughout the Middle Ages, the supports being fitted with cup rests or notches at intervals so that the height of the spit could be adjusted and, often with large fireplaces, more than one spit was held at any one time so that a pig or a sheep could be roasted simultaneously with smaller animals or birds. By the fifteenth century these fire-dogs were made with ratcheted spit rests and were known as cob-irons or cobbards (10, 12, 142, 155, 208).

Different designs of spit were made (mostly by the local blacksmith) to accommodate food of varied size. The straight spit was in general use (8, 12, 142, 155, 208, 213). Sometimes this was of the pronged variety in which a two-pronged fitting was attached at either end of the spit and these could be moved as needed to accommodate animals of different sizes. Such a design would hold a carcase without piercing it through the centre (151, 152). The basket or cradle spit was used for small animals or birds. These designs had removable bars so that the joint could be inserted and when these were re-affixed the meat was held securely (10, 142, 154, 211). Spits were stored in a rack above the fireplace when not in use (9, 10, 12, 151, 152, 154).

A large rectangular metal tray or trough was placed under the roasting meat to catch the fat and this became known as dripping (7, 8, 9, 10, 12, 142, 151, 154, 155, 208). This fat was then stored in a three-legged metal pan with a pouring lip and a handle; it was called a greasepan and the grease from it was used for making candles and rushlights (see chapter 8).

This manner of roasting by means of a revolving spit continued in use until the full development of the kitchen range in the nineteenth century. The basics of the operation remained unchanged, but a number of different methods were introduced, one after the other, to provide the motive power for turning the spit continuously and with a minimum of labour. Until the end of the Medieval period the spit was turned by hand, in larger houses usually by a kitchen boy who was known as a turnspit. He was responsible for seeing that the meat was evenly and fully cooked, 'done to a turn' in fact (208). In smaller homes turning the spit by hand was continued for a long time after this. It was necessary to protect the turnspit from the heat of a large fire and a screen was set up (212). This was made from various materials, often of wetted woven straw (208), alternatively of metal incorporating an aperture to look through and one through which could be inserted a long-handled basting spoon.

In the sixteenth century the dog turnspit began to replace the boy. Short-legged dogs were bred to work in pairs, taking turns to pad round and round a wooden dog wheel, the dog being forced to continue moving or he would lose his balance. These wheels were about two feet six inches in diameter and were fastened to the wall high up the side of the fireplace (216). The breeds of dogs used in this way varied in different parts of the country. The dog illustrated (214) is on display (taxidermied) in Abergavenny Museum. Of a now extinct breed, it is golden-haired and has a long body (about 22 inches). In order to turn the spit by this (and other means), it became necessary to replace the handle by a wheel. In the case of the dog turnspits the dog treadmill was connected to the pulley of the wheel spit by an endless chain (9, 12).

Dogs continued to be used as turnspits until well into the nineteenth century, particularly in country areas, but from the mid-seventeenth century onwards, a mechanical jack[12] was to be found in most larger homes. These mechanisms, which had been introduced into England in the late sixteenth century, consisted of a system of weights and gears. The weight was suspended from a cord which was wound round a cylinder by a handle. The power was transmitted via cog wheels to another cylinder and thence, via a pulley, to the spit. As the weight descended so the grooved wheel of the spit was turned. These contrivances were variously termed gravity spits, weight-driven spit jacks and mechanical jacks (10, 154, 215).

The smoke jack was introduced to England in the

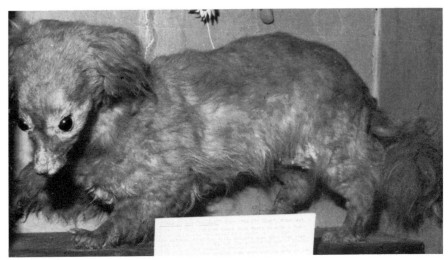

213 Medieval scene showing a man turning a spit on which are fowl and a suckling pig while his co-worker tends the fire, c. 1340. The Luttrell Psalter. British Museum

214 Dog which was bred to work the dog wheel. Now preserved in Abergavenny Museum, Wales

215 A mechanical weight-driven jack. Torquay Museum

216 Wooden dog wheel to turn the spit, about 2 ft 6 in. in diameter. Abergavenny Museum, Wales

second half of the eighteenth century, though it had been used on the Continent long before this. Its power was drawn from the uprush of hot air ascending from the fire. A vane or fan was fixed horizontally into the chimney at the point where it narrowed to ascend the shaft and the heated air caused it to revolve. The vane was connected by a system of gears to the power shaft and thence to chains which could turn the wheels of several spits (151, 155, 217, 218).

The smoke jack would not function satisfactorily unless it was fed by the heat from a large fire and so was criticised by Count Rumford,[13] among others, for wastage of fuel. It was, however, eminently suitable for the large roasting ranges of the eighteenth and nineteenth centuries which were established in great houses, clubs and halls and used for feeding considerable numbers of people. The roasting range in the kitchen of the Royal Pavilion at Brighton was one such example (219). It is of impressive size and carries several spits which could roast a large animal and many smaller ones. A copper canopy above took away steam and cooking smells. This was an advanced example for the time in that the dimensions of the fire-box could be adjusted by operating a handle at the side of the fireplace which would move the side cheeks.[14] Another fine example is that from Skinner's Hall at present on display in the Science Museum in London. In the drawing (220) the chimney breast is cut away to show the smoke jack with its vanes and attachment via the cog wheels and worm gear to the power shaft which turns the spit wheels.

The nineteenth-century kitchen range virtually eliminated the function of the open-hearth spit. Despite this one or two individuals continued to develop ideas for new means of motive power for spits. A patent was taken out in 1845 by a Mr Norton for a spit electrically-powered with the aid of two magnets. In 1852 Mr Suttie designed a water-powered mechanism comprising pipes, buckets and a wheel. In fact he was nearly a century late in this idea. James Boswell refers in his journal of 1775 to the impression made on him by a visit to the kitchen at Chatsworth in Derbyshire to see spits turned by water power. This was in a kitchen built there in 1756–63 which was superseded by another, larger one in the 1820s. Water power was, apparently, a tradition at Chatsworth due to its geographical situation. Overall, spits powered by water were rare.

At the beginning of the nineteenth century the bottle jack [15] came into use (209). This was a spring-driven mechanism which was wound up with a key, like a clock. The roast was suspended from a wheel under the jack which caused the joint to turn first one way then back in the opposite direction for about an hour. The bottle jack could be clamped to the mantelpiece above the fire but was often used in conjunction with the hastener[16]. This was a metal roasting screen which was polished to become a reflector of the heat from the fire and so 'hastened' or speeded up the cooking process. The joint to be roasted was suspended from the top of the hastener and was turned by the bottle jack. The hastener was made in more than one form, the most usual being half-cylindrical with a half-dome top from which the joint depended. One side was open to the fire and at the back was a door which could be opened to allow the cook to baste the joint. In the base of the hastener was a dripping pan and the whole device was generally supported on a metal stand (221, 222).

The chimney crane

In the early Middle Ages when the hearth was moved from the centre of the floor to a wall fireplace (page 54), various means were experimented with for suspending cooking pots over the fire. Iron bars or hooks were fixed into the wall structure of the chimneypiece and vessels hung from chains attached to these (224, 229). Several problems arose from this arrangement: only one or two vessels could be suspended at any one time, it was difficult to adjust the position of a cooking pot relative to the heat of the fire, and the cook tended to burn herself in hanging up one metal pot in place of another.

Solving these difficulties took a long time, though they were slowly dealt with between the twelfth and seventeenth centuries. First the ratchet-hanger was made, which enabled the cook to raise or lower the level of a cooking pot (7, 227, 228). Then the idea of a chimney crane gradually evolved. At first this was an iron bar fixed to the side or back of the fireplace from which a number of pots could hang (224). The next development was the crane with greater manoeuvrability. A vertical iron post was hinged to the side of the fireplace or sunk into the floor of the hearth at the side of the fire. From this extended at right angles a horizontal bar, making a bracket which could be swung like a gate through an angle of 90° enabling the cooking pots to be exposed to varying degrees of heat

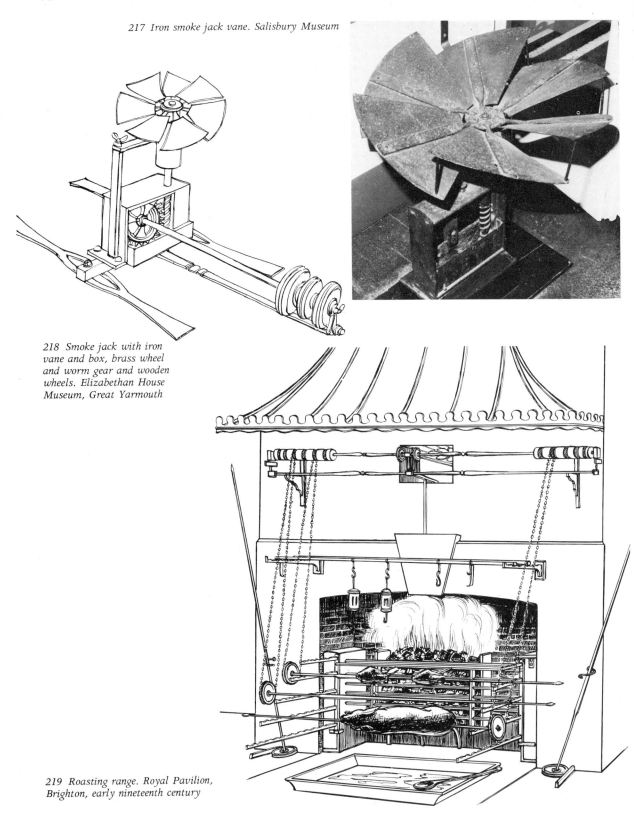

217 Iron smoke jack vane. Salisbury Museum

218 Smoke jack with iron vane and box, brass wheel and worm gear and wooden wheels. Elizabethan House Museum, Great Yarmouth

219 Roasting range. Royal Pavilion, Brighton, early nineteenth century

according to their position relative to the fire. More complex designs of crane were fitted with a mechanism which could raise or lower the level of the pots, and also move them along the bar towards or away from the centre of the heat source. Such cranes were three-motion designs which were fully developed in the seventeenth century. Some examples were plain, workmanlike contrivances, others were decorative, incorporating ornamental ironwork. Each customer ordered a design from his local blacksmith according to his taste, needs and pocket (10, 12, 151, 152, 154, 155, 223, 225, 226).

The Highland Scottish equivalent of the chimney crane was the swee (swey, sway). This began to replace the pot chain (*slabhraidh*) in homes where the chimney and hearth were built to accommodate it. Again, designs ranged from the starkly simple to the elaborate (223, 224, 229).

Even with a chimney crane which could be swung towards the cook and away from the heat of the fire, she was still liable to burn her fingers in taking a hot cauldron or kettle from the fire to pour from it. To ease this problem the kettle- or pot-tilter was devised. This was a rectangular iron frame with a projecting handle which was balanced so that when the cook pressed the tip of it the kettle tilted to pour without having to be

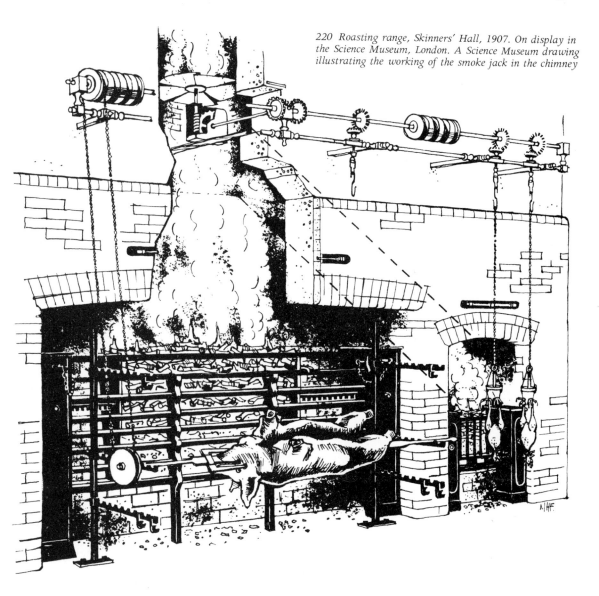

220 Roasting range, Skinners' Hall, 1907. On display in the Science Museum, London. A Science Museum drawing illustrating the working of the smoke jack in the chimney

lifted off its hanger. These tilters were known by various names in different parts of the country: lazy-back, idle-back, handymaid (154, 155, 230).

Ovens

Although roasting, broiling, stewing and boiling could satisfactorily be done over the open fire, the baking of bread, cakes and pies needed an oven. In Roman times it was possible to buy bread and cakes in large towns from the bakery but in country areas most households

221 Rear view of metal hastener or roasting screen. Bottle jack hangs from the top. Abington Museum, Northampton Museums

222 Metal hastener or roasting screen with brass bottle jack. Stranger's Hall Museum of Domestic Life, Norwich

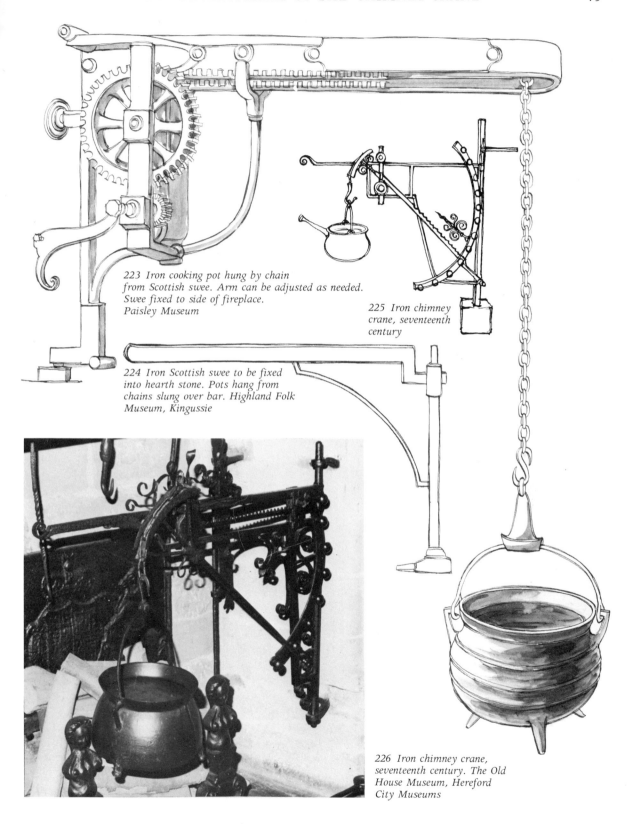

223 Iron cooking pot hung by chain from Scottish swee. Arm can be adjusted as needed. Swee fixed to side of fireplace. Paisley Museum

225 Iron chimney crane, seventeenth century

224 Iron Scottish swee to be fixed into hearth stone. Pots hang from chains slung over bar. Highland Folk Museum, Kingussie

226 Iron chimney crane, seventeenth century. The Old House Museum, Hereford City Museums

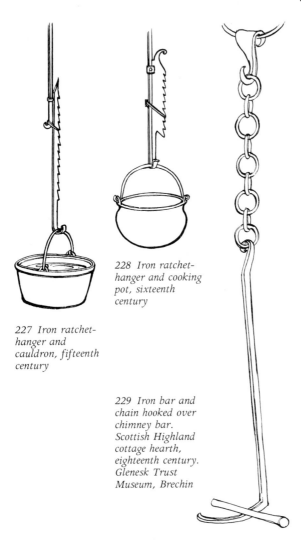

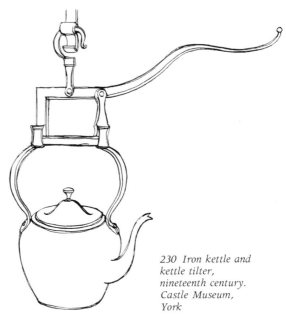

*228 Iron ratchet-
hanger and cooking
pot, sixteenth
century*

*227 Iron ratchet-
hanger and
cauldron, fifteenth
century*

*229 Iron bar and
chain hooked over
chimney bar.
Scottish Highland
cottage hearth,
eighteenth century.
Glenesk Trust
Museum, Brechin*

*230 Iron kettle and
kettle tilter,
nineteenth century.
Castle Museum,
York*

small quantities of food or for keeping food hot in the dining room. These small ovens were also domical in form; they were generally double-walled and -floored, charcoal being burnt in the cavities to provide the heat.

In the early Middle Ages when the log fire burned on a central hearth, baking was carried out at the side of the hearth under a domed metal cover; in summer this would be done out-of-doors. With the removal of the hearth to a wall fireplace, in larger houses the oven was usually built into the thickness of the wall at the side of the open hearth so that it shared the same chimney flue. From then until the advent of the nineteenth-century kitchen range (chapter 4), oven design changed little. In shape it was circular or oval and was lined with brick. The entrance was arched above and had a sill at floor level. It was sealed by a hinged door, first of hard wood, later of iron (7, 8, 14, 231, 232, 233).

The fuel was usually wood, faggots or brushwood which, as in Roman times, was burnt until the oven was hot enough, then the ashes raked out.[18] In small ovens the fuel was burnt on the floor of the oven and this was then thoroughly cleaned before inserting the dough; in larger ones there was a separate cavity below the oven floor with perforations between so that the heated air could rise into the oven. The dough or pies were put into and taken out of the oven by a peel. This was a flat, spade-like implement with a long

baked their own supplies (see page 39). In the larger Romano-British homes the kitchen would be designed with more than one oven. These were most often domed structures looking like a beehive and made from rubble and clay or stone and lined with bricks,[17] though some examples were lined with pebbles and stones. In some homes ovens were built into the hearth, in others they were sunk into the floor or were placed against the wall or in a corner. Many designs had elaborate flue systems.

A fire would be lit of charcoal or wood and when the air in the oven had reached the desired temperature, the ashes would be raked out, the food inserted and the entrance covered by a board or door.

Small portable ovens were also in use. Made of metal or earthenware, these were available for baking

231 Stone great oven in the Abbot's Kitchen, Glastonbury Abbey, fourteenth century

232 Brick oven with iron door built as part of a hearth at the side of a hob grate, early nineteenth century. Castle Farm Folk Museum, Marshfield

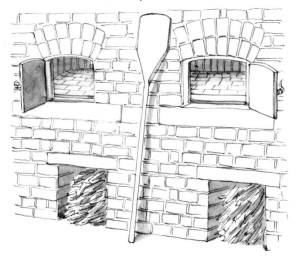

233 Brick scuffle ovens in the bakehouse of a large country house (Erddig). Note: doors, fuel beneath and wood peel, eighteenth century

handle (some six to seven feet) which would ensure that the baker did not get too hot by having to approach close to the heated oven. Bread, cakes and pastry were baked in the stored-up heat of the oven. After this the residual heat was used for drying herbs, also firewood, in readiness for the next baking. In larger homes a big baking was done about once a week.

In small houses and cottages which were built of half-timber or wattle-and-daub it was not possible to construct an oven in the wall thickness, and there was also danger of fire. In these cases the oven would be built to project externally from the wall in a hemispherical shape.

Many people were too poor to have an oven at all. In Medieval times they could take their dough to the bakehouse owned by the lord of the manor and have their bread and pies baked on payment of a small fee. Later, in towns, it was possible to use the municipal bakery in a similar way. It was also possible to purchase bread at the bakers, but this was too costly for most people. Many poor people baked at home without the aid of a proper oven, using a griddle or bakstone near the open fire (page 69) and covering it with an earthenware or metal cooking pot. They then piled hot embers or burning peat around it to maintain the heat.

Over the years were developed in different parts of the country designs of smaller ovens, some of portable type, which were separate from the hearth and not built into it. There was the dome-shaped earthenware oven, used widely in country areas and similar to the Roman pattern. Made until the early decades of the twentieth century in various sizes, these were heated on the oven floor by burning faggots and brushwood, then raked and cleared before inserting the food and sealing the door in place with wet clay (234).

There was also the metal camp oven. These oval or round ovens were made of cast iron; they had handles at the sides and were supplied with a lid. They stood on short legs and were put down into the hot ashes of

234 Dutch oven to hang on fire bars, nineteenth century, Tiverton Museum

235 Iron camp oven (in the USA often called a Dutch oven). Tiverton Museum

236 Earthenware oven. A Devon example, known in local dialect as a cloam oven. Barnstaple grit was added to the clay to improve its refractory properties. Tiverton Museum

237 Roasting or Dutch oven

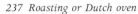

the open fire. Burning peat or hot embers could also be placed in the lid to speed up cooking (235). This type of oven is, in some areas, and notably in the USA, known as a Dutch oven, but this latter term in England is more generally applied to a partially enclosed version of the hastener (page 75), which could be set in front of the fire or hung on the fire bars and which contained a handled spit for roasting fowl or small joints of meat. This type is not really an oven at all (236, 237).

CHAPTER FOUR

The Cooking of Food 2

The Range, Stove and Cooker: 1780s to the Present Day

Cooking with solid fuel

During the nineteenth century the enclosed kitchen range, made of iron and steel and burning coal, gradually replaced the open fire for cooking purposes. This represented the logical progression from the hob grate which, developing from the dog and basket grates, had begun to enclose the fire-burning area and so create better draught conditions for burning coal. Over many years it became understood that a further enclosure of the fire would be more economical in use of fuel as well as giving better heat control and making it possible to provide an oven and a boiler for hot water as well.

It was in the second half of the eighteenth century that inventions were patented which led to the development of the kitchen range. A precursor of these was an iron oven designed by Hornbuckle which was intended to be set at the back of the open fire grate. It was warmed here by the fire and also by heat-carrying passages built in behind the grate. Thomas Robinson designed the first actual range in 1780. This roasting range was similar to a hob grate, having an open coal fire with removable bars, flanked on either side by metal hobs, but at one side he had built into the rectangular brick space an iron oven which had a hinged door and, on the other side, an iron tank for hot water. The oven was lined with brick and fitted with shelves. A hinged trivet which could be swung forward to take a kettle or pan was fitted to the top bar of the open fire-grate.

Robinson's range marked an important step forward: it was a landmark in the evolution of cooking means. There were, though, considerable drawbacks. The oven was only heated on one side, so that the food tended to be burnt on one side and undercooked on the other. The top of the fire-grate was open so making a good deal of smoke and burning coal extravagantly.

In the succeeding 20 years improvements were made, such as enclosing the open fire with a metal hot-plate and introducing passages for the circulation of warm air round the oven.

It was George Bodley, an Exeter iron-founder who, in 1802, patented the enclosed kitchen range which was the prototype of the many and varied designs used in homes large and small throughout the nineteenth century. Bodley's design retained an open-fronted coal fire-grate which could be used for roasting, but its top was closed by a metal plate which was fitted to accommodate pans and kettles for cooking and boiling water. The oven was still hotter on the grate side than on the other, but was heated more evenly than in Robinson's design due to the insertion of a firebrick next to the grate and flues built into the opposite side to convey the heat round the oven. Also, the bottom of the oven was level with the firebar so leaving a space below for the circulation of hot air.

It was Count Rumford (Sir Benjamin Thompson 1753–1814) who, at the end of the eighteenth century, applied scientific methods to the design of kitchen ranges. Benjamin Thompson – scientist, philanthropist, administrator – was born at Woburn, Massachusetts. His family had emigrated from England to America a century earlier. His interests and achievements were wide-ranging in America, Germany and England. It was in southern Germany, where he entered into civil and military service with the Elector of Bavaria[1], that he first designed some of his remarkable cooking and heating stoves. His studies of the motion of heated gases[2] had led him to consider the problems of stoves and cooking fires. He was strongly critical of the kitchen fireplaces of the late eighteenth century, especially those in Britain based upon Robinson's pattern, considering that they were in-

238 *Kitchen and cooking range in the house of Baron de Lerchenfeld in Munich designed by Count Rumford, in the late eighteenth century. From Rumford's original designs*

239 *Cast-iron open kitchen range with adjustable hob and fire-bars. Oven with draught control. Early nineteenth century*

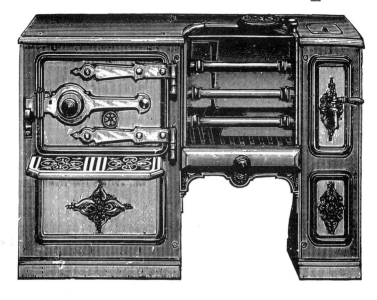

240 *Later iron and steel cottage range (catalogue)*

efficient and extravagantly wasteful of fuel. He set himself the task of devising a means of cooking and heating which would improve the efficiency of fuel consumption. His intention was to enclose the fire and design the stove and cooking vessels so that the maximum quantity of heat would be transferred from the fire to the food with the consumption of the smallest amount of fuel. The vessels and the stove were to fit so accurately together and the pan bottoms to be so shaped that the maximum amount of heat would be drawn from the burning fuel gases and efficiently utilised.

A major contribution to such heat conservation was his design for the fireplace in the kitchen of Baron de Lerchenfeld in Munich, Germany (238). In this the stove was a complex, inclusive unit fitted into the kitchen, the flues being concealed in the walls of the room. The stove structure was of brick with a flat top into which the covered pans and cooking boilers were sunk to fit exactly and were held in place by circular rings of iron so no heat was wasted. Beneath each vessel was its own fireplace with draught control. Pans had long handles; large cooking vessels one handle at each side. The stove was equipped for boiling, stewing and warming. The draught could be adjusted critically to be damped down at night or in warm weather and to brighten quickly the fire as required. Rumford also designed a roasting oven heated by a separate fire and a boiler for hot water.

Rumford was made a Fellow of the Royal Society in England in 1779. Twenty years later, with Sir Joseph Banks, he founded the Royal Institution in London which received its charter from George III the following year. A large house in Albemarle Street. Piccadilly, London, was obtained as premises for the new body and Rumford re-organised the basement floor, which had been used as servants' quarters, into a model kitchen planned to his own designs of the type which had been installed in Munich for Baron de Lerchenfeld. These included a Rumford kitchen range and roasters[3]. Rumford's theories on heat conservation were well in advance of his time. Coal-burning kitchen ranges continued to be built into British houses all through the nineteenth century, but these were more advanced models of Robinson's and Bodley's designs rather than Rumford's. It was after 1900 before his principles of producing heat only where and when it was required and of reducing fuel consumption by insulation were put into practice. His ideas lay dormant for over a century.

Between 1800 and 1900 progress towards more efficient, labour-saving kitchen ranges was painfully slow. In the first half of the century, particularly the 1840s, a number of different models became available, each manufacturer putting forward claims for the advantages, indeed virtues, of his product. Among the contenders for purchase by the public were Brown's Patent Universal Cooking Range (1840), Sylvester's Range (1842), Deane, Dray and Drummond's Cooking Apparatus (1844), Harrison's Economical Derby Range (1846) and the Newark Cottage Range (1848). As time passed new models became more numerous and varied and competition fiercer. Ranges were built into the kitchens of new houses, large and small, and were incorporated into existing properties, slowly replacing the open hearth, though the latter was still to be seen in cottages well into the twentieth century.

Most of the designs of kitchen range were of two main types, one being more enclosed than the other. The open design was in use from about 1800 until well into the 1920s. Developed from the late eighteenth-century prototypes, this had an open fire-box with bars across the front, the upper ones being fitted to swing down to act as a trivet for pans or kettles. Another set of hinged bars could also be adjusted over the fire to support further pans for cooking. At one side of the fire-box was the oven, at the other a small hot water boiler or warm closet, with a hob above for simmering. The oven was a great improvement upon eighteenth-century designs in that it was equipped with a damper-controlled flue which provided a passage for warmed air round the side away from the fire and over the top, so giving a more even heat to the oven interior (241).

This type of range with open fire-box was, in general, more popular in the north of Britain than in the south because it cooked the food and warmed the kitchen at the same time and so was more suited to a colder climate. Dampers were fitted to control both the oven and fire heat, but the fire had to be kept going for cooking and so the kitchen became overheated in summer. The greatest drawback to the open range, of which the cottage range and Yorkshire range were typical, was its extravagant use of fuel. Indeed, in early models especially, a housewife unskilled at managing the dampers could turn the fire-box into a furnace hot enough to melt the firebars (16, 22, 239, 240, 242, 244).

The second type of range became available about 1840. Known as a closed-range or a kitchener, this was based more closely on the theories of Bodley and Rumford that an enclosed heating apparatus would be

241 *Oven set in brick wall. Decorative cast iron front and door with fire below, behind cast iron door, c. 1850–60. Castle Museum, York*

more economical of fuel and more efficient to operate. The firebox was covered by a metal hot-plate on top which was fitted with boiling rings and the front firebars were enclosed by a metal door. Ovens were placed on either side of the fire-box or one of these could be substituted for a hot water tank. The kitchener was designed to cook or heat, but not to carry out both purposes simultaneously. When cooking was being done the fire-box was completely closed with door and hot-plate in place. When cooking was over and it was desired to warm the kitchen, the door could be opened and the hot-plate slid back. It is understandable that this design, the heat of which was more controllable than in the open range, was more popular in the south of England (13).

Some improvements were incorporated into range design in the second half of the nineteenth century. Larger ranges comprised two ovens, four to six hobs, a water boiler and a warming compartment for plates and dishes (17, 243). Regulation of heat and smoke control were improved. Expensive models included a back boiler which would provide a large quantity of hot water. Many of the old cooking aids which had been used with the open hearth continued in operation with the range. These included the roasting screen or hastener, the Dutch oven, the bottle jack from which a roasting joint hung turning in front of the firebars, trivets, kettle tilters and ale warmers.

Gas slowly became more popular in the later nineteenth century, but yet the gas cooker did not replace the solid fuel range because the latter, already installed in most people's homes, carried out more than one function. If one had a gas cooker, one needed also a separate water and space heating device. However, in well-to-do homes a gas cooker was installed for use in summer when the range, even the kitchener, made the kitchen unbearably hot.

A modern housewife would view with horror the idea of having to cook and heat her kitchen by means of a kitchener which was, by any standards, a large, dirty, coal-consuming monster. In contrast, to the nineteenth-century housewife, it was the last word in modern convenience but then, in middle and upper class homes at least, there was more than adequate servant labour available to keep it clean and functioning well. Every day the fire-box had to be cleaned out, the ashes removed and the soot brushed off the flue pipes. The oven had to be scraped, washed and dried before the whole iron case was black-leaded and

242 Yorkshire kitchen range. Open design of cast iron with steel and copper fittings. Late nineteenth century (catalogue)

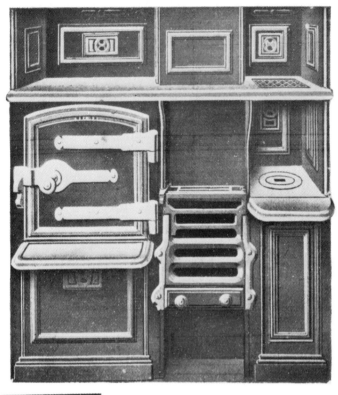

243 Patent Quadrant Kitchener. Cast iron with bright steel fittings. Tiled back. Double oven and hot closets with roll doors. Optional extras: thermometer on oven door, pedal opener to oven door, oven door insulated with packing, plate glass doors to hot closets, c. 1905–10 (catalogue)

brush-polished. The steel parts were then cleaned with emery paper and polished with leather and dry powder and the brass fittings made bright with paste and leather (see chapter 6). After cleaning the fender and fire-irons in a similar way the maid-of-all-work could then have her breakfast. Mrs Beeton[4] gives careful details of the duties of all house servants.

The kitchen range was also a temperamental mon-

244 *Working family's cottage hearth. Painted wood chimneypiece with brass rail under mantelpiece. Decorative cast-iron range with open fire-box and brick backing. Open range comprises one oven, hot water boiler with tap and warming cupboard. Brass fittings. Steel fender and fire-irons, 1880s. Derived from several similar cottage hearths*

ster to control and to use to best advantage. Experience was necessary to be able to handle the damper controls and to obtain good results in cooking. Molly Harrison[5] quotes some useful if imprecise advice on judging the suitable heat for one's oven given in a cookery book published in Vermont in the USA in 1845:

> For pies, cakes and white bread the heat of the oven should be such that you can hold your hand and arm inside while you count 40. For brown bread, meats, beans, Indian puddings and pumpkin pies it should be hotter, so you can only hold it in while you count 20.

Twentieth-century kitchen ranges were mostly much smaller than before, partly to cater for smaller families and partly to fit into smaller houses less well served with domestic help. Many of these ranges were combination designs which continued to be fitted into houses until the advent of the Second World War. A popular model had an oven at one side adjacent to a living room grate, while the hot water boiler was situated behind (245). Useful in small kitchens was the convertible range which was designed with its oven over the fire, and the latter was completely closed in when cooking was taking place. Where a kitchen backed on to a living room the back-to-back version was also convenient. In this the fire was in the living room while the oven was behind it in the kitchen.

By the 1920s the kitchen range was outdated in comparison with gas and electric cookers, but there were still many homes in Britain which had not yet been provided with gas or electric supply. The solid fuel method of cooking was then given a new lease of life by the Swedish Nobel prize-winner Dr Gustav Dalen who was responsible for the design of the Aga cooker. Dr Dalen was blinded in the 1920s because of an accident and, at home for some time as a result, he realised the need for an efficient, clean, attractive-looking cooker which would be economical in fuel consumption. Like Count Rumford more than a century earlier, Dr Dalen devised a cooker which, based on sound scientific principles, would produce guaranteed results, be economical and simple to manage and need a minimum of attention. The first Aga contained a cast-iron fire-box enclosed in an insulated[6] jacket. The fire-box was connected to cast-iron hot-plates and ovens, all designed so that the heat was conducted to the various parts at precisely the correct temperatures for the types of cooking required: simmering, boiling, baking, grilling, etc. The hot-plate heat was maintained at the correct temperature with the aid of insulated, hinged covers which were only lifted when the hot-plate was in use (246).

The Aga was introduced to Britain in 1929 and has continued to prove its worth even in competition with modern electric and gas cookers. It is costly to purchase but inexpensive to run, as in its heat-storage system of operation no energy is wasted. The modern Aga can function on solid fuel, oil or gas. It is thermostatically controlled, provides constant hot water and cooks varied foods simultaneously in any manner desired (247, 248).

Portable cookers

A number of different models were produced during the nineteenth century (249) primarily in North America and especially in the West where the settlers had had to manage up to this time with an open fire and brick oven. These cooking stoves began to be marketed about 1830 and by the time of the Great Exhibition in Hyde Park were becoming available in Britain where they were especially suited to small homes and cottages: they were inexpensive, did not take up much room and could be moved around as required. Typical was the design which stood on short legs and comprised an oven, enclosed fire-box and three or four hot-plates. Many models were sold, later in the century, complete with iron pans, kettle, baking tins and a few kitchen gadgets. Later designs were convertible and could be powered by coal or gas (250).

Pressure cookers

In this method of cooking a vessel is used which is designed to seal in and control the steam which normally escapes when cooking in an ordinary saucepan. As the steam is retained, the pressure rises and so does the temperature at which the water boils. The pressure forces the superheated steam through the food, so greatly reducing the cooking time required.

Denis Papin (1647–c.1712), the French physicist, invented such a pressure cooker, which he called 'A New Digester or Engine for softning Bones', in 1679. In 1681 he demonstrated its use to the Royal Society in London, apparently to the satisfaction of the members. According to Papin's own description, his

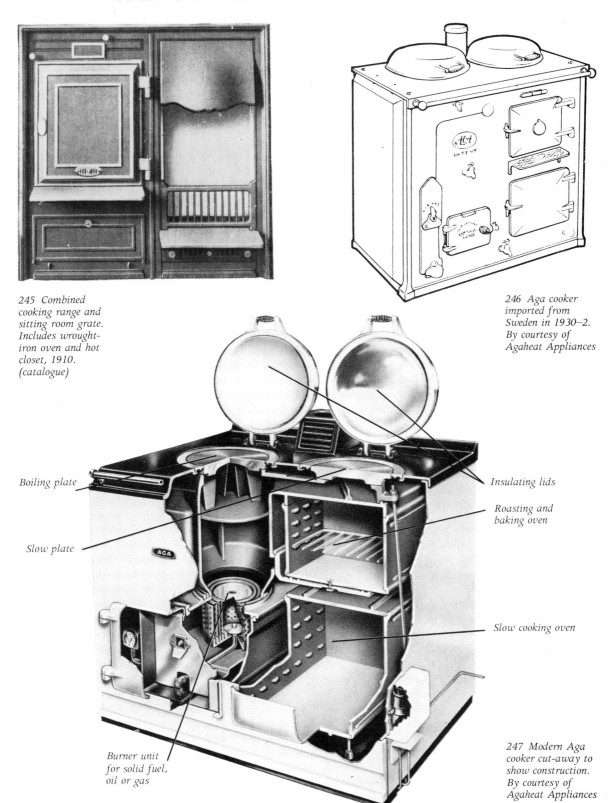

245 Combined cooking range and sitting room grate. Includes wrought-iron oven and hot closet, 1910. (catalogue)

246 Aga cooker imported from Sweden in 1930–2. By courtesy of Agaheat Appliances

Boiling plate

Slow plate

Burner unit for solid fuel, oil or gas

Insulating lids

Roasting and baking oven

Slow cooking oven

247 Modern Aga cooker cut-away to show construction. By courtesy of Agaheat Appliances

248 Modern Aga cooker. One insulating lid raised. By courtesy of Agaheat Appliances

'digester' was intended to assist in cooking at sea, for use in chemistry, for making drinks but mainly for softening bones to make stock. The vessel was designed with a tight-fitting lid and a safety valve to guard against excessive rise of pressure.

After Papin the idea of pressure cooking languished until it was revived in the nineteenth century. This digester, as it was still termed, was a cast-iron pot with handle, a conical, fitting lid and a valve (251). By the 1930s cast aluminium models were available which were fitted with pressure gauges on top (252). Modern pressure cookers are made of aluminium or stainless steel and have a non-stick finish. They can be used on any type of heat. They were very much in demand until about 1960, but are now less so, partly due to the ready availability of convenience and frozen foods and partly because of the introduction of auto-timer devices on cookers and of slow-cookers (253).

Oil cookers

Like the portable cookers these were much more popular in America than in Britain and became common there in the later nineteenth century. This was because the fuel – paraffin (kerosene) – was plentiful and cheap. Also, there were so many homes in remote areas which had no hope of obtaining a gas or electricity supply. The cookers were mostly small and inexpensive and many different designs were marketed. Some were exported to Britain in the years 1880–1930, but, due to less abundant supplies of the fuel and a greater availability of gas or electricity, the use of oil cookers was, in general, confined to rural areas (254, 255).

Cooking by gas

Although simple experiments had been made in Europe in the sixteenth and seventeenth centuries with gas produced from various substances (and, it is believed, by the Chinese long before this), it was not until the late eighteenth century that the idea of using gas for illumination became a serious proposition.

Professor Jean Pierre Minckelers (1748–1824) experimented with lighting his lecture room at the University of Louvain in 1784 and published in that year his paper on the preparation of coal gas for ballooning, but the first public exhibition of the possible use of gas for lighting and heating took place in Paris in 1801. The gas was generated from the distillation of wood, a process developed by Philippe Lebon (1767–1804), a French inventor and engineer. Lebon was brought up in a charcoal-burning area and this had aroused his interest in combustion and led to his research in the subject. In his experiments in Paris in 1798–9 he built a gas-making plant which he intended to be used for lighting and heating. Lebon was well aware of the potentialities of gas in this field and after his public demonstration continued his work, but this was tragically cut short when he was stabbed to death at the age of 37 in a mugging attack in the Champs Elysées in 1804.

It was the work of William Murdock (1754–1839), researching in coal gas, which pointed the way finally to its commercial application. Murdock was a Scottish mechanic who worked for the engineering firm of Boulton and Watt. He became interested in the possibilities of coal gas for illumination. This led to a successful experiment in 1792 when he lighted his home at Redruth in Cornwall with gas produced in large iron retorts conveyed through metal pipes. In 1798 he installed a lighting system in his firm's works near Birmingham.

Murdock's experimentation was followed by others: Zachaus Winzler (1750–c.1830) from Moravia, who worked in the field of gas lighting and heating;

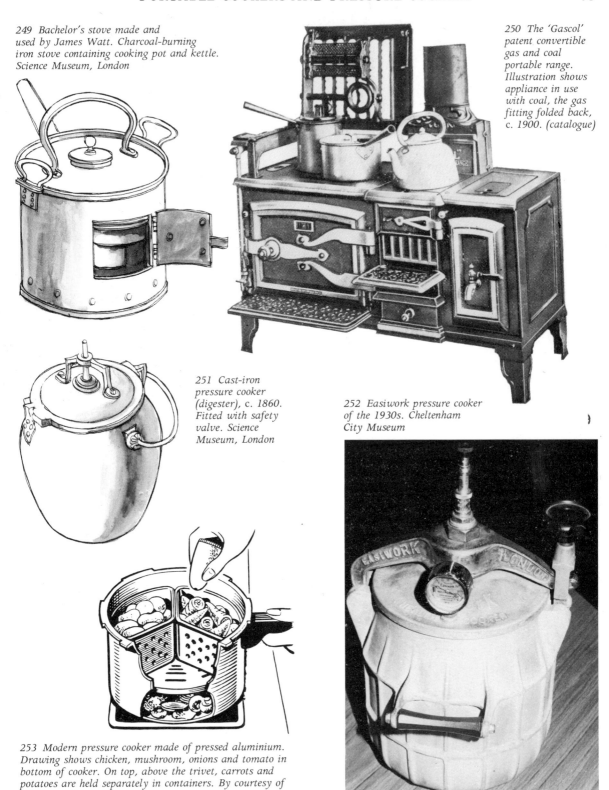

249 Bachelor's stove made and used by James Watt. Charcoal-burning iron stove containing cooking pot and kettle. Science Museum, London

250 The 'Gascol' patent convertible gas and coal portable range. Illustration shows appliance in use with coal, the gas fitting folded back, c. 1900. (catalogue)

251 Cast-iron pressure cooker (digester), c. 1860. Fitted with safety valve. Science Museum, London

252 Easiwork pressure cooker of the 1930s. Cheltenham City Museum

253 Modern pressure cooker made of pressed aluminium. Drawing shows chicken, mushroom, onions and tomato in bottom of cooker. On top, above the trivet, carrots and potatoes are held separately in containers. By courtesy of TI Tower Housewares Ltd

254 'Veritas' paraffin cooker with oven, c. 1930. Two burners. Oven has glass window in the door. Oven is placed on hotplate for roasting. Science Museum, London

255 Paraffin table cooking stove, c. 1880. Made of decorative cast iron. 12 in. high. Science Museum, London

256 Below, left Hand-made cast iron gas cooker encased in a wooden external box and packed with fire-clay, c. 1850. Science Museum, London

257 Gas cooker designed by James Sharp, made of sheet iron, 1839–50. Intended chiefly for roasting. By courtesy of Tube Investments Ltd.

Samuel Clegg (1781–1861), who tried to purify the gas; and the German Frederic Albert Winsor (1763–1830), who foresaw the possibilities of piping gas long distances to light the streets. It was Winsor who formed the National Light and Heat Company and demonstrated in London on George III's birthday in 1807 the first public installation of gas street lighting illuminating part of the Mall. In 1812 the company gained its Royal Charter under its new name, the Gas Light and Coke Company. By the 1820s it had lit miles of London streets and gas illumination was being installed in shops, banks, churches, theatres, clubs and public buildings.

As the supply was extended experiments were made to use coal gas for cooking and heating, but the problems which confronted designers and inventors in making it commercially viable were formidable. The cost of gas was much greater than coal, there were no meters and the difficulties in measuring the gas were considerable, and, greatest of all, the public were firmly prejudiced against the use of gas, believing it to be dangerously explosive and the fumes and impurities in the gas to be harmful to any food which was cooked by this means.

However, inventors continued trying. An early cooking appliance was adapted from a laboratory furnace which included its own gas generator worked by bellows: a hard way to do one's cooking. The first workable appliance dates from 1824 when a griller was made at the Aetna Ironworks near Liverpool. This was a gun-barrel twisted into the shape of a gridiron which had holes pierced in it: the prototype of the modern gas griller. The 1824 version was used horizontally, with the pan placed on top, to fry or boil. If it was desired to roast it was placed vertically and the meat was hung in front of it, a reflector or hastener being used to help the cooking process.

In the 1830s James Sharp (1790–1870), assistant manager of the Northampton Gas Company, demonstrated gas cooking in his home and designed cookers which were sold commercially. Other designers followed suit; for instance there were cookers by Hicks and by Weller.

A detailed description of a new gas cooker was given by A.A. Croll in a paper which he read to the Royal Society of Arts, London, in 1847 entitled 'The Domestic Uses of Gas'. Much of this deals with gas lighting and the author's work on a possible meter to measure the quantity of gas, but, at the end of the paper, he refers to the advantages of using gas domestically for cooking. He suggests that if the gas jets are enclosed in a sheet-iron case and cooking vessels are fitted inside, no heat would be wasted. He describes the method of roasting by gas, where the joint is surrounded by small jets of flames, so making it unnecessary to turn the meat, and the dripping would be collected in a pan at the bottom of the apparatus. He recommends gas-stands for cooking that provide even, unvarying temperatures suitable for soups, pies or stews. He also refers to the economy of using gas which can, unlike coal, be turned off when not needed.

Mr Croll also comments on extending the use of gas in cooking for large numbers of people and refers to Mr Soyer. Alexis Soyer was a famous French chef who took the lead in promoting cooking by gas because he believed it to be clean, efficient and economical in comparison with coal. He introduced it into the kitchens of the Reform Club in London in 1841. Soyer's enthusiasm for gas cooking for large numbers of people was not abated a decade later when he designed an apparatus called the Phidomageireion which was able to roast, boil, stew, steam, fry and broil for about 70 people at an economical cost. Later designs were able to cater for hundreds of diners.

Domestic cooking by gas finally began to come of age in the 1850s (256) when a number of designs were produced on the lines of a cast-iron black box standing on four legs containing an oven, a grill and a hot plate with burners. Pioneer models of such cookers included Charles Ricketts' Economic Gas Cooking Stove 1849, Alfred King's Liverpool Gas Cooking Range 1850 and the latest designs of James Sharp, now manager of the Southampton Gas Works (257). A new design of cooker, by Ebenezer Goddard, engineer with the Ipswich Gas Company, was advertised in 1851. This had a porcelain-lined oven and possessed a pilot-lighting attachment in the way of a flexible tube with a gas jet termination. In 1851 an exhibition of gas cooking stoves was held at the Polytechnic Institution in London. This had been intended to be shown at the Great Exhibition in Hyde Park, but, due to the rules of the Exhibition which stipulated that 'no apparatus should be exhibited which was in practical operation through the agency of gas', this was not possible.

By 1855 gas cooking had been demonstrated to be a practical proposition, but it was not for more than 20

258 *Locally made cast-iron gas cooker with single burner, c. 1870–80. Dawlish Museum Society, Devon*

259 *Below, left* Black Beauty *gas cooker, 1878. Made by R. and A. Main of Glasgow. Cast iron, four burners, front taps. Science Museum, London*

260 *Cast-iron gas cooker made in Leeds, 1864. Three burners, side taps. Castle Museum, York*

years that these cookers became a viable competitor to coal ranges. Prejudice and fear remained strong deterrents and cost was still high. An important factor in the development of the technology of the gas cooker was the invention of the Bunsen burner. An idea, generally attributed to the German chemist Robert Wilhelm von Bunsen (1811–99) led to the burner introduced in 1855. This was so designed that in the pipe there was mixed – by very simple means – a predetermined quantity of air with the stream of gas before it was ignited, so resulting in a hot, non-luminous flame. This burner produced a more efficient and safer combustion.

During the 1860s and 1870s improvements were made in gas cooker design. The multi-burner hot-plate was introduced, also the independent gas ring; the cooker taps, which had generally been fixed to the side of the oven in earlier models, were brought round to the front for easier access and to save space. These factors, together with the incorporation of Bunsen-type atmospheric burners, helped to popularise gas cookers, but the biggest stumbling block for most people to the adoption of gas cooking was the higher cost. Gas was still more expensive than coal and, since they already possessed a solid-fuel range, to purchase in addition a gas cooker was too costly for the majority of the population (258, 259, 260).

Two important incentives were then offered by the gas companies which tipped the scales in favour of gas cooking. The first was the introduction from the 1870s by a number of companies of facilities for hiring cookers instead of insisting on purchase. During this decade large numbers of people took advantage of this offer. Then in the 1890s came the prepayment slot-machine system which brought gas within reach of the poorer members of the community. The coin used was a penny[7] and the scheme was such a success that by 1911 the Gas Light and Coke Company were taking over 230 million pennies from their machines annually, an amount which weighed nearly 2,000 tons.

From this time onward, gas cooking largely took over from the use of solid fuel but there was little improvement or innovation in the cooker itself between the 1870s and the 1920s. It seems strange in retrospect that, in introducing a cooker using a different fuel, it did not seem to occur to the designers and inventors from the 1840s onwards that such a new technology deserved an equally revolutionary re-think of the materials used for the equipment itself.

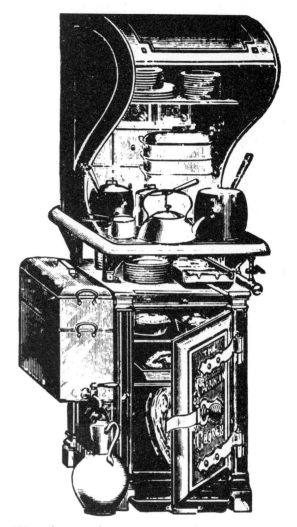

261 Parkinson cooker, c. 1890. Made of cast iron with silicate packing for insulation. Water heater at left side. Plate warming hood over hotplate. By courtesy of the Gas Council

The fact is that all gas cookers continued to be made of the same materials as the solid-fuel kitchen range and were, therefore, just as laborious to keep clean and unlovely to look at. Granted that a gas cooker did not produce soot and ash, but its cast-iron case had to be black-leaded and its taps and fittings of brass and steel needed emery paper, paste and a great deal of elbow-grease (258, 259, 260, 261).

As in the case of kitchen design (see chapter 2, page 29), it was the First World War which forced a change on to the designers and manufacturers. The smaller family and the disappearance of the ample supply of servants aroused housewives to become

262 'Stimex' combination gas range, fire and water circulator. By Stimex Gas Stove Co., London, c. 1920. All purpose gas appliance. Cooker has a lagged oven, three boiling burners and a grill. Hot water circulator is at the bottom on the left. There are two flues at the back. Science Museum, London

263 Iron gas ring, 1900–10

264 Radiation 'New World' gas cooker, 1923. First cooker to incorporate 'Regulo'. Science Museum, London

265 Eureka cooker by John Wright and Co. Ltd. Produced c. 1898, model in continuous production until 1916. By courtesy of Tube Investments Ltd

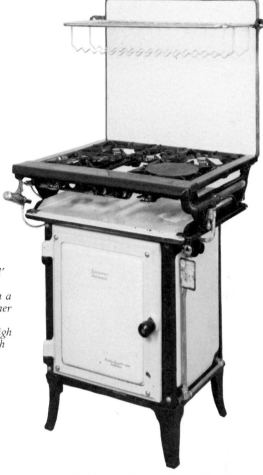

266 Above left *Regulo 'New World' table model gas cooker, 1951. The cooker was mounted on a stand with a pot-rack. The oven had a single burner and removable grid guides. The hotplate was equipped with a central high speed grill and four burners, one high power and two with simmer control. Coloured vitreous enamel finish. By courtesy of Tube Investments Ltd*

267 Above *'Kingsway' New World gas cooker, c. 1935. Enamelled in blue and cream. Science Museum, London*

268 *Modern New World gas cooker, 1971. Finished in white and coloured vitreous enamel. Comprises two ovens, storage drawer and hot plate equipped with four burners with varied heat control and automatic ignition. Splashback incorporates fluorescent light fitting and controls, automatic oven timer, electric clock and minute minder. The wind-away sola grill is situated to be flush with the hot plate when not in use. When required the grill rises at the turn of a handle to the height most suitable for individual cooking. When fully extended it becomes a rotisserie with three spits and three heat settings. By courtesy of Tube Investments Ltd*

vocal in demanding easier-care surfaces and more attractive and colourful equipment. Manufacturers began to introduce cookers clad in white or cream enamelled iron panelling. At first this was only applied to the top of the oven and the splashback, but in 1927 R. and A. Main had marketed the all-over enamelled cooker[8] and in the 1930s coloured vitreous enamel was introduced (265).

Other improvements were also made. Ovens were better insulated, the cooker was stream-lined and stripped of extraneous decoration and enamelled iron sheets lined an easier-to-clean oven. Some cookers became multi-purpose, for example, the Stimax combination gas range (262) which incorporated an oven, grill, boiling rings, a hot water circulator and a gas fire.

The most notable innovation was the introduction in 1923 of the oven thermostatic control. This was developed and introduced by Radiation Ltd. (now TI New World Ltd.), a company which was formed as a result of a merger in the years 1919–21 of six major, long-standing cooker manufacturers[9]. The thermostat was called Regulo and was first fitted to the Radiation New World H16 cooker (264). It was the forerunner of all such thermostatic controls and the name regulo has long since passed into the language in this context (267). The manufacturers also initiated the custom of supplying a cookery book with each cooker.

In the post-war years the 1950s saw the standardisation by manufacturers of their thermostat settings so that whatever the make of cooker, the same foods needed to be cooked at the same mark. The high-level grill was introduced, also automatic ignition to burners, thermostatic hot-plate burners and lift-off oven doors. The cooker became more stream-lined and easy to clean (266). It lost its legs and the space at the bottom was utilised as a storage drawer or a warm cabinet. The Sola Grill was introduced in the 1960s; this gave a balanced, even heat at all settings. In the same decade there became available rotisseries, spits and cookers which were being designed to blend and fit in with kitchen units.

Innovations and improvements in the 1970s, in line with other types of cooking appliances, have included self-clean oven linings. Automatic oven-timing devices (introduced into its cookers in 1965 by Radiation Ltd.) have made it possible for the working housewife to leave her dinner in the oven at breakfast time secure in the knowledge that the oven will switch itself on and off as she has set it, the food being ready to eat when the family returns from work and school. Electric spark ignition has been introduced for burners and graduated simmer control is available on some cookers. An important safety feature has been the introduction of the flame failure device to the oven burner. Country-wide conversion to natural gas, begun in 1966, has been achieved in a remarkably short time (268).

Cooking by electricity

The fourth of the major cooking fuels, electricity, was a late starter. The phenomenon of static electricity produced by friction was known to the ancient Greeks. As long ago as 600 BC they observed that after a piece of amber had been rubbed it would attract materials of light weight. They also knew that the torpedo fish produced (electric) shocks. It was William Gilbert (1544–1603), Queen Elizabeth's physician and man of science, who referred to such attractions of materials due to friction as 'electric', after the Greek word for amber which is 'electron'. Gilbert spent many years studying and experimenting on magnetism: an important contribution in the sixteenth century to safe navigation on the high seas.

Great advances in the understanding of electricity and magnetism were made by Michael Faraday (1791–1867) in his experimental work which led to his electrical discoveries, the crowning one of which was his successful induction of electric currents in 1831: an experiment which he described to the Royal Society in London on 24 November of that year.

During the next 40 years the work of scientists from a number of European countries and America contributed to a wider comprehension of the subject, but the technology lagged behind and it was not until, in the 1870s, the generation of electricity was developed sufficiently to provide a practical source of current that electricity could be used as a means of illumination. As in the development of gas, electricity was used for lighting for several decades before it was adapted as a power source for heating and cooking.

One of the leading pioneers in Britain in the field of electrical engineering was R. E. B. Crompton (1845–1940), who designed one of the early arc lamps. In his factory at Chelmsford he manufactured these as well as electric generators and meters measuring and recording electricity. In 1879 Crompton was responsible for illuminating the Henley Regatta and

269 Above, left *GEC 'Magnet' electric
toaster. c. 1920. Three heating elements.
Science Museum, London*

270 Above *GEC electric cooker, 1895.
Cooker has no hotplate. Oven heated by
three electric elements of Archer
system. Science Museum, London*

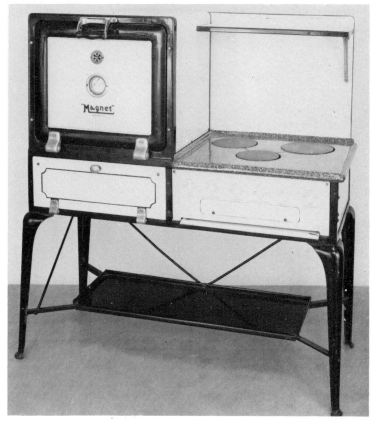

271 *GEC eye-level cooker on split-level
pattern, 1927. Vitreous enamel-covered
iron. Science Museum, London*

later the grounds and lakes of Alexandra Palace with Crompton lamps powered by Gramme generators. It was Sir Joseph Wilson Swan (1828–1914) who had first produced the carbon filament lamp in 1860.[10] Twenty years later Crompton and Swan met. This led to co-operation between two enterprises, the Swan United Electric Light Company and Crompton and Company to manufacture Swan lamps and fittings with generators to supply them.

During the 1880s electric lighting was slowly adopted. It was introduced at the Mansion House and the Law Courts in London and a new housing estate in Kensington. The first power station at Holborn Viaduct began to supply domestic consumers, but these were few as yet as most buildings were not so far wired for electricity. The possibilities of cooking by this means were being explored in the 1890s. In 1891 an electric cooker was demonstrated at the Electrical Fair held at Crystal Palace. Two years later a model electric kitchen was displayed at the Chicago World Fair.

In the meantime Crompton, in collaboration with H. Dowsing and E.J. Fox, was designing and manufacturing a range of electrical appliances. In 1900 the Crompton Company catalogue was advertising ovens, hot-plates, saucepans, frying pans, kettles, coffee urns and hot cupboards. By 1894 the Crompton electric cooker was being made for sale. An 1895 cooker of similar type is displayed in the Science Museum (270). Like most early electric cookers, it resembles a safe. Made of metal sheeting on a metal frame, it has no hot-plate. The oven is heated by elements placed at the top and bottom and controlled by the four brass switches at the side of the cooker. The heating elements were made of wire coiled round cylindrical ceramic formers. Most of the early cookers were like this, consisting of an oven and a number of separate appliances – griller, kettle, frying pan, hot-plate – which were put on top of the oven or set on the floor beside it. They were all wired separately and plugged in to a panel of switches on the wall above.

By 1900 the electric cooker had become a practical proposition, but until the 1920s few people wanted one. The cookers were not attractive to look at nor were they easy to keep clean: in fact, they looked just like gas or solid fuel cooking appliances, black, cast iron, ugly monsters. They were, of course, cleaner to use since there were no dirt-making burners, but this very quality was the one which made most people distrust electric cooking. The heat was not visible. The

cooker became hot, but it was only too easy to burn oneself inadvertently. The elements were as yet unreliable; they easily burned out, they were very slow to heat up and, therefore, expensive to use. But the most important factor mitigating against electric cooking was that most people already possessed a solid fuel or gas stove and few homes until the 1920s were wired for electric current.

The electric supply companies and the cooker manufacturers mounted vigorous advertising campaigns stressing the cleanliness of electric cooking, its convenience and qualities of heat conservation. The supply companies followed the earlier example of the gas companies and offered their cookers for hire at low rentals in order to popularise them. For example, the City of London Electric Lighting Company advertised in their leaflet of 1894 electric ovens for hire at 7s (35p) to 12s (60p) per quarter and a current charge of 4d. ($1\frac{1}{2}$p) per unit: half the usual price. Despite these inducements, sales and rentals were only marginally increased.

Between 1900 and 1914 a number of designs of electric cooker were put on the market. These were nearly all based on the gas models. The manufacturer produced a gas cooker without its gas taps and burners and substituted electric switches and burners. Like the gas cookers the electric ones were made of cast iron finished with black stove enamel. They had no flat hob surface but were fitted with open-type boiling plates instead of gas burners. The appliance was not efficient as the oven ventilation had been designed for gas not electricity. Elements continued to burn out quickly until after 1906, when nickel-chrome alloy was adopted for making resistance wire. It was found, with experience, that the oven elements were more effective if they were placed at the oven sides instead of at the top and bottom as in early models. Generally these elements were bonded to the underside of a cast-iron plate; they took a long time to heat up and to cool down. One needed to switch on the oven at least half an hour before wishing to cook the food. Heavy cast-iron pans had to be used on the boiling plates, another factor which put housewives off using electricity: they preferred the new, lighter-weight aluminium pans when they became available.

Among the cooker designs produced in these years the 'Plexsim', made by Simplex Electric Cooker Ltd. (now TI Creda Ltd.), was marketed in 1912. It was very similar to the type just described. In the same

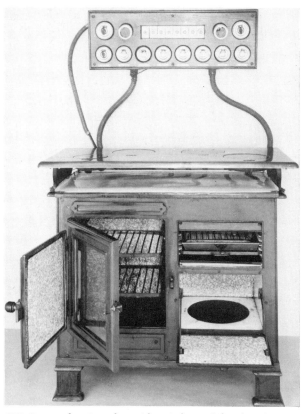

272 Carron electric cooker with switches and fuse-board, c. 1912. Made of cast iron with mottled grey enamelling to line oven and doors also has glass inner door. Circular elements mounted on fire-brick base are placed at top and bottom of the oven. Four hot-plate heaters, each enclosed in an iron box. Cooker 4 ft wide. Science Museum, London

273 'Modernette' Belling electric cooker, 1919. Made of light steel. Hot plate has three heaters and a grill, all with three heat settings. Coiled wire elements exposed. Plate warmer at side. Science Museum, London

year the Carron Iron Company brought out its large, double-door cooker, the outer door being lined with a sheet of grey enamelled iron and the inner one made of glass. This is a massive iron cooker, about four feet wide (one is displayed in the Science Museum, 272), typical yet an advanced model for its time. The hot-plate has four heaters enclosed in an iron box. Number one is designed with on/off positions, but the other three have three settings each. There is an oven, a grill and a hot cupboard. The large control switches – one for each section of the appliance – were fixed to a wooden board on the wall above the cooker. Each switch had its own fuse and an indicator light glowed red when that part of the appliance was switched on. The cooker is an impressive piece of apparatus. Only one feature of the design seems to spell disaster. In order to switch on or off any part of the appliance, one

had to lean over the heaters and steaming saucepans upon them.

From 1908 Mr A. F. Berry, founder of the British Electric Transformer Company (later Tricity and now Thorn Domestic Appliances Ltd.) endeavoured to persuade housewives through lectures and demonstrations to cook by electricity. The Tricity oven and separate boiling plate of 1917 (274, 275) helped to popularise cooking by electricity as the appliance was smaller and more convenient than massive cookers such as the 'Carron' and could be adapted to cook for a variable number of people by using a suitable range of ovens.

Mr C.R. Belling also encouraged the use of electricity for cooking by marketing his smaller cookers. The 'Modernette' of 1919 was made of light steel. It had two boiling burners and a grill, each with three

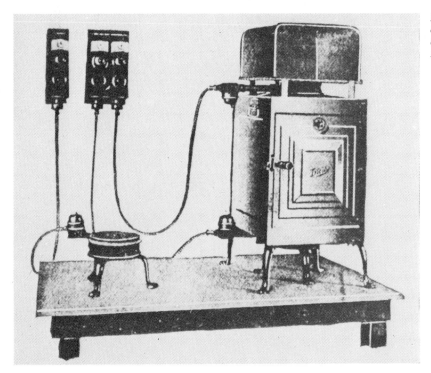

274, 275 Tricity electric cookers, 1917. By courtesy of Thorn Domestic Appliances (Electrical) Ltd.

In this illustration the cooker is installed in a country cottage

heat settings, also a plate warmer. As in most cookers of this time, the burners were of the open type so that, if the contents of saucepans boiled over, the spillover ran straight down into the coiled wire heating element and often caused a short circuit (273). In the mid-1920s Belling brought out the prototype of the famous Baby Belling; a small table model with an oven and a single boiling plate which could alternate as a grill.

The split-level cooker made its appearance in 1917. In this the oven was placed at the side of the hot-plate boiling burners and the whole appliance was mounted on a stand to obviate stooping (271).

It was not until the decade of the 1930s that electricity began seriously to compete with gas for the housewife's favour. By then the majority of households were wired to mains supply and the cost of consumption had been markedly reduced. At the same time a number of significant improvements were made in cooker design and utility. As with gas cookers the easy-clean vitreous enamel finish, first in white and cream then in colours, replaced the old black iron stove.

The great step forward was the introduction by Creda of automatic oven control in 1933 (281). This was the electric cooker manufacturer's answer to Radiation's gas 'Regulo'. At this time a thermometer was fitted to the oven door so that the cook could check how the oven temperature was faring. The thermometer continued to be fitted until the thermostatic control was later fully reliable (276, 277). Before this the cook had to keep opening the oven door to check on the progress of her cakes, to the detriment of the food and the size of the electricity bill. Improvements were also made in insulation and ventilation of the oven, in the positioning of burners and the design of the elements.

One of the features which changed most radically was the boiling plate on the hob. As mentioned previously, early models had open-type heating elements which 'shorted' when food boiled over. These were followed by the solid cast-iron plates which were slow to heat up and cool down. Such plates were cheap and reliable but wasted time and electricity. The elements, of coiled wire wound into ceramic moulds, were covered by the iron plates. The heat generated by the coils had to permeate the plate before it could warm the saucepan. In order to utilise the electricity to the best advantage the housewife had to organise her cooking in a careful programme, both on the hob and in the oven, so that she made full use of all residual heat in the elements. This was a deterrent to would-be converts to electric cooking: gas was so much quicker and cheaper. The fast-heating tubular-sheathed radiant rings were introduced in the 1930s, but for some time tended to wear quickly. When the teething troubles of manufacture had been overcome they were greeted with enthusiasm and electric cooking was at last competitive with gas. By 1939 over a million households were using electricity for cooking, though this compared with nine and a half million which preferred gas.

In the post-war years the picture gradually changed as boiling rings heated up still more quickly – a simmerstat was introduced for them which gave a wide range of heat control and split rings enabled only the centre part of a radiant to be used if only a small pan was required. The auto-timer controlled electric cooker was introduced with automatic switch on and off for the oven.

Electric cookers marched in step with gas designs with regard to replacement of the legs with a storage drawer or hot compartment, the introduction of spits and larger grills and the removable, self-clean oven linings. Also adopted have been the fan-assisted ovens and the two-oven design with one large oven and one smaller one which can serve alternatively as a grill compartment with split-grill heating elements (280). There was, too, the combined grill and spit which was able to cook a complete meal in a portable appliance.

In the 1970s have come the ceramic hob and cool-top-hob. The former is made of toughened heat-resistant glass; patterned marked heating areas are incorporated beneath this surface and these become hot while the surrounding area remains cool. The hob is pleasant in appearance and easy to keep clean. The cool-top-hob type of cooker functions by induction heating. Under the hob a wire coil creates an oscillating magnetic field. This induces an eddy current in the metal saucepan or dish placed on the cooker and so heats the food while the ceramic surface of the hob remains cool.

These last two products of modern technology represent the Rolls Royce level of electric cooking. But even for the average housewife electricity is now more attractive than at any previous time. The cost of electric current is still higher than the supply of gas, but the new cookers are so fast, clean and efficient in conservation of energy that the running costs are not

276 GEC electric cooker, 1927. Stoved black cast iron and polished steel. Polished steel hot plate has three heating plates each with three heat settings. Grill switch is only on/off. On left side of cooker is a 2-pin socket for plug which can be used for a kettle or a toaster. Science Museum, London

277 Enamelled iron electric cooker, 1935. Hot plate has three heating plates. Theremometer fitted on the exterior of the oven door. Castle Museum, York

278 Morphy-Richards toaster, c. 1970. (Author)

dissimilar. A further advantage is that an electric cooker is, model for model, a much cheaper appliance to purchase than its gas counterpart.

The sum of these factors, added to the fact that a proportion of new houses built since the last war are 'all-electric', has dramatically altered the cooking preferences of the nation: in 1979 41% of the population were cooking by electricity.

Microwave ovens

Traditional means of cooking using solid fuel, gas, electricity and oil all involve the transference of heat. Microwave cooking is a new and different method which makes use of radio waves of length as short as 12 cm. The electronic devices which were first used to generate these very short radio waves for radar purposes were developed during the Second World War both in Britain and the USA. The first microwave cooker was produced in America soon afterwards and this method of cooking was introduced into Britain in 1959.

In all forms of cooking, the effect of the heat is to raise the temperature of the material (the food, in the present case), i.e. to increase the agitation of its molecules. In the microwave cooker, the very high frequency radio waves (the microwaves) penetrate easily to the centre of the food and, by agitating the water molecules within the food, raise its temperature, i.e. heat it. Thus, the heating effect is produced within the food itself and is not – as in conventional cooking – transferred to the food's surface by radiation from a source exterior to the food, although in the oven. The design of the inside of the microwave oven assists the concentration of the microwaves at the food by having reflecting polished interior surfaces to the walls and by the use of a rotating fan attached to its roof from the blades of which the microwaves are scattered. Microwave cooking will not 'brown' food, so if it is desired to brown steak or cheese, for example, the food must be placed, after microwave cooking, under a conventional grill.

The chief characteristic of microwave cooking is the immense reduction in the required cooking time. An example is given in the label on the Philips' oven displayed in the Science Museum, London (279), indicating that the cooking time for a sausage is about 10 seconds, a cutlet or rissole 15 seconds and a chicken only 45 seconds. These ovens are now extensively used by the catering trade for quickly re-heating

prepared, frozen meals. They are slowly being introduced into homes, but the high cost of purchase is an inhibiting factor.

Electric toasters

The first step towards a self-heating method of toasting slices of food was the toast crisper of the early years of the twentieth century. The bread had to be toasted in the old-fashioned manner with a fork in front of a fire or under a gas grill, but it was then put into the crisper to keep it from becoming cold and soggy. The crisper was 'powered' by a spirit burner and had a covering hood.

The electric toaster proper was a feature of the 1920s. Typical was the 'Magnet' (269), which had three heating elements consisting of bare wire wound on flat sheets of mica. The slices of bread were held against the sides by spring-loading. In order to cook the other side the slices had to be turned by hand. When cooked they were put on top of the toaster to keep warm. The 'Universal' electric toaster of 1923, an American model made by Landers, Frary and Clark, was a more advanced design which turned the bread round to cook the second side. Both these models, like most electric appliances of the time, were not earthed (278).

Materials for cooking vessels

Before the nineteenth century such vessels had been heavy to handle and difficult to keep clean. Iron, brass and copper were the metals chiefly used and with iron, the commonest and cheapest material, rusting was a great problem. By the early nineteenth century a black varnish was used to coat the exterior of such utensils and this reduced the cleaning labour. During the century a process of vitreous enamelling was developed to improve such exterior finishes. Vitreous enamel, also known as porcelain enamel, is made from particles of glass fused on to metal at very high temperatures.[11] The process has been used as a decorative medium for jewellery and armour over 2,000 years, but was developed for applying to sheet iron in Germany just after the middle of the nineteenth century. Nowadays the enamel, which can be coloured and patterned, is applied to aluminium, cast iron and steel vessels.

Aluminium is the third most abundant element found in the world after oxygen and silicon, but in nature it does not occur as a metal but in various

279 *Philips microwave cooker, 1968.
Science Museum, London*

280 Below, left *Creda 'Carefree'
cooker, 1976. Enamelled sheet metal
and stainless steel. Hob has four
variable radiant rings (one fast). Two
ovens with auto-clean liners. Top oven
alternates as a large, split grill. Auto-
timer, minute minder and electric clock. (Author)*

281 *Creda electric cooker, 1933. Model
in which thermostatic control was
introduced into electric cookers. Fully
enamelled cooker. Hot plate has two
heaters; the one on the left is the newly-
introduced spiral tube element which
glows when hot: on the right, the
square heater has an open, coiled wire
element which heats the grill beneath.
The thermostat works on the oven only.
Science Museum, London*

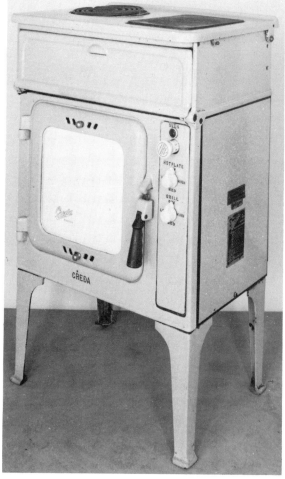

282 Aga cookware, 1979. From left to right: Cast-iron enamelled casserole, cast-iron enamelled omelette pan and omelette dish with non-stick finish, and aluminium double boiler, pans and percolator. By courtesy of Agaheat Appliances Ltd

compounds. Today, it is most commonly derived from the naturally-occurring ore, bauxite, which contains much aluminium hydrate. The name 'aluminium' comes from the Latin word *alumen*. This was the term applied by the Romans to salts which they found in volcanic areas around the coasts of the Mediterranean Sea and which they used both in medicine and in dyeing. It is believed that these salts were mixed sulphates of iron and aluminium.

From the middle of the eighteenth century attempts were made in a number of countries to reduce and separate alumina (as it was called in Britain) by means of smelting and in both chemical and electrical experiments. Small quantities of the metal were produced. The manufacture of aluminium only became a commercial proposition after the successful electrolytic process was developed independently in the 1880s by the Frenchman Paul Héroult and the American Charles Hall. By the 1920s aluminium had become a popular material for cookware due to its lightweight quality and ease of cleaning.

Stainless (rustless) steel became a viable proposition for cutlery after 1916 when the English metallurgist Brearley patented his process of alloying steel with chromium. Stainless steel cooking vessels were slower in development and were not produced in any great quantity until after the Second World War. Modern stainless steel cookware is produced from a steel alloy in which 18% chrome plus 8% nickel are added to low carbon steel[12]. It is hard and durable but expensive because of the high cost of both material and manufacture. Because it is a poor conductor of heat, better quality saucepans are clad externally with copper or aluminium.

The twentieth century has brought a number of new materials and processes which have given variety and convenience in cookware (282). Borosilicate glass was introduced in America from whence it has become familiarly known to us as Pyrex. At first made only in transparent glass form, but later in colours and patterns, this glass with high silica content, which is resistant to thermal shock and therefore may be transferred without delay from the heat of the oven to rinsing in cold water, is widely used in all homes for oven-to-table ware. More expensive and less ubiquitous is the ovenproof and flameproof ceramic glass made from pyroceram, a material developed in the USA in the research carried out for making nose-cones of guided rocket missiles. It was introduced to Britain in the early 1960s under the trade name of pyrosil.

Probably the advance which has brought the greatest advantage to post-war housewives is the non-stick coating of cookware and bakeware. This material, polytetrafluoroethylene, usually shortened to PTFE, was produced at the Du Pont laboratories in the USA in 1938 in research into refrigerants. It was not until the 1950s that work on it was adapted for cookware. This coating finish was marketed widely in the USA in the early 1960s and introduced to Britain in 1967.

PTFE is an inert organic material resistant to a wide range of temperatures and chemicals so food will not adhere to it and it is easily cleaned. Du Pont supply the coating to manufacturers under the trade name of Teflon and Silverstone. The surface of the interior of an aluminium vessel is roughened and a primer coat of PTFE is sprayed on it and fired at a temperature of about 200°C. A further coat is given to quality cookware. In the Silverstone finish there are three layers, a hard filler material being inserted between to give a greater durability.

The easy-clean non-stick coatings have also been introduced for cooker ovens. The auto-clean oven appeared in Britain in 1968. This interior was treated so that if the oven temperature, after cooking was finished, was raised to 480°C, any splashes were burnt to an ash which could quickly be swept up. This was followed in the 1970s by the self-cleaning or stay-clean oven. Here the detachable oven linings are coated with a catalytic substance which enables the splashes to be burned off as they are made.

CHAPTER FIVE

The Storage and Preservation of Food

The storage of food

Careful thought has always been given to the keeping of food which, before the advent of the modern domestic refrigerator, presented a considerable problem. This was particularly so in the days when every particle of edible meat, fish, fruit, vegetables and grain had to be stored to last the community through the winter from autumn until next season's growing time (chapter 2 page 52).

From the Middle Ages on the larger households living in monasteries, castles and great houses were served by separate storerooms of all kinds: the larder or pantry, stillroom and buttery (chapter I page 15). As time passed these larders were extended and in large houses there were two or three, one being reserved to contain meat and game which was being hung prior to cooking.

Food was also kept in wooden cupboards which had ventilation holes pierced in the panels. Such livery cupboards[1] or ambries (aumbries)[2] were often decoratively carved, a design feature being made out of the need to provide air holes (283, 284). Cupboards were in use, especially in smaller homes, to contain fresh food such as milk and butter. In the western Scottish Highlands, where basketwork was a skilled craft and the materials were to hand, the ventilation was frequently provided by basketwork or wickerwork panels let into the sides of a wooden-framed cupboard. These were known as 'larders' (285).

By the nineteenth century nearly all houses had a pantry or larder adjacent to the kitchen (chapter 1 page 21). These were spacious, walk-in rooms containing utensils and food. Shelving was often of stone or marble in order to keep edible foodstuffs cool. After the First World War, in the 1920s, some foods were kept in the kitchen cabinet (chapter 1 page 29 fig. 23), when drawers were lined to store bread and flour. The larder continued to be of vital importance until the coming of the household refrigerator, but the contemporary kitchen no longer has need of such storage facilities.

Various types of containers have evolved from earliest times because of their suitability in shape or material for storing different foodstuffs. Characteristic of the ancient classical world around the shores of the Mediterranean were the great earthenware storage jars known as *amphorae*.

An *amphora* is shaped with a slender neck which has a handle at each side. At the lower end of the vessel the swelling body narrows towards a spiked base. *Amphorae* were designed in this way so that they were equally useful for transportation and for storage. They were used to contain oil, wine, grain or salted fish and when filled were sealed with a wood, cork or clay bung made airtight with pitch. *Amphorae* were transported by sea and, packed in straw, were economical in storage space in a ship. On land each jar could be carried easily by two men with ropes suspended from a pole across their shoulders. In the home they were stored in special racks or by inserting their pointed bases in sand on the storeroom floor. *Amphorae* came to Roman Britain in quantity from Mediterranean countries; many survive and can be seen in museums (1, 2, 286, 288). The carrot *amphora* (descriptively named) is a variation in design. It usually contained dried fruits imported from the eastern Mediterranean (1, 289).

Earthenware storage jars of more familiar shape

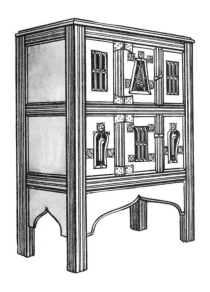

283 Left *Standing ambry or livery cupboard. Carved wood, c. 1500. Victoria and Albert Museum, London*

284 Right *Carved wood ambry, late fifteenth century. Victoria and Albert Museum, London*

285 *Scottish 'larder' of wood and wickerwork*

286 *Roman amphorae. Colchester and Essex Museum*

287 *Roman earthenware jar. Salisbury Museum*

have been in use through the centuries in Britain for containing all kinds of food and liquids (287, 295). Wooden and glass vessels were also suitable, but before glass was available in general supply, liquids were stored in vessels of skin and hide and this led to the characteristically English leather bottle. These containers were hand-sewn from pieces of tough ox-hide (291). The large size black jack or bombard was a wide-mouthed jug often made of jack leather[3], The name bombard derived from its resemblance to the bombard cannon (294). With the ready availability of glass and stoneware at the end of the seventeenth century the leather vessels were made only rarely.

Different types of container were found to be suitable for different foodstuffs. For example, vinegar was stored in wood or glass (later stoneware) vessels, wooden tubs were best for butter, sugar and flour (290), herbs were kept in paper bags. Yeast was stored in wood, jam, jellies, preserved fruit and salted foods were best in salt-glazed stoneware. Cabinets with storage drawers were in use for spices, rice and dried fruit (138).

Eggs and cheeses needed to be kept cool. The eggs were stored pointing downwards and the cheeses needed daily attention (chapter 2 page 52). Meat, which had to be hung before cooking, and bread had to be stored safely out of reach of vermin. The meat was hung in a large safe which was suspended from the ceiling. Bread was similarly stored in a suspended bread car (chapter 1 page 18 and fig. 9).

Various types of seals to make glass jars airtight were patented in the second half of the nineteenth century, and in 1908 came the 'Lightning Closure' which was sealed with the aid of a rubber ring which fitted inside the glass lid then was held in place by a metal screwband.

A serious and constant problem was how to keep the various foods secure from pests. In a community which was largely agricultural, its transport and power based on the horse and before the days of pesticides, a variety of means of destruction and deterrent were sought and tried out. Recommended remedies included sprinkling with fine tobacco to keep away moths, fumigation with brimstone (old name for sulphur) to deter fleas, leaving containers around the house which were filled with sweetened water and cobalt to kill flies. Some of the suggested cures sound worse than the disease.

There are a variety of traps on display in museums in Britain for catching and/or killing flies, wasps and mice. These are mainly of nineteenth-century date, though the designs are traditional. The usual fly or wasp trap is a corked glass vessel which is supported on short legs raising it half an inch or so above the surface on which it stands. The bottom of the vessel is open to admit entry of the fly, but this entrance is above the base of the trap so leaving a surrounding channel which is between it and the exterior walls. This channel is filled with a sweetening agent such as honey to attract the insect which, having crawled in, cannot get out (296). There are also several designs of wasp tongs, one of which squashes the insect between the two blades, while another has a fabric bag attached to one blade which traps the wasp there (292).

Mouse-traps were generally made of wood. A common design (293) was rectangular in shape, having a base and two sides. A heavy block of wood was made to fit precisely into the rectangular receptacle. In the set and baited trap, the heavy block was supported above this receptacle by a string attached to a catch containing a release pin. When the mouse nibbled at the bait, the catch was released, the pin was removed and the block fell, killing the animal. Such traps could be made of correct size for either mice or rats. Some were multiple, designed for mass murder. An alternative mechanism (297) trapped the mouse without squashing it and poisonous bait could be used here.

The preservation of food

There are six principal ways to preserve fresh food: by pickling, drying, salting, smoking, canning and freezing. The first four of these methods have been in use since classical times; the last two were not developed until the nineteenth and twentieth centuries. These first four means of preservation alter the flavour of the food; the aim of the last two is to retain the natural flavour, though there is a certain loss of taste even by use of the most modern techniques and processes.

The various traditional methods of *pickling* involved the use of chemical preservatives such as vinegar, salt and vinegar, sugar and, by the eighteenth century, borax and formalin. The use of sugar, in the case of preserving cheese, wines and beers, usually involved a process of alcoholic fermentation. The action of borax, formalin and, later, sulphurous acid, were, towards the end of the nineteenth century, found to be harmful for human consumption as well as inhibiting the activity of micro-organisms, and their

288 Roman amphorae. Colchester and Essex Museum

289 Carrot amphora, Roman. Rougemont House Museum, Exeter

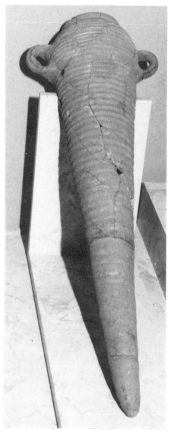

291 Leather vessels, seventeenth century. Blaise Castle House Museum, Bristol

290 Wooden flour container. Christchurch Mansion Museum, Ipswich

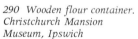

use was forbidden in the Food Acts of 1875 and 1899.

Dehydration (or drying) is probably the oldest way of preserving food. Sun-drying was the ancient classical method, used especially for meat and fish. If the drying process could be carried out quickly under a hot sun, the food would keep for quite a long time. Examples are the South African *biltong* (strips of sun-dried meat) and the North American Indian's *pemmican*, which is dried and pounded meat mixed into a cake with the aid of melted fat. Fish was also dried in this way, but in the cooler, northern countries was air-dried. From the Middle Ages onwards in the north of Scandinavia, for example, fish was gutted and washed, then hung in the open air for several weeks until hard.

From the second half of the nineteenth century ideas were developed to dry food artificially. Experiments made with eggs and milk were the most successful.

Salting food as a means of preservation was a custom almost as ancient as drying. Over the centuries, until it was discovered how to refrigerate ships and packing stores, fresh fish was only available in coastal districts and inland where fresh water sources, such as rivers and lakes, were available and these were kept stocked for the well-to-do. It was early discovered that salt, either powdered or in brine solution, acted as a preservative for both fish and meat provided that the quantity of salt in relation to the food was adequate – generally one part salt to three parts fish – and that the food was completely fresh and undamaged before salting.

It was the Romans who developed by experience scientific methods of salting. The fish caught in the Mediterranean sea was quickly salted and transported to all parts of the Empire. In the Middle Ages also fish was widely salted and pickled in brine. The merchants of the Hanseatic League organised large-scale operations in the North and Baltic Seas catching, for example, herring and later, cod. Quickly after landing they gutted the fish, washed it in sea water, then packed it in wooden barrels with salt between the layers and topped up with brine. By the end of the fifteenth century Dutch and English fishermen were salting the fish on board the moment the nets had been drawn up. It was discovered by experience that the sooner the fish was immersed in salt and the cleaner it was at the time, the longer would it last to be fit to eat. Strict regulations were enforced regarding the use of clean barrels, the quantity of salt and the quality of the fish. Under such careful conditions the fish would keep for at least a year.

An alternative method of preserving fish which has been in use for centuries is *smoking*. There are various ways of doing this. One common way, known as cold smoking because the fish is not fully cooked, is to gut, split and wash the fish, then pickle it for a while before hanging it up in rows over a fire in which the flames have been damped down. Oak chips, peat or sawdust are used to impart colour and flavour. In some other methods the fish can be simultaneously cooked and smoked.

These means of preservation of food, drying, pickling, salting and smoking continued to be the only widespread, satisfactory methods until the second half of the nineteenth century. The arrival of railway transport made it possible to move the food more quickly from source to towns but it was still not fast enough, especially in summer, to keep food fresh.

Various efforts had been made to preserve fresh food in other ways, the chief of which was to cover or coat it in order to exclude the air, but these had a marked lack of success. The difficulty of keeping food on long voyages by sea had always been a great problem and experiments were made from the seventeenth century onwards in cooking meat then packing it in containers and pouring melted butter over it before sealing. Alternative substances included gravy and melted paraffin wax.

Canning

In 1795 Napoleon was so concerned about the difficulty of feeding his armies in their extensive European campaigns that he appealed for anyone to come forward, who could find a way to preserve fresh food so that it could be transported for use with an army on the march. As an inducement Napoleon offered 12,000 francs. This was eventually won by a Paris confectioner, Nicholas Appert, who had the idea of heating food in glass jars and sealing them. Appert was successful in his experimentation with this process in 1809. He put the fresh food into the glass jars, corked them loosely then immersed them in a container of boiling water. After a period of time, which he judged by experience, the corks were pressed home and sealed. Appert is generally recognised as the pioneer in this method of preservation by heating food in vessels which were then hermetically sealed. The following year, in 1810, his treatise was published, entitled *The Art of Preserving Animal Substances for Many Years.*

This was the first step, but glass jars are not too convenient for transportation. The second advance came from Peter Durand, an Englishman who took out a patent in 1810 for the idea of using canisters[4] made of iron or steel thinly coated with tin for packing heat-sterilised food. Durand does not seem to have made use of his idea commercially but within a year or so more than one firm was producing such tin cans and marketing food contained in them. By 1814 Donkin and Hall were supplying the Royal Navy and canned food was included in the provisions for Sir Edward Parry's third Polar expedition in 1824.[5]

By the 1820s canned food was on sale in the shops and soon both the Navy and the Army began to order large consignments for their Services. As yet, though, the principles by which the food was preserved in these canning processes were imperfectly understood and there were a number of instances of food which went bad in cans and of cans which 'blew' or exploded. In the later 1840s and early 1850s several large consignments of food, intended for Service personnel, suffered in this way. As a result the public became suspicious of all canned food and a government enquiry was ordered into a particularly serious case of a large Navy order.

The research work on bacteria carried out in the 1860s by Louis Pasteur brought a greater understanding of the scientific principles involved in this method of food preservation. Previously tins used had often been of too large a size for the food contained in them and had been heated at temperatures too low to sterilise completely the food in the centre of the cans. The size of cans was reduced and the contents heated for longer at higher temperatures.

The canning process proved especially valuable to countries such as Australia and America which needed to transport their large quantities of meat to Europe. A canning factory had been opened in Sydney in Australia as early as the 1840s and most of its production supplied ships intended for Britain. By the 1860s, triggered off by steep rises in the cost of home-produced meat due to a serious loss of cattle suffering from disease, sales of canned meat from Australia rose markedly. America had been slower to develop the canning business in the first half of the nineteenth century than either Britain or Australia

but, after the Civil War, took up canning in a big way. Large-scale research was undertaken into the failure of some processes[6], the results of which made canning safer and finally set at rest the doubts of the purchasing public. The familiar baked beans in tomato sauce were being canned by 1880. Heinz introduced them to Britain in 1905.

A modern housewife, equipped in her kitchen with an easy-to-work hand- or wall- tin-opener, would probably be surprised to learn that, as late as 1860, one of the great problems of canned food was how to open the can. Early cans were made by hand, the lids soldered on and helpful instructions were printed on them suggesting that the best method of opening was by hammer and chisel. The domestic opener was introduced in America in the 1860s and was supplied with tins of bully beef. It was characterised by being made of painted cast iron in the shape of a bull's head, the handle finished in the form of his tail. A two-part steel blade was fastened to the bull's neck; one end was intended for piercing a hole in the lid and the other for cutting round the tin. The bull's head tin-opener was on sale well into the twentieth century (298, 302). Other, plainer designs followed (300) after the double-sealed ridged can lid was introduced during the first decade of the century. The wheel-turning type of cutter became popular in the 1930s (299).

Preservation by chilling: refrigeration

Since very early times it has been known that fresh food will keep longer if the temperature is lowered. Over the centuries the natural means of cooling, by cold water, ice and snow, have been employed where they have been available. Ice cellars were in use in China as long ago as 1000 BC. In ancient Greece food was contained in earthenware dishes which were then immersed in cold water. The Romans used snow and ice to cool drinks and keep food.

In Britain, from the Middle Ages onwards, large establishments, such as monasteries, castles and great houses, built storage places for ice. There was then no means of making ice so it was collected from lakes and rivers in winter-time and stored underground to use for chilling food. In monasteries deep wells were dug where the ice would remain solid for as long as possible.

From the seventeenth century large country houses were equipped with ice-houses, many of which can

292 Wooden wasp tongs

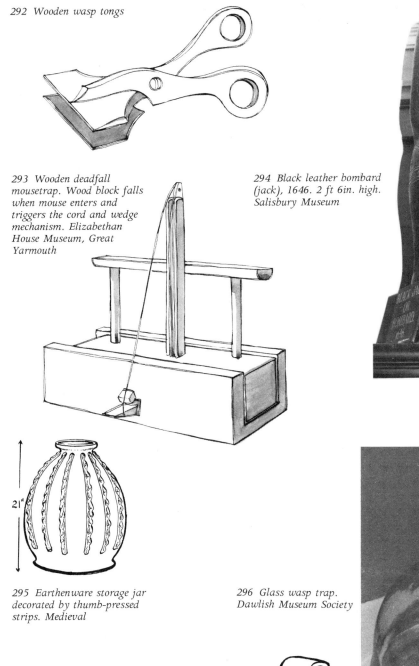

293 Wooden deadfall mousetrap. Wood block falls when mouse enters and triggers the cord and wedge mechanism. Elizabethan House Museum, Great Yarmouth

294 Black leather bombard (jack), 1646. 2 ft 6in. high. Salisbury Museum

295 Earthenware storage jar decorated by thumb-pressed strips. Medieval

296 Glass wasp trap. Dawlish Museum Society

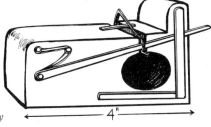

297 Wood mousetrap with metal bar and spring, eighteenth-nineteenth century

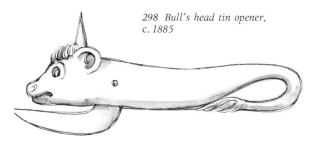

298 Bull's head tin opener,
c. 1885

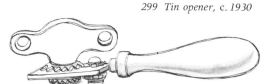

299 Tin opener, c. 1930

300 Tin opener with
beechwood handle, 1929.
Price 7d. (3p) in Harrods'
Catalogue, 1929

301 Refrigerating cabinet.
Harrods' Catalogue, 1929
Price £6 19s. 6d. (£6.97½p).
Wooden cabinet, insulated
and lined with steel

302 Bronzed metal bull's
head tin opener. Harrods'
Catalogue, 1929. Price 8d.
(3½p)

303 Seeger patented dry air
siphon refrigerator. A
refrigerating cabinet made
c. 1890 in USA. Cabinet
made of wood insulated with
zinc and porcelain. Blocks of
ice kept in top right hand
section. Science Museum,
London

still be seen today in the grounds of such houses open to the public. Some were still in use well into the twentieth century. These ice-houses were tunnelled into a hillside and lined with brick for good insulation. They were fed in winter with snow and ice and some were built by the side of running water which could be diverted into the ice-house during the winter months and supply the ice. Vents were constructed in some vaults, angled towards the north-east to direct the colder winds into them. The idea also had commercial possibilities. Ice-houses were built in towns and cool drinks were sold in the summer months from an adjacent stall.

By the early nineteenth century the demand for ice had grown enormously. The urban population had increased greatly and there was a growing need for ice to keep fish which the fleets were bringing in larger catches from further afield than ever before. There was still no satisfactory method of making ice artificially so it had to be collected and transported over considerable distances. In Britain many farmers flooded their fields in winter, collected the ice and sold it to country estates, trawler fleets and port warehouses.

By the 1830s great insulated ice-warehouses were being built in the large ports to store ice which was being imported, first from the USA and later from Norway. In America the population was growing rapidly and many communities lived in areas which were very warm in summer. Ice was needed urgently in ever-increasing quantity. Cutting ice on the ponds and rivers of the northern parts of the country and transporting it all over the USA as well as exporting it in quantity became big business.

In Britain ice was used to preserve fish from the later eighteenth century when salmon was despatched in ice-filled boxes from Scotland to London. By the 1860s it was being used in the holds of trawlers and there was increasing demand from the railways carrying food.

In the home, demand for ice was also rapidly growing where, as the century progressed, more kitchens possessed an ice-box, ice-chest or ice-safe. Insulated boxes cooled by ice were in use in American homes as early as 1830. By the late 1840s these were wooden cupboards or chests lined with zinc or slate and insulated with various substances: charcoal, ash, felt, asbestos, cork or slag wool. The insulation was contained between the outer casing and the zinc lining. The ice was delivered daily by an ice-man and the food placed upon it.

By the second half of the century it had been realised that the best use of the ice-box could be made if the ice was kept in a compartment in the upper part of the cupboard where the air could circulate around it and the food stored in the lower section. The heat from the food warmed the air which rose and melted some of the ice, the water from which then drained away down a special channel. The cooler (heavier) air then circulating round the ice descended to the food and cooled it. The process continued until all the ice had melted and had to be replaced. So successful were these ice-boxes that sophisticated models of chests and cupboards (known as refrigerators) were still shown in the 1929 Harrods' catalogue, alongside gas and electric refrigerators. The ice-boxes were much cheaper than the gas and electric refrigerators (301, 303).

For centuries ways had been sought to lower the temperature artificially and so make ice, but satisfactory equipment to do this was not developed commercially to pack and transport foodstuffs in bulk until the late 1870s and the domestic refrigerator is an appliance of the twentieth century.

Marco Polo is said to have returned to Venice with a recipe for making water ices which he had obtained on his travels in China. In sixteenth-century Venice it was discovered that a mixture of one-third salt and two-thirds snow would lower the temperature sufficiently to freeze water. This mixture of salt and snow was widely used after this in Europe to maintain the cold in ice-houses. In 1755 the Scottish physician William Cullen (1710–90) devised a means of evaporating water with the aid of an air pump and thereby he obtained temperatures low enough to make ice. Sir John Leslie (1766–1832), Scottish physicist and mathematician, made Cullen's apparatus more effective by introducing a saucer of sulphuric acid which absorbed the water vapour.

The basis of modern commercial refrigeration was laid by the contribution of a German professor of thermodynamics, Karl von Linde (1842–1934) when, in 1876, he introduced an ammonia vapour-compression system of refrigeration. Ammonia (studied experimentally amongst others by the great Michael Faraday in 1823) has a critical temperature of 132.4°C – well above that of the room, as was, no doubt, appreciated by von Linde. This work led to the wide-scale development of plant which came to be used for carrying food-stuff cargoes in ships.

The greatest incentive for the development of such plant came from the need for transporting by sea the large quantities of Australian, New Zealand and South American meat to Britain and Europe. Even before von Linde's contribution, two Australian emigrés from Britain were setting up business there. Dr James Harrison was a Scot who went to Australia in 1837. He became interested in the possibilities of refrigeration in the 1850s and developed a sulphuric ether machine. He set up a refrigerating plant in Melbourne where in 1870 he was successfully freezing mutton, beef, poultry and fish. He tried to ship the frozen carcases to England in 1873 but the experiment failed. Thomas Sutcliffe Mort (1816–78) came from Lancashire. He emigrated to Australia in 1838. In 1861 he opened his first freezing plant in Sydney and, in 1876, like Harrison, attempted to send frozen cargoes of meat to England. Also like Harrison, he failed. But success was soon to come. In 1879 the first shipment of artificially chilled meat arrived in satisfactory condition in England from America. Within a few months this was followed by a shipment from Australia. By the 1890s chilling and freezing were being successfully used in shipments of eggs and fruit as well as fish.

The household mechanical refrigerator was marketed in the early twentieth century. There are two types of domestic refrigerators: the compressor design and the absorption model. The compressor type evolved from the work of Karl von Linde. In this process the vapour (usually Freon nowadays, not ammonia) is compressed and becomes a liquid when it is passed through a condenser. It has to be powered by a motor which drives the compressor. At first the energy source for this motor-drive was steam, later electricity or gas. The absorption design derives from the work of the Frenchman, Ferdinand Carré, who built an apparatus designed to operate with ammonia as refrigerant and water as the absorbent in 1859. Further contributory work was carried out by the German physiologist August Julius Geppert. An absorption refrigerator has no moving parts to wear out or make a noise. It needs no gas or electricity from the mains supply as only a small amount of heat is needed to act upon the refrigerant; this is provided by a small gas flame or electric element. There can be no leak of the refrigerant as this and the heating element are sealed in one unit. Both types of domestic

refrigerator have been made during much of the twentieth century. The compressor design is probably more common nowadays because it is more efficient and so suited to the modern 'fridge-freezer' models which demand lower temperatures.

The chief stimulus towards the production of a suitable household refrigerator came from America. The climate made such an appliance desirable and the population was sufficiently wealthy to be able to pay for it. The Domelre model[7] was sold from 1913 in Chicago. The Kelvinator came out in 1914 in Detroit. Like a number of early designs, this was powered originally by steam but later by electric motor. Due to the large size of the motor and the fact that sulphur dioxide was often used as a refrigerant, both motor and compressor were usually housed separately from the ice-box, probably in the cellar, because of the noise of the former and the smell of the latter. For many years after this the cooling unit was frequently set on top of the refrigerator, outside the food compartment, because it was so large (305, 306).

Britain lagged behind America in accepting the refrigerator. The climate was more temperate, the population was less wealthy and more conservative. The first model sold in Britain was of French compressor design in 1921. The Guardian Frigerator Company was producing refrigerators in the USA by 1919. Later known as Frigidaire Corporation, it began manufacture in Britain in 1923.

Meanwhile, in Sweden, two students Balzer Von Platen and Carl Munters, were experimenting with refrigeration at the University of Stockholm School of Technology. Though ignorant of the earlier work of Carré and Geppert, they developed in 1922 a continuous absorption unit, an invention which was then acquired by Electrolux[8]. This company spent four years in research and development of the appliance and brought out the first Swedish-made water-cooled absorption refrigerator unit in 1926. The same year this was marketed in Britain. It had a capacity of 10 cubic feet and cost £48 10s. (£48.50p).

In 1927 Electrolux began manufacturing this type of refrigerator in a new factory at Luton. These models still had wooden cabinets; they were insulated with cork and lined inside with painted sheet metal. They were cooled by a continuous flow of cold water. Soon the wooden cabinets were replaced by ones of sheet steel (304).

At this time the domestic refrigerator was still a

304 *Electrolux absorption refrigerator, 1927. Wooden cabinet, insulated with cork and lined with painted sheet metal. This model originally supplied to King George V and used at Sandringham until the early 1950s. Science Museum, London*

305a *Kelvinator refrigerator, 1925. One of the first models to incorporate all the moving parts within the cabinet — motor, pump, condensing unit. Wood and metal cabinet. About 5 ft 6 in. high. Science Museum, London*

305b *White Mountain Freezer ice cream maker, made in USA, 1923. Science Museum, London*

luxury only to be seen in well-to-do homes, but in the 1930s demand became greater, partly because of the passing of the Food Preservation Act of 1926 which forbade the use of chemical preservatives and partly because, with mass-production methods, refrigerators became cheaper as well as smaller. (By 1932 Electrolux had produced a one-cubic-foot model selling for £19 10s. (£19.50p).

After the Second World War many more people began to regard refrigeration as a necessity rather than a luxury. Both in government-planned 'prefabs', and in private housing, 'fridges' were being built-in to modern kitchens and these took up less space than the pre-war larder. By 1969 56% of the population in the UK possessed a refrigerator and sales topped a million per year. In recent years the household refrigerator has become more efficient and offers greater facilities. Insulation is better, automatic de-frosting has been introduced, also door storage capacity. Freezer compartments are larger and incorporate a 'star' rating system. The idea of the separate home freezer, in chest or cupboard form, is a miniature version of the larger equipment used for bulk freezing in food container storage and in supermarkets. A later development domestically than the refrigerator, it has taken off in Britain since 1960.

In the USA the desire to make ice-cream at home acted as a strong incentive for inventors to design and develop a machine to do this. A patent was taken out for an appliance as early as 1848, but the practical, working equipment dates from the 1860s. In the later 1880s smaller, convenient-sized domestic ice-cream makers were being produced by several manufacturers and the idea began to spread to Europe. Most of these designs consisted of a wooden staved bucket which contained a freezing mixture of ice and salt[9]. Inside the outer bucket, surrounded by the freezing mixture, was an inner pail, generally of metal, fitted with a paddle which could be turned by a crank handle. The cream was poured into the inner bucket and the turning action (on the same basis as a butter churn, chapter 2 page 49) beat and churned the cream as it froze (305b).

306 Electric refrigerator made by B.T.H. Co. of Rugby, 1932. Compressor and cooler set on top of cabinet. Science Museum, London

CHAPTER SIX

Cleaning in the Home

General cleaning

Before twentieth-century technology brought labour-saving appliances into the home, keeping the surfaces and utensils in a house clean and bright was extremely hard work. It was monotonous unremitting labour. From earliest times brooms and mops were used for floors and walls. At first sweeping brooms were natural brushes and these were soon bound together and often wound tightly round a wooden handle. These were usually besoms, that is brooms made of heather, birch or other twigs such as myrtle; they continued in use over the centuries to sweep out the cottage floor of beaten earth, brick or wood (313). In Roman times brushes were manufactured and could be purchased; these had multiple knots of bristles made in a traditional form which changed little in the succeeding centuries. By the later sixteenth century a wide variety of brushes and brooms were available to the housewife. Some of these had long handles, others were hand-brushes. Some were made of stiff bristles suitable for scrubbing or scouring, others were soft for use on decorative wall surfaces or furniture.

While more sophisticated brushes and brooms were being made commercially for sale to the housewife (307, 312, 314, 315, 317, 319, 320, 321, 322, 324), in country areas natural materials continued in use until the later nineteenth century. Writing in 1775, Gilbert White[1] describes 'neat besoms which our foresters make from the stalk of the *polytricum commune*, or great golden maidenhair, which they call silk-wood and find plenty in the bogs. When this moss is well combed and dressed, and divested of its outer skin, it becomes a beautiful bright chestnut colour; and being soft and pliant, is very proper for the dusting of beds, curtains, carpets, hangings, etc.' Later, feather dusters became popular for a light flicking to keep ornaments and pictures free from dust. These were particularly in use in nineteenth-century homes where rooms were so overcrowded with furniture and a wide variety of decorative articles (309).

Many surfaces, especially in the kitchen, required scrubbing and washing and, before about 1800, the means of getting various utensils clean were limited and crude. The unsealed wood surfaces in the kitchen had to be scrubbed daily. Mops were used to wash tiled and painted surfaces. These mops were made of natural fibres – wool, cotton, linen – attached to a stick or handle (316, 325). Cooking vessels were scoured out with the aid of sand or a 'black soap' which was made from a mixture of ashes, sand and linseed oil. Where it was important not to scratch a metal utensil, one made of pewter for example, it was boiled in water in a cauldron to which a mixture of wood ash and unslaked lime had been added. Home-made polishes were used for silver, brass and copper. These recipes generally included charcoal or bone-ash.

By the mid-nineteenth century the labour of keeping a house clean was very great but many more recipes and aids to such cleaning were then available and these could be bought or made at home. A vivid impression of the immense labour involved in keeping a well-to-do or middle class home bright and furbished and for the appliances and substances used for this are described by Mrs Beeton[2] in her sections on 'Duties of the Housemaid' and 'Duties of the Maid-of-all-Work'. The descriptions also present a horrifying picture of the long hours and onerous duties worked by these girls.

Mrs Beeton begins section 2292 on the housemaid's duties by the words 'Cleanliness is next to godliness, saith the proverb.' She goes on to tell us of how the

124

housemaid should clean out the fireplaces early in the morning:

> She sweeps the dust towards the fireplace, of course previously removing the fender. She should then lay a cloth (generally made of coarse wrappering) over the carpet in front of the stove, and on this should place her housemaid's box, containing black-lead brushes, leathers, emery-paper, cloth, black lead[3] and all utensils necessary for cleaning a grate, with a cinder-pail on the other side (330).

> She now sweeps up the ashes, and deposits them in her cinder-pail, which is a japanned tin pail, with a wire-sifter inside, and a closely-fitting top. In this pail the cinders are sifted, and reserved for use in the kitchen or under the copper, the ashes only being thrown away. The cinders disposed of, she proceeds to black-lead the grate, producing the black lead, the soft brush for laying it on, her blacking and polishing brushes, from the box which contains her tools. The housemaid's box should be kept well stocked. (308, 310).

Mrs Beeton continues:

> Bright grates require unceasing attention to keep them in perfect order. A day should never pass without the housemaid rubbing with a dry leather the polished parts of a grate, as also the fender and fire-irons. A careful and attentive housemaid should have no occasion ever to use emery paper for any part but the bars, which, of course, become blackened by the fire.

Mrs Beeton recommends a recipe for polishing bright stoves and steel articles. This is composed of turpentine, sweet oil and emery powder.

Further advice is given regarding sweeping carpets, where it is recommended to be good practice first to sprinkle the carpet all over with tea leaves as this will lay the dust and lend a fragrant smell to the room. The sweeping should then be done with a hand whisk brush made of coconut fibre (323). Advice is given in detail on the subject of dusting, especially the staircase balusters and banisters (311, 318). Furniture may be dusted with a soft cloth or a brush made of long feathers or a goose's wing. There are also special recipes for furniture polishes and pastes. The bases of these are mainly linseed oil, turpentine, vinegar and spirits of wine or salts; alternatively, for paste, beeswax, curd soap, turpentine and boiled water.

Mrs Beeton gives wide-ranging advice on the biennial spring and autumn cleaning[4] which includes carpet beating (on the line, outside) (328) and shampooing (with bullock's gall mixed with cold water), scouring, washing and re-furbishing the paintwork and the polishing of all furniture. Ceilings had to be washed and re-whitened. All draperies were shaken and clean curtains and covers replaced them for the new season. Suggestions are given for the brightening-up of gilt frames, for cleaning glass and polishing floor coverings with milk. Linoleum appeared on the market in 1860. Made by coating canvas with a preparation of oxydised linseed oil and cork (compressed and dried) this was the first inexpensive, mass-produced floor-covering available to a wide range of homes; it was also easy to keep clean. Parquet flooring was recommended to be polished using a cotton mop and home-made polish.

The easy-to-clean wall and floor surfaces of the twentieth century have brought a new range of appliances. Particularly since the Second World War the new coverings of vinyl sheeting and squares, thermoplastic tiling and ceramic surfacing can be cleaned quickly and without effort. Since the 1950s the housewife has been able to use the lever-operated squeeze mop with a head of cellulose sponge (326) which did away with the need to get her hands wet. In more recent years a range of interchangeable heads have become available for such mops, enabling the housewife to sweep, wash, scrub or polish (see also shampooer page 136 and fig. 348).

Table silver and knives

According to Mrs Beeton the household silver should be cleaned thoroughly once a week with hartshorn powder and rubbed daily with plate-rags. The powder, which was derived from shavings from a hart's antlers, was purchased in powder form and made into a thick paste by mixing it with spirits of wine or water. The paste was applied to the silver, left on for a while to dry, then rubbed off with a brush and polished up with a dry leather. The plate-rags were soft rags (the tops of old cotton stockings were considered ideal) which had been boiled in a solution of new milk and hartshorn powder to impregnate them.

Before the advent of stainless (rustless) steel in the home, steel knives needed careful regular cleaning to keep them bright and unmarked. The traditional

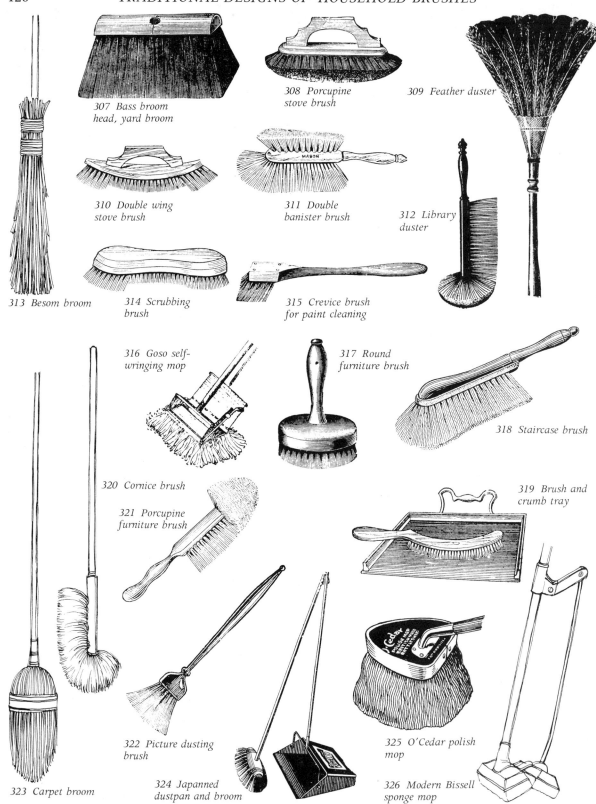

307 Bass broom head, yard broom

308 Porcupine stove brush

309 Feather duster

310 Double wing stove brush

311 Double banister brush

312 Library duster

313 Besom broom

314 Scrubbing brush

315 Crevice brush for paint cleaning

316 Goso self-wringing mop

317 Round furniture brush

318 Staircase brush

320 Cornice brush

321 Porcupine furniture brush

319 Brush and crumb tray

322 Picture dusting brush

323 Carpet broom

324 Japanned dustpan and broom

325 O'Cedar polish mop

326 Modern Bissell sponge mop

method in use over the centuries was by means of a knife board. The knives were first washed in a strong solution of washing soda and water. They were then polished by stropping the blades, with the aid of emery powder, on a board covered with leather or an india rubber compound.

In the later nineteenth century the rotary knife cleaning machine was introduced which could clean, without due labour, several knives at once; some machines took four knives, larger ones up to twelve. The most common design was like the Kent Knife Cleaner, of which improved patents were taken out in 1870, 1882, 1887 and later. This machine consisted of a circular wooden drum mounted on a cast iron stand. Inside was an inner wheel fitted with leather leaves or alternating felt pads and bristle attachments. The washed knives were inserted into holes fitted around the drum and, when the crank handle was turned, the inner contrivance cleaned and polished the knives. To assist this process a special abrasive powder was poured into the machine; a popular product was Oakey's Britannia Knife Polish (329). The action of these machines was so drastic, however, that the knife blades became progressively thinner and shorter.

By 1890 alternative designs of knife cleaning machine had appeared on the market. Typical was the Uneck model, made by Spong, which resembled a metal miniature mangle with india rubber rollers. This could be clamped to a table and when the handle was turned the rollers revolved and polished the knives (331). A smaller version, cleaning one knife at a time, was the Vono knife cleaner. Most of these and similar appliances (327) continued to be manufactured and used until stainless steel knives became more readily acceptable in the late 1930s (chapter 2 page 37). For many years stainless steel knives were used with reluctance because they were not sharp, and it is only comparatively recently that improvements in this respect have been achieved by the use of new stainless steel alloys, such as vanadium steel, so effecting a virtual disappearance from the home of the ordinary steel knife, which required so much cleaning and polishing.

Cleansing agents: detergents, soap, soap powder

A number of different cleansing agents, or detergents,[5] have been used over the centuries for cleansing and washing the home and the household and personal linen. In the classical lands round the Mediterranean fuller's earth (hydrated aluminium silicate) with an alkaline solution was used to clean garments and household linen. This mixture formed a soluble compound which absorbed the dirt and grease from the material. Alkalized water was known as lye. This could be made by adding urine to the water or by pouring water through wood ash and so producing an alkaline solution.

It is not known precisely when or where soap was first made and used, but the Phoenicians are generally credited with the discovery and development of its possibilities. These sea-faring and -trading people are believed to have passed on their knowledge and experience of a primitive type of soap-making to the Gauls, though it appears that the substance was used more as a pomade and unguent than as a cleanser. Pliny the Elder tells us in 77 AD in his *Historia Naturalis* that the Gauls used it as a hair tint and dressing.

The Oxford English Dictionary defines soap as 'a substance formed by the combination of certain oils and fats with alkaline bases and used for washing and cleansing purposes.' Through the ages, from the Phoenicians and Gauls until its commercial production in the nineteenth century, soap has been made from a variety of substances, but the two basic constituents had to be some type of fat combined with an alkaline solution, the two substances being mixed and boiled together, then left to cool until the mixture thickened.

The 'soap' produced in Gaul was (according to Pliny) made by boiling together goat fat and lye, the latter produced by running water through wood ash (usually beech). This produced a soft potash soap which could then be rendered harder by salt treatment. Knowledge of the method of making this primitive form of soft soap, suitable as a salve and pomade, spread to Germany and Italy and was taken up by Rome: a 'soap factory' has been excavated at Pompeii.

The earliest reference to soap being used as a cleanser comes in the second century AD from Galen, the famous Greek physician from Pergamum and again in the fourth century from the physician Priscian. It was expensive, a luxury commodity. By 800 soap-boiling establishments had been set up in many European centres. Soft soap was made in these for several centuries. This was derived from tallow

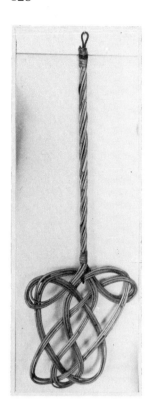

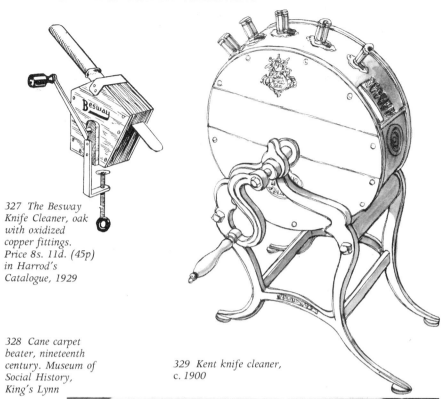

327 The Besway
Knife Cleaner, oak
with oxidized
copper fittings.
Price 8s. 11d. (45p)
in Harrod's
Catalogue, 1929

328 Cane carpet
beater, nineteenth
century. Museum of
Social History,
King's Lynn

329 Kent knife cleaner,
c. 1900

330 Housemaid's box
(Harrod's Catalogue)

331 Spong's Uneck knife
cleaner, c. 1890. Gustav
Holst's Birthplace Museum,
Cheltenham

(animal fat) or whale oil boiled with caustic potash which had been made by running water through a mixture of wood ash and lime. This soft soap was used chiefly for industrial needs such as the cleansing of fleece and textiles. A hard soap intended for home and personal use was made first by the Arabs and later in certain centres, notably Castile in Spain, Marseilles in France and Venice in Italy. Though animal fats were traditionally used, it was discovered that vegetable oils (in the Mediterranean areas olive oil) were better and the stink of production was less offensive. The olive oil was boiled with soda ash to make this hard soap which was then perfumed for toilet use. It was still very expensive.

Soap was made in England from the early Middle Ages and there were famous soapworks (sopehouses) in Bristol and London, but these made chiefly soft soap for commercial use. Hard soap for domestic and toilet needs was largely imported from European countries and a heavy tax was levied on this in the seventeenth and eighteenth centuries. Because of this most households made their own soap, using rendered-down animal fats and making their own lye. For this a lye dropper was needed. This was a wooden box with holes in the bottom boarding. A layer of twigs or brushwood was laid in the bottom, covered with a muslin cloth and the box was filled to the top with wood ash. The dropper was then set on top of a large tub and water was poured over the ashes so that the solution dripped into the tub. The process was repeated several times until the alkaline solution was strong enough. The melted fats were then stirred while being boiled together with the lye. The boiling was a lengthy process, lasting most of a day, and it was not one for fastidious noses. The result was, by modern standards, unattractive. It was greasy and of the consistency of putty. It also smelled unpleasant so, for toilet use, flower perfumes were added. Home recipes were varied, experiments being made with different fats. By experience it was found that different woods produced ash which imposed characteristics on the lye. Personal preference led to the use of one wood ash or another. Beech was popular, oak made a strong solution but apple-wood often gave the best washing results.

In the first half of the nineteenth century methods of making soap became cleaner and more efficient. The work of two French chemists led to this great improvement. In 1789 Nicolas Leblanc (1742–1806)

discovered a means of making soda from salt. In 1791 he set up a factory to carry out his process in which sodium sulphate, together with chalk and charcoal, were heated and from this 'black ash' was dissolved out soda. This was a great help to the soap-makers who now did not need to produce their alkaline solution from wood ash. A few years later the researches of Michel Eugène Chevreul into the constituents of oils and fats led to a clearer understanding of the chemical reactions which took place when the fats and alkaline solution were boiled and so improved the quality and processes of soap-making.

Manufacture was then established on a large scale and, by mid-century, the tax was repealed, so soap became more plentiful and cheaper. In the later nineteenth century it was only in the more remote country areas that people still made their own soap at home. In Britain William Hesketh Lever (1851–1925), later Lord Leverhulme, contributed greatly to the widescale purchase of soap by his extensive, imaginative advertising and his flair for giving the customer what she wanted, in this case, an attractively packaged and perfumed commodity.

In the nineteenth century also there was an attempt to give the housewife a convenient soap powder or flakes for domestic washing needs. She was accustomed to making her own product for dealing with the weekly wash by mixing shredded soap with soda. In the 1860s a product on these lines made of ground soap with alkalis was put on the market. Lux soap flakes were available from 1900 and Persil soap powder nine years later.

The synthetic or soapless detergent, now used in every home for all forms of washing and cleansing, has only been produced on a large scale since the Second World War. This detergent possesses remarkable cleansing properties which give it a notable advantage over soap because of its molecular structure. The surface tension of the water is reduced, thus increasing the wetting power of the cleanser. A synthetic detergent will also, unlike soap, produce a good lather in hard or salt water and rinses more easily from dishes and fabrics.

Some of these compounds with long-chain molecules have been known for many years, but it is only since 1930 that they have become a commercial proposition. Most modern synthetic detergents are made from oil or by-products of coal and it was the development of the oil industry in the early 1930s which led to the research on detergents made from mineral sources. Work on this was accelerated during the Second World War because of a deficiency in the supplies of natural oils and fats. In 1942 came the liquid detergent Teepol, which was suitable for washing up or cleaning floors, and in the 1950s appeared the detergent powders for washing clothes. Biological detergents, developed in the 1960s, contain enzymes which help to remove protein stains on garments by reacting upon them.

Mechanical cleaning devices

The sweeper

Several attempts were made during the nineteenth century to produce a machine which would sweep floors and carpets, collecting the dust and not just spreading it around. Up till this time the only possible methods had been dusting, sweeping and beating, and all of these raised the dust only to allow it to settle in a different place.

A machine to sweep floors was patented in the early 1800s. This comprised a brush fitted inside a box. The brush could be made to revolve by means of a pulley connected by a string to the long handle of the device. By the 1860s a number of designs of carpet sweeper had appeared. These generally consisted of a cast-iron box carried on two rollers and containing a roller-brush which was rotated by means of a belt pulley fixed to the rear roller. These machines were not very efficient because, although the rotating brush satisfactorily swept some dirt into the box receptacle, the belt drive was insufficiently powerful to counteract the frictional resistance of the brush in contact with the carpet.

It was Melville R. Bissell of Grand Rapids, Michigan in the USA who produced the first satisfactory carpet sweeper. Mr Bissell and his wife owned a china shop in the town. Mr Bissell, unfortunately, was allergic to the dust which arose when he removed the pieces of china from the sawdust and straw in which they had been packed for transportation. He decided to make a machine to take up this irritating dust and in September 1876 was granted a patent for his design which, though heavier and more cumbersome, worked on the same principles as modern sweepers. In these the rotation of the brush is achieved by the friction of four rubber-faced carrying wheels against the drums which are fitted to the brush. In order to reduce the frictional resistance of this brush the tufts

of bristles are traditionally set in four of five spiralling rows so that only a few tufts are in contact with the carpet at any one moment.

The early Bissell model also had a rotating spiral of bristles, a friction drive from the four sprung wheels and a dust box which could be opened and released for emptying by depressing a lever. It also incorporated a knob to adjust the brush to various floor levels (332). Some of the early designs had 'sidewhiskers', that is leading rotary brushes to clean the edges of skirting boards and alongside furniture. In the latest model this idea has been revived (335).

The production of the Grand Rapids carpet sweeper was at first a semi-cottage industry, the wooden cases and the castings being made by small local firms and the brushes and rollers being produced by girls working at home. Bissell himself went out to demonstrate his sweeper, throwing handfuls of dirt on to the floor in order to sweep them up before an astonished customer. By the 1880s the Bissell Carpet Sweeper Company was housed in a purpose-built factory. So successful did it become and widely known in the western world that other manufacturers produced their models. In Britain the best-known of these has always been Ewbank Ltd. The Ewbank sweeper (a similar design) was selling in 1911 for 10s. 6d. (52½p) (333).

The suction cleaner

A number of experiments were tried out in the second half of the nineteenth century to remove dust and dirt by some form of pump which blew or sucked. The machines which were made were large and cumbersome and, if at all practicable, were only used by commercial carpet cleaners. One such American device, powered by a rotary engine, swept up the dust by brush and carried it away to a water tank by means of a current of air produced by bellows. Another, powered by steam, beat the carpets with wooden flails.

The first successful, practical, powered suction cleaner was devised in 1901 by Hubert Cecil Booth (1871–1955), a construction engineer. Mr Booth's interest in the subject was aroused in 1900 when he attended a demonstration at St Pancras Station of the cleaning of railway carriages by a new dust machine. The machine was a compressed air device which blew the dirt from one end of the carriage to a container placed at the other end. Mr Booth was not impressed

333 Ewbank 'Success' Carpet Sweeper. Rubber corner buffers, ball bearing wheels. Japanned fittings. 34s. 3d. £1.71p) in Harrods' Catalogue, 1929

332 Bissell Grand Rapids Carpet Sweeper, 1895. Made in USA. Wooden case, rubber cased wheels, protective furniture guard. Science Museum, London

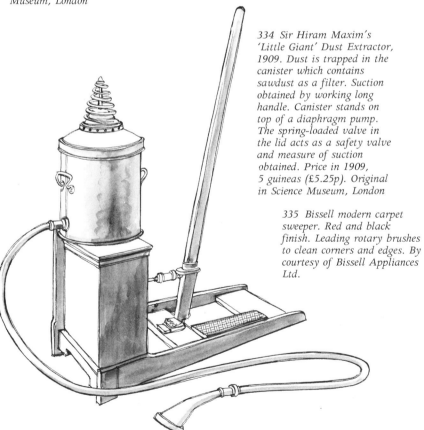

334 Sir Hiram Maxim's 'Little Giant' Dust Extractor, 1909. Dust is trapped in the canister which contains sawdust as a filter. Suction obtained by working long handle. Canister stands on top of a diaphragm pump. The spring-loaded valve in the lid acts as a safety valve and measure of suction obtained. Price in 1909, 5 guineas (£5.25p). Original in Science Museum, London

335 Bissell modern carpet sweeper. Red and black finish. Leading rotary brushes to clean corners and edges. By courtesy of Bissell Appliances Ltd.

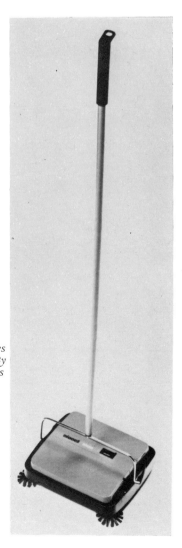

by this technique of cleaning; it seemed little improve-ment on carpet sweeping, but the problem interested him. When he reached home he damped a piece of material, placed it over the arm of a chair and sucked: a ring of dirt had appeared on the cloth. Suction, clearly, was the answer and for this Mr Booth coined the term vacuum cleaner. He translated his domestic experiment into practical mechanical terms and paten-ted the device in 1901. He formed the Vacuum Cleaner Company Ltd. (now Goblin BVC Ltd.) to manufacture his machines.

For some years the cleaners made by the Vacuum Cleaner Company Ltd. provided a cleaning service to town houses. The vacuum cleaner itself was large and costly. Painted bright red, it measured 4 ft 6 in. × 4 ft 10 in. × 3 ft 6 in. and cost £350. Powered by a petrol-driven 5 horse-power piston engine, it was trans-ported through the streets on a horse-drawn van. A team of white-uniformed operators then parked the

apparatus outside your house, festooned the façade with several hundred feet of flexible hose which reached every room and sucked the dirt of decades from your carpets, curtains and upholstery. In the first cleaning the weight of many such carpets was reduced by 50% (336). One major problem arose. The cleaning operation took some time and the firm was summonsed more than once and fined for causing an obstruction in the narrow streets. The company appealed and the Lord Chief Justice upheld their right to work from the streets.

In general the company carried out commercial carpet cleaning rather than selling their costly mac-hines. There were two royal exceptions to this. In 1902 Westminster Abbey was being prepared for the Coronation of King Edward VII and Queen Alexandra. Mr Booth was invited to demonstrate his vacuum apparatus on the Coronation carpet. This was so successful that the King and Queen requested a

336 Mr Booth's vacuum cleaner in use outside the Metropolitan Theatre. Note: white-suited operative and hoses festooned from windows of building. The operation

was still sufficiently unusual to attract a crowd of onlookers. Photograph reproduced by courtesy of Goblin (BVC) Ltd.

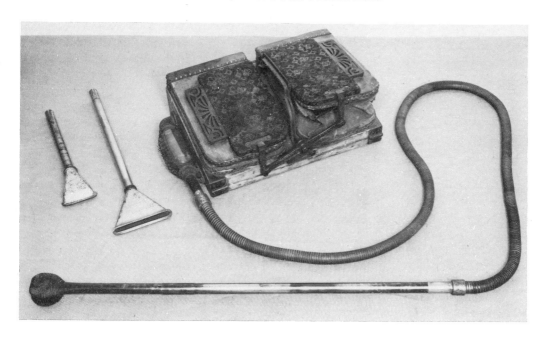

337 Griffith foot-operated vacuum cleaner, 1905. Two persons needed to operate cleaner. Note glass cylinder at left side where dust being sucked in can be seen. No dustbag. Dust passes through cloth filters into box beneath. Science Museum, London

338 Trolley domestic vacuum cleaner, 1906. Made by British Vacuum Cleaner Company. Powered by electric motor. Operated by one person (see fig. 340). Science Museum, London

further demonstration at Buckingham Palace. As a result two machines were sold to the Royal Household, one for Buckingham Palace and one for Windsor Castle.

Soon afterwards a series of legal actions took place as attempts were made by other designers and manufacturers to cash-in on the vacuum cleaner. Mr Booth's patent was upheld in the House of Lords and in 1903 he was granted world patent rights for his invention. The company embarked upon an advertising campaign to sell their apparatus. Demonstrations were organised at fashionable homes and public institutions[6]. Sales were made to the Palace of Westminster, a number of hotels and theatres and to a few wealthy families, but the cleaner was too costly to achieve wide sales.

Meanwhile great efforts were being made on both sides of the Atlantic to produce a smaller convenient vacuum cleaner which could be purchased and used in the home. The incentive to do this was rather greater in the USA because it was more difficult there to obtain cheap servant labour. Many models of cleaner were produced by various inventors and manufacturers, but they all suffered from the same drawback; the lack of a small electric motor to power them. The alternatives were a large, heavy, expensive machine powered by a large electric motor or a smaller machine powered by hand and needing two people to operate it.

The chief British example of the former alternative was the Trolley Vac designed by Booth and produced in 1906 by the Vacuum Cleaner Company. This elaborate equipment comprised a sophisticated electric motor which drove a rotary vacuum pump by means of a belt. The dust was trapped in a cloth filter within a metal canister which, for doubting Thomases, was fitted with a glass section of tubing to show the dust being sucked up. There were adequate hoses and an impressive array of attachments for different cleaning purposes. The whole equipment was contained on a tray of a trolley which could be pushed around the house. When not in use a mahogany case fitted over the whole machine. This was a magnificent vacuum cleaner. Its drawbacks were the price (35 guineas) and the weight (nearly a hundredweight) and the consequent difficulty of getting it upstairs (338, 340).

There were many ingenious models produced both in Britain and America which were hand-operated. An early and typical one was the Harvey cleaner for which a patent was taken out in the 1890s. The suction was produced by bellows hand-operated by a lever. One person pushed this lever backwards and forwards while another used the hose with attachments on books, pictures, curtains, etc. The model was on wheels and light enough to be transported around the house. Made of metal, wood and leather it sold successfully in the first decade of the twentieth century (342).

Notable alternative designs included the Griffith foot-operated cleaner (1905) where one person, often a child, marched up and down on the pedals and pumped while the other cleaned. This also was fitted with a glass cylinder at the side to show the dust being absorbed (337). Another foot-operated model was the Cyclone (*c.* 1914) which was cumbersome but had the advantage of only needing one person to operate it. The Baby Daisy (*c.* 1910) (341), Sir Hiram Maxim's 'Little Giant' dust extractor of 1909 (334) and the BVC model of 1912 all worked on a similar bellows and lever principle to the Harvey design. A little different was the model where the bellows were operated by turning a wheel. The Wizard, patented 1912 by Maguire and Catchell of Dublin, was typical (343). Some of the American models were more ingenious. The Sweeper-Vac (1915), made in Boston, combined the advantages of a carpet sweeper with those of a vacuum cleaner (339). In 1908 came the version where the bellows were incorporated into a rocking chair so that one operator just sat and rocked while the other did the cleaning. For some reason the husband was depicted in the former activity, his wife in the latter.

Efforts were being redoubled to make a small, inexpensive cleaner which only needed one operator. The answer to this, valued chiefly in America, was the pump which resembled a garden insect spray. It comprised a plunge suction pump, a dustbag contained in the cylinder and an attachment nozzle at the end (346). These overgrown bicycle pumps (but they sucked; they did not blow) were very hard work to use. They were about five feet long, so unwieldy to handle, and it was not easy to pump and at the same time keep the nozzle firmly pressed on to the carpet; this one had to do in order to maintain the suction. A slightly easier version was the popular Star cleaner (1911), which was shorter and with a cylindrical bellows of greater diameter. The dust bag was contained in the same cylinder (344).

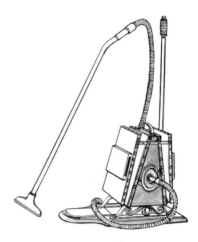

339 Sweeper-Vac Carpet-Sweeper, 1915. Made by Pneuvac of Boston, USA. Price 2 guineas (£2.10p). Single wheel at rear operates with cranks bellows in box. Sweeper brushes driven by other wheels. Science Museum, London

340 Maid using Booth's Trolley-Vac, 1906. Note: clean patch of carpet just vacuumed and apparatus connected to electric light fitting. Photograph reproduced by courtesy of Goblin (BVC) Ltd

341 Baby Daisy Vacuum Cleaner, c. 1910. Price £4. Operated by two persons. Cloth dustbag

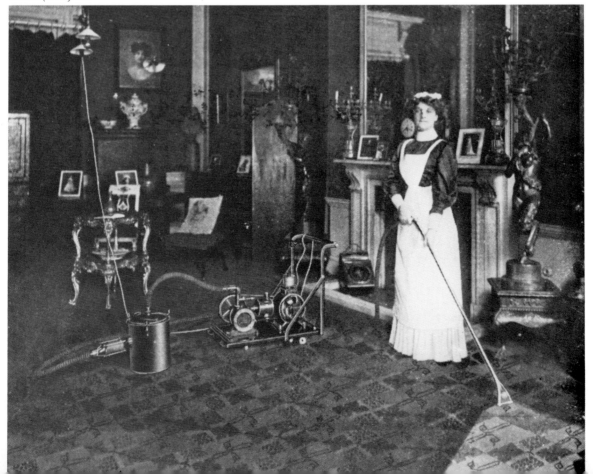

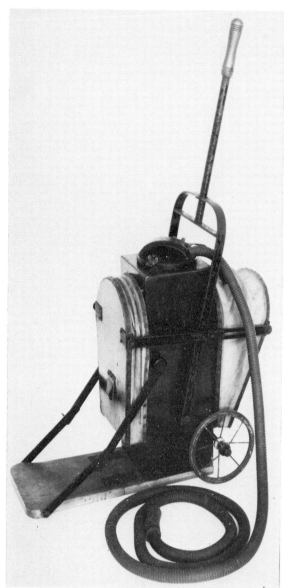

342 Harvey Vacuum Cleaner, 1910. Requires two persons to operate cleaner. Science Museum, London

These mechanisms and many more were soon outdated[7] when it became possible to marry a small electric motor to a conveniently-sized vacuum cleaner. The man who did this was J. Murray Spangler of Ohio, who in 1907 devised a prototype which comprised an electric suction sweeper in a tin can with a dustbag supported on a long handle. The machine worked and Spangler sold the rights for it to a successful firm of saddlers who, with the growing interest in America for motor cars, found this affecting their leather saddle trade and were looking around for a new venture to invest in. They developed Spangler's idea and produced the first electrically-powered upright domestic vacuum cleaner with exterior dust-bag in 1908. The machine was an instant success and a few years later was selling widely in America and Europe. By the 1920s (347) it was so well known that the name of the firm became accepted for the machine's function. If Mr Spangler had not sold out to W.H. Hoover we might well have talked about 'spanglering' the carpet instead of 'hoovering'.

By this time, also, the characteristic Hoover triple action had been incorporated into the machine, which vibrated the carpet to loosen the dirt deep in the pile. This agitating action was achieved in 1920 by combining the suction with a revolving brush. In 1926 the idea was further developed by the addition of revolving bars which helped the brush action by gently beating the carpet on a cushion of air. This gave rise to the company's well-known catch phrase, 'it beats as it sweeps as it cleans'.

Hoover's success led to the upright model being adopted by other manufacturers. The Magic was available in 1915, the British Vacuum Cleaner Company version came out in 1921 and the Bustler was popular in 1931 (351). The horizontal canister shape was pioneered in the 1920s. This was lighter in weight, quieter and cheaper. Electrolux introduced their Model 10 in 1927. The canister, which was held by a pistol grip fitting, contained dustbag and electric motor (345). BVC quickly followed with a canister model, their cleaners now selling under the trade name of Goblin.

Today three main designs of domestic vacuum cleaner are available: upright, cylinder, sphere. There are also smaller hand models suitable for stairs and car interiors (349, 352).

Carpet shampooers and floor polishers
After the Second World War wall-to-wall carpeting and modern floor coverings led to the introduction of the upright carpet shampooer. First developed in 1958 under the presidency of Melville R. Bissell, grandson of the inventor of the Grand Rapids carpet sweeper and founder of the firm (page 130), this was quickly followed by the Hoover version. Both designs[8] have made home cleaning an easy task. Some models (348) are now fitted with interchangeable heads which enable the machine to shampoo, polish or scrub.

343 Bellows-type vacuum cleaner. operated by turning a wheel, c. 1912. Requires two persons to use the cleaner. Abbey House Museum, Leeds

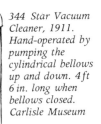

344 Star Vacuum Cleaner, 1911. Hand-operated by pumping the cylindrical bellows up and down. 4 ft 6 in. long when bellows closed. Carlisle Museum

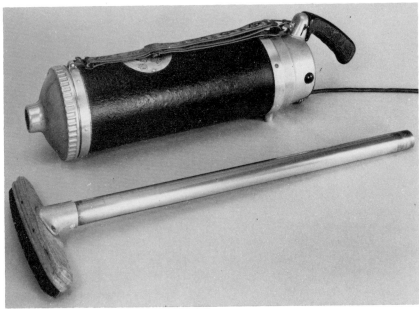

345 Electrolux Vacuum Cleaner, Model 10, 1927. Pistol grip handle model. Canister may be slung over the shoulder. Science Museum, London

346 Good House-keeper Vacuum Cleaner, 1913. All metal. Dustbag inside cylinder. 5 ft long. Science Museum, London

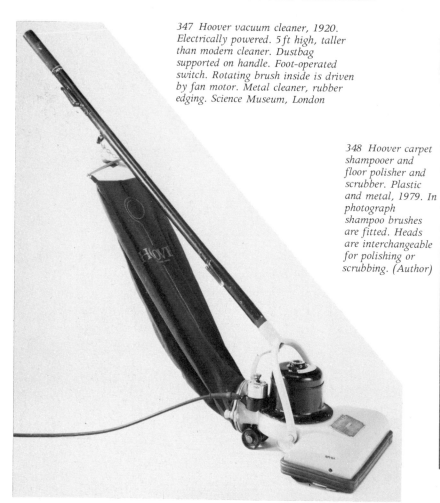

347 Hoover vacuum cleaner, 1920. Electrically powered. 5 ft high, taller than modern cleaner. Dustbag supported on handle. Foot-operated switch. Rotating brush inside is driven by fan motor. Metal cleaner, rubber edging. Science Museum, London

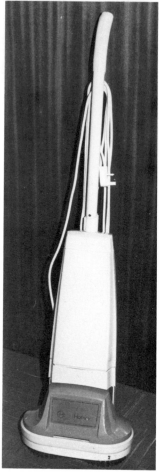

348 Hoover carpet shampooer and floor polisher and scrubber. Plastic and metal, 1979. In photograph shampoo brushes are fitted. Heads are interchangeable for polishing or scrubbing. (Author)

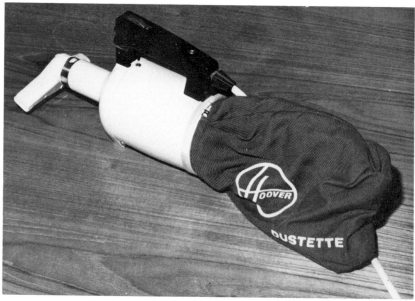

349 Hoover dustette, electrically powered, for stairs and cars, 1965. (Author)

350 Colston dishwasher, 1976. By courtesy of Mrs Jean Naylor

351 Bustler vacuum cleaner, 1931. Science Museum, London

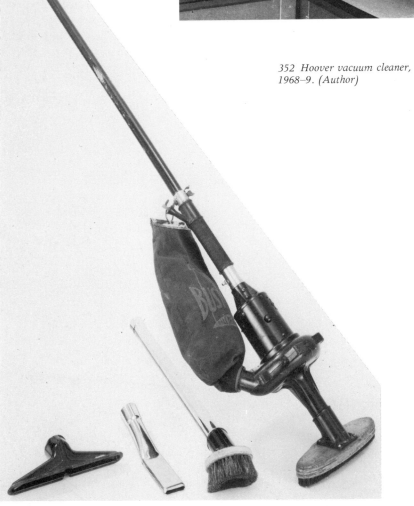

352 Hoover vacuum cleaner, 1968–9. (Author)

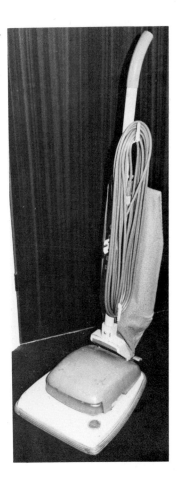

Dishwashers

The history of development in this field was similar to that of so many domestic appliances in the nineteenth century. American ingenuity, spurred on by a need to find a labour-saving mechanism, produced a variety of ideas and workable gadgets but, because of the lack of motive power not yet developed for the small household machine, the mechanism required almost as much labour as the old-fashioned method of carrying out the task. For example, patents were issued for dishwashers as early as the 1850s and 1860s, all of which incorporated ideas such as paddles to splash water over the dishes or propellors to agitate the water and so splash the dishes or plungers which forced the water up over the dishes. But, in all instances, most of the work still had to be carried out manually. Water had to be heated on the kitchen range. The machine had to be filled by hand with jug or bucket. Home-made soap had to be shredded or cut up for use in the dishwasher. The dirty water from the machine had to be emptied by hand. A handle had to be turned to operate the paddles, propellor or plunger.

It was 1914 before a dishwasher powered by an electric motor was available and still some years before most of the processes could be carried out mechanically. Many improvements were made between 1920 and 1940 in America. Machines were plumbed in and an increasing automation was incorporated.

In Britain the dishwasher was not accepted until the 1950s and even as late as 1965 criticisms were being justly made by research organisations showing that the machines were not functioning adequately and that food was not being completely removed from dishes by the superheated water jets. The dishwasher here is still an exceptional item in the home rather than the norm. For a working wife with several children it is a blessing. To a couple without children or with only one child it does not rate high on the list of home essentials.

The modern dishwasher can be free-standing on the floor or can be accommodated on a draining board or fixed to a wall. It is generally programmed to work a heating cycle (i.e. to heat the water to a desired temperature), a washing cycle, two rinsing cycles and one drying cycle. Some dishwashers are programmed to give special treatment to different problem dishes such as casseroles and pans (350).

CHAPTER SEVEN

Laundering of Personal and Household Linen

Washing

In the years before the later eighteenth century the cleaning of fabrics, whether in household or personal use, presented great problems. It was hard work heating up enough water, then carrying it in vessels to fill tubs and cauldrons. Soap was very expensive so was mainly made at home from kitchen-produced fat and lye (see chapter 6 pages 127, 129). Also many of the fabrics were not suitable for any form of washing. The heavier coverlets, curtains and garments – many of them of velvet or brocade and lined with fur – were shaken and beaten at intervals. Marks were removed by means of various cleaning fluids made from, for example, wine or fresh grape juice. The most general cleaning agent was fuller's earth combined sometimes with lye. In the Middle Ages personal and household linen made of cotton, linen or similar washable material, was communally washed at open streams or riversides or in large tubs, the fabric being beaten with battling stones or wood battledores.

In the sixteenth and seventeenth centuries the washing of personal and household linen was a regular event but one which in most households only took place once a month or even at two- or three-monthly intervals. Only the aristocracy enjoyed the luxury of a frequent change of linen which was made ready for them by personal service. The ritual of the infrequent wash was carried out, if weather permitted, in the open air. Large households would have a laundry room for winter washing and, in such establishments, professional washerwomen would be employed for the occasion to help the servants to carry out the work. For poorer people an open-sided washhouse was erected near to the stream for all the villagers to use.

Water was heated in immense iron cauldrons over a fire, lye was added and the clothes were steeped or boiled in it. For particularly dirty fabrics, these were piled into wooden tubs which had holes in their base. Lye water was poured over the material which was beaten or stamped upon with bare feet then more lye water was poured on top. The action was repeated until the clothes were clean. The process of boiling or steeping the clothes in a solution of lye was known as bucking or buck-washing.

After washing, the clothes would be rinsed in clean water, wrung out by hand and, weather permitting, spread on the ground or over bushes to dry.

These methods of washing, used for centuries from Roman Britain onwards, were not only hard work for the people involved but also had an unfortunate effect on the garments. Linen and cotton stood up to it reasonably well but the processes were disastrous to wool. The combination of hard work and wear to the fabrics did not encourage a more frequent washing cycle.

In the eighteenth century washing was still largely done at home but now at more frequent intervals; usually a two-day washday followed by two more days for pressing and ironing took place every four or five weeks. Large country houses contained permanent accommodation where water could be heated and clothes washed, dried, starched and ironed (353). A typical example in the most remarkable state of preservation is the laundry at Erddig in Clwyd (354). The laundry yard here was constructed in the 1770s

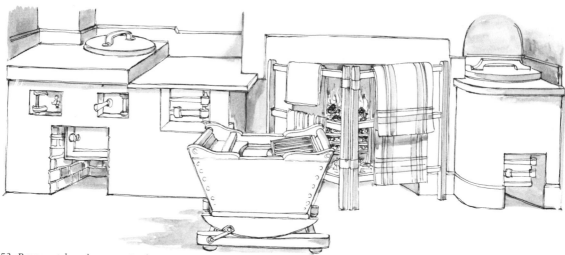

353 Basement laundry room in the Georgian House, Bristol, c. 1790. Coalburning grate in the centre airs the clothes. To left and right wash boilers with draught-controlled fires. Wooden lids lift off. Rocker-washer with fitted washboard in front. The room also contains a box mangle. All the water had to be pumped up from the tank in the sub-basement which filled with rainwater collected by pipes from the roof

354 The dry laundry, Erddig, Clwyd, eighteenth century. Note: left, drying racks which run on wheels into heated chamber. Centre, box mangle. Background, ironing tables and blankets, clothes horse and irons. Front, laundry basket

355 *Drawing of laundry at Aynho House,
Northamptonshire, 1847 by Mrs Cartwright (see also fig.
15). Note: left, box mangle and laundry baskets. Above,*
*airing frame suspended from ceiling. Background, maids
ironing on ironing tables fitted with drawers. Right,
laundry airing on clothes horse in front of fire*

and the two laundries, one wet, one dry, were built then and the facilities have survived almost unaltered since, though much of the equipment is of a later date.

The wet laundry is the smaller of the two rooms at Erddig. The floor is stone-flagged. In the centre of the pitched roof is a vent to let out the steam from the coppers in which the clothes and bed linen were boiled. There are two coppers of brick with fires below and the water is supplied to them by pipe from a pump in the wall. Nearby are fitted six wall sinks of brown glazed earthenware supported on glazed brick pillars.

The larger, dry laundry next door is well-equipped (354). It measures about 20 feet by 15 feet and is about 15 feet high. On one side are immense drying racks of wood and metal, capable of holding blankets, sheets and curtains, which run on wheels in and out of a ceiling-high drying compartment which is heated from a brick fireplace. A large square creel or wooden airer is suspended by pulleys from the ceiling. Wooden tables extend round two sides of the room, which were used for starching, ironing, finishing and crimping. A box mangle stands in the middle of the floor (see page 154).

In smaller homes the washing was for a long time still done outside in the cottage courtyard, where water was boiled in an iron cauldron over a brick hearth. Gradually this became enclosed and roofed and the cauldron or copper[1] was built into the wash-house. Communal wash-houses were still in use in villages until well into the nineteenth century.

By the nineteenth century in large towns the heavier washing could be sent out to be laundered[2] professionally by the new laundry companies which were then being established. The custom was generally only adopted where there was inadequate space in a town house for the facilities of washing, drying and ironing because the mechanical and chemical processes used were thought to injure the fabrics. In country and suburban areas all washing was done at home and in towns all the finer, decorative materials were handled there also. Washday had become more frequent as cotton and linen were less expensive than before and the numerous layers of be-frilled underwear and nightwear worn by everyone produced quantities of garments to be laundered.

Middle and upper class households employed a large staff of servants and these included a full time laundry staff. Mrs Beeton,[3] in her section on 'Duties of a Laundry Maid', gives us a complete and vivid account of the laundering process which was carried out weekly and took nearly a whole week to do before it all began over again.

Mrs Beeton first outlines the ideal laundry establishment and its equipment which is notably similar to that at Erddig (page 141). She recommends that the establishment should consist of a washing room and a drying one, the latter including a drying closet heated by furnaces. The floor should be of York stone, sloping to a drain. A shaft or vent in the roof should carry off the steam. Running water and hot and cold taps were more common by the mid-nineteenth century and Mrs Beeton recommends taps and drains to all sinks, tubs and coppers. Adjacent to the washing and bleaching house should be a room for drying, mangling and ironing. This should include tables with drawers to hold the ironing blankets, clothes horses and creels for airing, mangles and starching facilities (355).

Mrs Beeton says:

'The laundry maid should commence her labours on Monday morning by a careful examination of the articles committed to her care, and enter them in the washing book; separating the white linen and collars, sheets and body-linen into one heap, fine muslins into another, coloured cotton and linen fabrics into a third, woollens into a fourth, and the coarser kitchen and other greasy cloths into a fifth'.

She then says that all the articles must be examined for ink, grease, fruit or wine stains and recommends chemical fluids for getting these out before washing begins. The various sorted piles of washing are then put into different tubs to soak at suitable water temperatures in a lye solution which varied according to the fabric, using soda, unslaked lime, etc. Coppers and boilers were then filled and fires under them laid ready to light.

Early on Tuesday morning the fires were lit and the washing process began and, again, this varied according to the fabric concerned. Each was carefully removed from the lye solution in which it had been soaking, was rinsed, wrung and then put into clean warm water. Some fabrics were then boiled and all were rubbed, soaped and washed more than once, then rinsed a number of times. Whites were bleached and were treated with 'fig-blue'[4] to improve the colour. Woollens were liable to shrink so the water should not be too hot and garments should be well rinsed. After this they were often stretched out to dry on tenterhooks.[5] Silks had to be washed separately and handkerchiefs which had been used for snuff needed special treatment.

The washing process for the different fabrics, whites and coloureds, continued through Tuesday and Wednesday. Mrs Beeton then explains the processes of mangling, starching and ironing which occupied Thursday and Friday (pages 152–9).

By the middle of the nineteenth century, although washing still involved excessive physical labour, several aids and appliances had become available to make the process a little easier. More houses possessed piped water, so relieving the immense labour of carrying pails of water from pump to cauldron or boiler.

The idea of the wash boiler was gradually developed. Generally housed in an out-house, at first this was a cast-iron cauldron set on a brick plinth with space beneath for a fire. Then wash boilers were made with the fire-place incorporated into the cast iron body (364). As gas was piped into more homes, gas boilers or coppers gradually became available. These were usually designed to be free-standing, on legs, and the later examples were fitted with taps which would empty the boiler, though it still had to be filled by hand (366). In the twentieth century came the galvanised copper which was coated with zinc to resist rusting (365). Enamelled models followed in the 1930s and some designs were powered by electricity as an alternative to gas.

The dolly stick and the posser were aids to alleviate the drudgery of washday. The dolly stick, also known

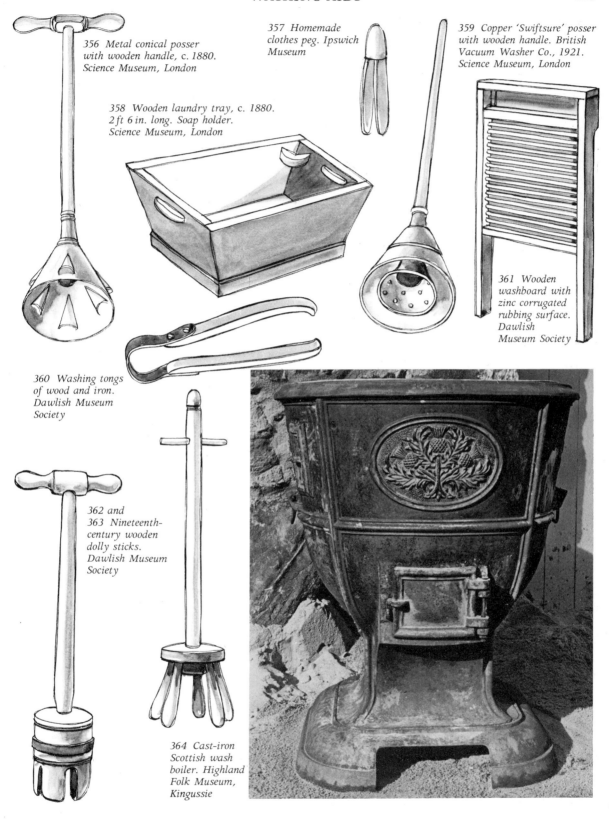

356 Metal conical posser with wooden handle, c. 1880. Science Museum, London

357 Homemade clothes peg. Ipswich Museum

358 Wooden laundry tray, c. 1880. 2 ft 6 in. long. Soap holder. Science Museum, London

359 Copper 'Swiftsure' posser with wooden handle. British Vacuum Washer Co., 1921. Science Museum, London

361 Wooden washboard with zinc corrugated rubbing surface. Dawlish Museum Society

360 Washing tongs of wood and iron. Dawlish Museum Society

362 and 363 Nineteenth-century wooden dolly sticks. Dawlish Museum Society

364 Cast-iron Scottish wash boiler. Highland Folk Museum, Kingussie

365 Steel portable gas-fired boiler, c. 1915

366 Cast-iron gas-fired wash boiler, brass top, copper lid. John Wright and Co., c. 1900. Science Museum, London

as a peggy stick, dolly pin or clump dolly, varied in design from region to region, but the most usual form was that of an upside-down wooden milking stool with a long handle attached to the centre of the seat. Many dolly sticks were fitted with a cross bar at the top to make them easier to use. The washing was pounded up and down in the washtub by this appliance, so forcing the soapy water through the fabric and easing out the dirt (362, 363). A slightly different appliance was the posser (posset) or vacuum clothes washer. This consisted of a cone-shaped metal head, with holes in the base, attached to a long wooden handle. When pumped up and down in the washtub, the water was driven through the fabric of the clothes and sucked back up again (356, 359).

Dollies and possers were in use for several centuries, but an especially typical nineteenth-century aid was the washboard. Made of wood, this was faced with a zinc-covered corrugated surface against which the clothes were rubbed to remove the dirt (361).

The washing machine

During the nineteenth century many and varied attempts were made to design a washing machine. Such appliances were not in any way comparable to the modern washing machine because the motive power still depended upon human energy. Also, the filling and emptying was, to a large extent, still carried out by human hands and the water had to be heated first then poured into the machine and chopped up soap added. Nevertheless nineteenth-century appliances were appreciated and, if the family could afford it, were purchased and used. It should be mentioned, though, that until after the First World War in Britain it is doubtful if these machines were available to more than five per cent of the community.

A patent for a machine to 'wash, press out water and to press linen and wearing apparel' was taken out as early as 1780 by a Mr Rogerson from Warrington, but it is not clear if such a machine was ever made. Two years later Mr Sidgier introduced an idea for a machine which worked on the modern rotary principle, where a cylindrical drum, constructed inside a larger vessel which contained water, was turned by a geared handle.

After this, efforts seemed to languish and it was the 1850s before serious attempts were made to solve the problem. In the succeeding 50 years many washing machines were designed, made and put on the market.

367 *Wooden washing machine with mangle. William Sellers of Keighley, c. 1890. When the large wheel is turned a five-legged dolly is agitated backwards and forwards. Although the wheel is turned continuously in one direction, an ingenious motion automatically reverses the direction of the dolly at every stroke. The mangle (wringer) is operated by the handle on the right. Science Museum, London*

368 *Wooden washing machine, late nineteenth century. Handle is moved backwards and forwards to agitate washing by means of a swinging wooden gate. Rubbing boards fitted on each side. Large mangle with wooden rollers turned by handle on wheel. Totnes Museum*

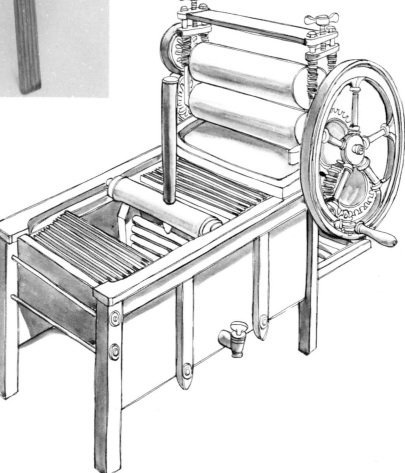

369　Vowel Y washing machine and mangle (wringer). Thomas Bradford, 1897. A popular model made in many sizes. This one is in cast iron painted red and black. Washing in hexagonal tub is tumbled by wooden slats when handle is turned. Handle on right operates mangle. Science Museum, London

370　Lever-operated washing machine and wheel-operated mangle (wringer), c. 1880. The clothes are put in the wooden box in warm soapy water. Pulling the lever rotates the wooden roller and its perforated blades agitate the clothes. Science Museum, London

They all followed the traditional method of washing clothes but presented a marginal improvement in that the housewife only had to turn a handle or a wheel or push a lever backwards and forwards instead of pounding a dolly stick up and down. The aim of the washing machine designer was to produce a mechanism which would agitate the soapy water in which the clothes were soaking, pushing it through the fabric and so easing out the dirt.

Most of these machines, often referred to as dolly washers, were made of wood in the form of a round tub or rectangular box. Only the wheels, handles, taps, legs and fittings were of metal. Many of them had a dolly stick or posser attached to the lid or the base and incorporated a mechanism that operated this stick when a handle, wheel or lever was used (367). Some designs included corrugated walls and base which increased resistance and acted like a rubbing washboard on the clothes (371). Others were made with a wooden roller with pegs projecting from it; this turned when the handle was operated and the pegs churned the washing round and round (370). A variant of this type was fitted with fins or paddles to move the washing. In yet another instance a lever operated a wooden gate which swung backwards and forwards to agitate the clothes in the water. This model was also fitted with removable washboards (368).

The 'Faithfull' washing machine ingeniously harnessed the motive power of the rocker, traditionally employed from early times to send a baby to sleep in its cradle and later adopted for churning butter (chapter 2 page 49). In this cradle washing machine the legs could be folded up and tucked away when it was not in use. The washing in the wooden tub was set in motion by the minimum of effort; the housewife could sit in a chair rocking the machine with her foot while, at the same time, carrying out another household task (373).

One of the best-known manufacturers of washing machines in the nineteenth century was Thomas Bradford, whose hand-operated machines were being made from the 1860s. His Vowel Y model of 1897 (369) was marketed in considerable numbers and, like most of the washing machines made from 1875–80 onwards, was fitted with a mangle (page 154). Bradford took a lead in pioneering the smaller mangles or wringers with rollers of reduced diameter.

Hand-operated washing machines continued to be made and sold until well into the 1930s. The wooden tub had been replaced in the 1920s more and more by galvanised steel or copper and the design of the machine had become smaller and neater (372). Many of these machines still had to be filled by hand with hot water and, in some cases, had to be emptied as well. But machines were being designed as early as the 1880s which would heat the water in the washing tank. Morton's Patent Steam[6] Washer (1884), made in Glasgow, was a successful example and Howarth's design of 1889 was another. These were both heated by gas jets, as was Howarth's Coronet model of 1920. Some machines were designed to heat the water by burning coal. The Krauss design of 1923 was one of these, the fire being contained beneath the galvanised boiler which was equipped with a flue to carry away the smoke. Two different designs were produced, one which operated the washing action by hand, the other by electric motor.

The electrically powered washing machine was pioneered in the USA in the first decade of the twentieth century. Until after the First World War this was simply a matter of adding an electric motor to the wooden, hand-operated models, probably as an optional extra (374). The machines were rarely earthed and since the motor was generally sited beneath the tub and the tubs often leaked, the equipment was not only liable to short-circuiting but was distinctly unsafe. Possibly the small number of accidents reported was only due to the restricted number of machines in operation.

By the later 1920s in the USA the washing machine was re-designed to take advantage of electric power and to be suitable for production for a mass market. The wooden tub machine was replaced by an all-metal design (375), which before long was enclosed in a white enamelled cabinet. There were several methods of providing the mechanical washing action of which two were most popular and successful. One was the agitator or impeller design where a revolving disc fitted with fins was mounted in the bottom of the tub and was operated by a driving mechanism beneath. The other was a rotating cylinder type. This cylinder, which rotated first in one direction then back again was perforated and contained in an outer tub of water.

Electrically-powered washing machines were being imported into Britain in small numbers by 1920, but these were costly and few were sold. Even by the late 1930s, when the price was more reasonable, the

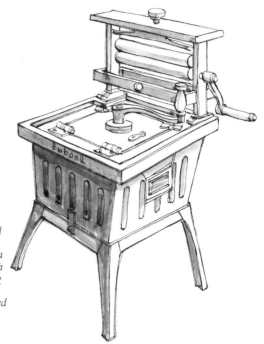

371 Wooden tub machine, the inner walls and base corrugated to increase resistance. The handle is pushed backwards and forwards to make the central posser rotate, c.1900–10. Carlisle Museum

372 Ewbank washing machine, c.1930. Metal and wood. Handle is turned to operate a metal beater which swirls the washing round. Wringer with rubber-covered rollers. Carlisle Museum

373 Faithfull cradle washing machine, 1906. Made of wood and rocked like a cradle. The hatch on top is removed for filling with soapy water and clothes. The legs are positioned as in photograph to stabilise cradle while it is being filled or emptied. They are pulled up in order to rock. Science Museum, London

374 *Wooden washing machine with metal wringer and rubber rollers. Beatty Bros. Canada, c. 1920. A hand-operated machine adapted to be powered by electricity. Electric Motor sited beneath tub. The drive to the dolly is automatically disconnected when the lid is raised. Mangle drive is engaged by the small handle at the rollers. Science Museum, London*

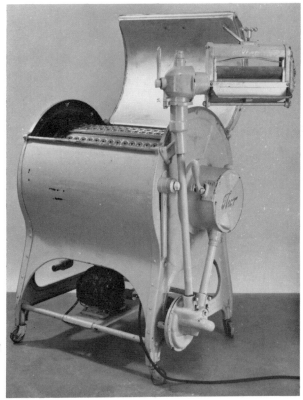

375 *Thor electric washing machine and wringer, c. 1929. Green enamelled metal machine, with motor sited beneath tub. Washing tumbled inside perforated metal cylinder. Science Museum, London*

washing machine was still thought of in Britain as a luxury. It was 1947–50 before the marketing campaign began to show results. At this time most models were fitted with small hand-wringers. Soon they were powered by electricity and immersion heaters were introduced.

The automatic washing machine, incorporating a spin drier, became a great success in the 1960s when it was programmed to provide a full wash, rinsing and spin cycles automatically. Since then the machines have become more sophisticated, incorporating hot water drawn from the house heating system, pre-washes, biological washes and a choice of eight programmes suited to different fabrics. Most modern washing machines provide agitator or tumble action. The former is usually adopted for a top-loading machine, the latter for a front-loader. The agitator design is fitted with a rotating bladed-spindle, the tumble with a cylinder, rotating first one way then the other and allowing the clothes to fall through the water.

Drying

Until the nineteenth century washed clothes and household linen were wrung out by hand then, weather permitting, dried in the open air. When it was cold or wet the washing was draped over clothes horses around the fire or hung from wooden frames (creels) which were pulled up out of the way towards the ceiling by means of ropes and pulleys. In large houses the laundry room was often equipped with drying racks heated by coal-burning stoves (page 143 and figs. 353, 354, 355).

Mangles were primarily intended for smoothing and pressing (page 154), but during the nineteenth century the smaller version for expelling water from clothes was developed. Known as a wringer, this could be clamped to a table or washtub or was supported on its own stand. The majority of washing machines were made with a wringer as part of the design. Most models were fitted with a screw adapter which would adjust the pressure of the rollers to be suitable to press out water either from fine garments or heavy blankets.

Many attempts were made from the later eighteenth century onwards to design equipment which would extract water from material by mechanical means. The urgent need for this stemmed from the textile and dyeing industries and during the nineteenth century efforts were made to develop machines which would

do this by making use of centrifugal force[7]. The idea is that the water in the clothes is released as the clothes are revolved rapidly – as in a modern 'spin-drier'. An early instance of this method being applied to the problem of drying clothes was the drying machine built to the order of Angela Burdett Coutts in 1855 and sent out to the Crimea to handle the linen for hospital army casualties. The machine, which was made of iron encased in wood, measured six feet square and was seven feet high. It cost £150 and was shipped out in parts and reassembled on the spot. It contained a copper for washing and a drying closet including a spin drier which worked on the centrifugal principle, drying 1000 articles of linen in 25 minutes.

It was not until the 1920s that, with the aid of the electric motor, the spin drier was developed on this principle in the USA for a small model suitable for domestic use. In this the washed, still wet clothes were revolved at speed in a cylinder, which had holes in its walls. As the washing was spun round the centrifugal action pressed the fabric against the walls of the cylinder, so expelling the water through the holes and away down a drain.

After the Second World War the market for spin driers expanded rapidly and sales in Britain began to rise. Further improvements followed: the twin tub machine with washer and drier side by side was followed by the automatic models which programmed washing, rinsing and spinning cycles. The tumbler drier, which worked on the same principle as the tumbling action in a washing machine (page 149), made its appearance also. In this the drum revolves in one direction only and hot air is drawn in and permeates the washing. Tumbler driers are most effective but costly to run as the time taken to fully dry a load is considerable.

Pressing and mangling

Various ideas have been generated and made use of over the centuries to press and smooth the fabric of household linen and garments after they had been washed. In Britain the clothes press, which was used chiefly for heavy and household linen, had been operated for this purpose since Roman times; the Romans called it a *prelum*, the same word being coined for a wine- or oil-press. Such linen presses would only be customary in larger homes where there was a quantity of household linen to be pressed. Different sizes were in use for sheets, tablecloths and smaller

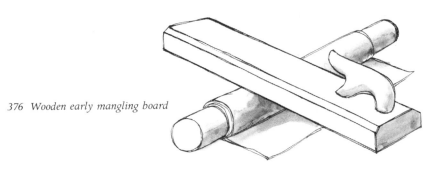

376 Wooden early mangling board

377 Wooden linen press, late eighteenth century. Georgian House Museum, Bristol

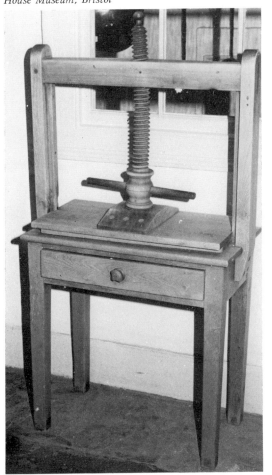

378 Typical mangle of the late 1880s. Note also yellow bar soap, water dipper and bowl. Gustav Holst's Birthplace Museum, Cheltenham

items. The press might be made with its own wooden stand or to rest upon a table. Many designs incorporated drawers to hold the finished linen. Most presses consisted of two heavy, smooth wooden boards; the upper board was raised and lowered as necessary to adjust the pressure on the material by a wooden turnscrew. By the seventeenth and eighteenth centuries many presses were fine pieces of furniture made of polished oak or mahogany (377).

From the late sixteenth century developed the idea of mangling clothes. At this time it was done by use of a mangling board and roller, a system which came from northern Europe where it was in operation in Danish, Dutch and German hoi   The word mangle derives from the Dutch and Middle High German *mangelen*, which itself stemmed from the older Greek word for an engine of war[8]. In sixteenth-century Italy the word *mangano* was used to refer to the 'pressing of cloth in order to give it a lustre or shine'.

In using the mangling board or bat, the fabric was rolled as smoothly as possible, while still damp, on to a cylinder (about 20 inches long) which resembled a rolling pin. This was then placed upon a smooth-topped table. The mangling board (a flat board about two feet long and three to four inches wide with a handle on top at one end) was pressed on to the roller, moving it backwards and forwards on the table until the fabric was smoothed out. This was then unrolled and left to dry (376). Some mangling boards had smooth under surfaces, some were corrugated. Many had decoratively carved upper surfaces and handles. This system of smoothing and pressing fabric obtained quite a high standard of laundering. It was widely used in all classes of home in northern Europe until well into the nineteenth century and the idea was exported by colonists to North America and South Africa.

During the eighteenth and nineteenth centuries the mangle as a machine was evolved. This process of mangling was almost a dry one. The eighteenth-century version was the cumbersome box mangle which exerted heavy pressure on the clothes and which was only suitable for large houses or for communal laundries where there was a great quantity of washing to be handled; it continued in everyday use throughout the nineteenth century.

The box mangle (354, 379) measured some six feet in length, three to four feet in width and was about three feet high. It consisted of a large wooden box which was filled with stones[9] and which was incorporated into a stout wooden frame standing on the floor. In a space under the box were a number of wooden rollers which ran on a flat bed of wood or slate. The washing fabric to be pressed was carefully wound round the rollers, the smaller items being enclosed inside and the whole being enclosed by a covering of plain brown Holland mangling cloths; these helped to impart a shine to the finished linen. The wood rollers were then inserted in place under the box and the crank handle of the mechanism was turned so that the box full of stones slowly trundled backwards and forwards till the clothes were sufficiently pressed. It was heavy work to overcome the inertia and get it moving, but after this the fly wheel at the rear made it easy to keep going. An elaborate system of stops was incorporated so that the box did not run off its bed under this momentum and crash to the floor. A tipping or lifting device was built in to the machine so that the rollers full of washing could be lifted out easily when they were ready.

By the mid-nineteenth century the standing mangle with two large-diameter wooden rollers supported in a cast iron framework stand had appeared. There were a number of designs, some which were incorporated into an early washing machine or a dolly washer (368, 370), but most were of standard form. These had a wooden tray to support the fabric as it was mangled and a wooden shelf below to hold soap, bowls and pegs. The rollers were operated by a handle on a large wheel and the pressure could be adjusted by a turnscrew at the top of the mangle (378). Towards the end of the century wringers of a similar or smaller pattern were made to expel water from the washing as well as to press it (367, 369, 372, 374, 375).

Smoothing and ironing

In Europe, before the advent of heated irons, various types of rounded artefacts were used to smooth fabric after washing. It is not known exactly when such aids were brought into use, but certainly in eighth-century Scandinavia several different types were being employed. These rubbing stones (*gnidestein*) were fashioned from rounded pieces of rock or they could be spherical, made in glass or wood. Some were formed in the shape of a mushroom with the stalk used as a handle and the smooth rounded cap would 'iron' the fabric (380). Many different versions have been found in Viking graves and this type of 'cold-iron' instru-

379 *Box mangle (Baker's Patent Mangle), early nineteenth century. Stranger's Hall Museum of Domestic Life, Norwich*

ment continued in general use in Europe, especially in country areas, until after the eighteenth century. Shaped, polished stones (called slickstones or slykestones) were widely used in England from the Middle Ages. No heat was used; the instrument was applied directly to the damp material.

The ancestor of the European heated smoothing iron is the Oriental pan iron which was in use in the Far East from very early times and has continued to be made to this traditional pattern ever since. A twelfth-century Chinese painting[10] in the Museum of Fine Arts in Boston, USA shows a group of Chinese ladies smoothing silk with such a pan iron. The brass or bronze iron is shaped like a shallow saucepan and

contains burning charcoal or coals. The handles of such pan irons needed to be of materials resistant to heat so were of teak or other hard wood, bone, ivory or even jade. Many pan irons survive in the West, but in most cases the handles have had to be replaced by later ones (381).

In Europe it was the early sixteenth century before household and personal linen was made of sufficiently fine fabric to need and to benefit from smoothing with a heated iron and it was later in the century that metal irons began to be made which could be heated to do

380 Viking glass smoothing iron, eighth century.

381 Chinese pan iron, Ch'ing Dynasty. Bronze iron with modern wood handle. By courtesy of Mrs Sheila Simmons of Eyhorne Manor, Kent

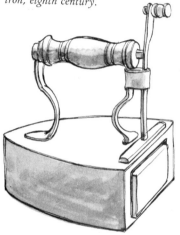

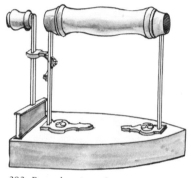

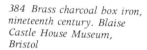

383 Brass box iron, late eighteenth century

382 Iron box iron with wood handle, nineteenth century. North of England Open Air Museum, Beamish Hall

384 Brass charcoal box iron, nineteenth century. Blaise Castle House Museum, Bristol

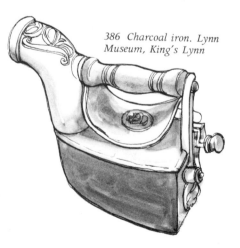

385 Cast-iron sad iron, 1900. North of England Open Air Museum, Beamish Hall

386 Charcoal iron. Lynn Museum, King's Lynn

this. The Dutch were the leaders in making beautifully decorated brass irons, but soon the rest of Europe followed suit, the designs varying characteristically with each nation. Cheaper, everyday models were produced by the local blacksmith in iron; most costly, elegant ones were fashioned by master craftsmen in brass. British irons were being made from the early seventeenth century and most of these were of iron or steel.

From the seventeenth century onwards until the emergence of the self-heating iron in the second half of the nineteenth century, there were two basic types of iron: the box iron and the sad iron. It is not known precisely which of these designs came first, but since the majority of the earlier surviving irons are of the former type, it seems likely that these were of earlier origin.

The principle of the box iron (also known as a slug iron and with a variant in the charcoal iron) was that it was a large hollow container designed to hold the heating agent. Box irons were similar in shape to the modern article, having a point in front and a square rear end, but they were much deeper because they were designed to contain a cast-iron heated slug. Slugs were provided in pairs, one in use in the iron and one heating on the stove or in the fire. The slug, of similar shape to the iron, was left in the fire until red hot and was then placed in an opening in the back of the iron by means of a pair of tongs. A hinged gate was swung open or was lifted up in order to open the aperture for the slug to be put in (382, 383).

The charcoal or ember iron was similar in appearance to the slug-heated box iron, but the top plate was hinged to lift up so that the burning charcoal or coals could be inserted using the small tongs provided. It was designed either with a row of holes along each side (some of these were decoratively shaped) or a chimney set in the top plate rose up in front. Both of these features were intended to provide a draught of air which would make the charcoal burn well and act as an escape for smoke (384, 386). Nineteenth-century improvements to charcoal iron design included the provision of a pair of bellows, the tip of which was inserted into a hole in the back of the iron in order to pump in air and improve the burning rate of the charcoal. A disconcerting disadvantage of doing this, especially with the chimney type of iron, was that it tended to project a shower of smuts on to the newly-washed linen awaiting ironing.

The other type of iron was the solid one. Most of these designs were made entirely of cast iron, sole and handle. This is known as the sad, smoothing or flat iron (385). Various explanations have been put forward for the use of the term 'sad'; the most likely seems to be that from the Middle Ages on alternative meanings for the word 'sad' were solid and heavy.

Sad irons were made in all sizes from small ones to smooth edges and delicate garments to large ones for heavy fabrics. Early sad irons were heated by standing them on their blunt ends on the hearth near the glowing coals of the open fire. Under these circumstances it was not easy to keep the sole clean and it had to be wiped before applying it to the washed clothes. The problem was eased with the introduction of the kitchen range (page 84), when the iron could be placed on the hotplate to heat up. One always needed at least two irons, one heating while the other was in use. Later still, the gas ring or cooker top was used for this purpose. If a quantity of ironing needed to be done regularly a laundry stove was used where a number of irons could be kept heating ready for use (389).

Using any of these designs of iron was skilled work. The handles became very hot and needed to be grasped by a padded holder. It required experience and careful judgement to know exactly when an iron was heated to the correct temperature suited to a given fabric. This was judged by holding the sole near to one's cheek or forearm – but not too near! Alternatively a few drops of water (or spittle) were allowed to fall on to the heated sole. A skilled operator would judge the temperature accurately by the strength of the hiss. Trivets of iron or brass were kept by the hearth and on the ironing table on which the iron could be rested for a moment while the fabric or awkward frills, collars, hems, etc. were adjusted on the ironing table ready for the next section to be smoothed. Such trivets varied greatly in design from plain iron ones to the highly decorative models (392).

Surprisingly, it was not until the nineteenth century that the detached wooden handle was developed for holding irons, so making the work less exhaustingly hot. The best-known was the sad iron designed by Mrs Potts[11] of Iowa in the USA, who patented her iron in 1870 (393). This was supplied with three clip-on walnut handles which could be transferred from iron to iron as the newly-heated iron was taken from the fire into use. Known as Mrs Potts Patent Cold-

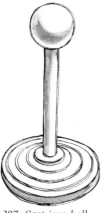

387 Cast-iron ball iron. Torquay Museum

388 Cast-iron mushroom iron

389 Cast-iron laundry stove for keeping sad irons hot. Shaftesbury Museum

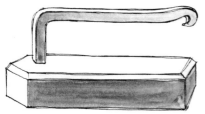

390 Cast-iron goose iron

391 Polishing iron with convex sole

392 Cast-iron trivet. Elizabethan House Museum, Great Yarmouth

393 Potts' sad iron, 1870s

394 Sleeve and bustle iron. Dry laundry, Erddig, Clwyd

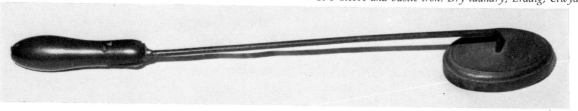

Handle Sad Iron, this model continued on sale in America until the 1950s.

Over the years a number of special-purpose irons were made, particularly in the nineteenth century, when such a quantity of garments were worn, many of which required special treatment to smooth the flounces, frills, pleats and difficult shapes of sleeves, collars, bustles, etc. Particular irons were produced to press bonnets (these were small and were known as bonnet irons) and to iron lace (these had no sharp point in front to catch in the intricate threadwork and the ends were rounded upwards). Standing irons made in different shapes were designed to smooth specific parts of garments. Widely used were the mushroom iron, the ball iron and the egg iron (387, 388), all intended for getting into awkward parts of the garment. The rounded end of the iron was heated and the fabric of cap, puff sleeve or bustle was drawn over it. There were also long-handled sleeve irons for similar purposes (394).

In the second half of the nineteenth century it was fashionable to give a glazed finish to starched garments. This was achieved by using an iron with a convex sole. The idea was that the smaller the surface area of the iron in contact with the material the greater would be the pressure and so the higher the sheen. Some of these irons, which were known as polishers or polishing irons, were two-handled so that still greater pressure could be exerted (391).

The goose iron was a particularly heavy one used chiefly by tailors (390). It was long, narrow and deep and so-called because its handle was shaped forward in a curve resembling a goose's neck; this formed a hook so that it could be hung up on a bar over the fireplace. Referred to as a goose iron by Shakespeare as early as 1605, it was also known in nineteenth-century slang as a weasel[12].

One of the most characteristic of the special-purpose irons were those developed over the centuries for crimping and goffering. This need arose in the second half of the sixteenth century to shape, dry and finish the starched ruffs and sleeve and collar ruffles. The word goffering derives from the French verb *gaufrer*, to crimp or flute. Both goffering and crimping produced a corrugated edging to the fabric, but crimping gave a finer, tighter wave.

From the sixteenth until the early twentieth century some form of heated iron was needed for making and finishing ruffles. The most characteristic design,

of which literally hundreds survive in museums, was the tally iron. This was invented in Italy in the sixteenth century, the word tally being an English corruption of Italy. This device, most commonly referred to as a goffering iron[13] followed the same traditional pattern continuously until the 1920s. Made of metal, it consists of one or more cigar-shaped barrels of differing diameter. Iron poking or setting sticks, made to fit into these barrels, were heated in the fire then placed inside them. They transferred the heat to the barrels, but the garment was protected from any soot or charcoal marking. The damp starched material of the ruff or other garment edging was held in both hands while the thumbs pressed it over the heated barrel till it was smooth and dry. Each convolution of the ruff had to be treated separately in this way (395, 399).

Though the fashion for ruffs went out in the early seventeenth century, the tally or goffering iron continued in use. It was employed for finishing ruffled or frilled edges of any garment but particularly collars, cuffs, aprons and caps. Small diameter tally irons, used for finishing dainty edging were known as piping irons.

From the late eighteenth century onwards alternative devices were beginning to become available for making flutes in material. First there were the fluting or quilling tongs which were scissor-like instruments closely resembling metal curling tongs (398). Later designs were multi-pronged, so creating more than one flute at a time. In the nineteenth century appeared the fluter and fluting board. This consisted of a hard wood or metal board which was finely corrugated with sharp-edged ribs and a roller which had ridges exactly matching those on the board. The damped starched material was placed on the board and crimped by working the roller backwards and forwards. The material was then left to dry (397).

A traditional means of goffering, in use for many years, was the goffering stack or stack pleater. This consisted of two wooden slotted posts fixed into a horizontal board at an interval of about 12–13 inches apart. The damped starched material was then threaded in and out of some 20–30 wooden spills or slats which were afterwards slotted into the posts. These were secured in place by a top wooden bar and the whole stack was put in front of the fire to dry (396).

The final phase in the saga of goffering was the

395 Tally iron used for finishing starched ruff

396 Goffering stack. Two rows of quills. Cylinder used to store quills. National Museum of Welsh Antiquities, Bangor

397 Fluting iron and board

398 Goffering tongs. Elizabethan House Museum, Great Yarmouth

399 Polished steel tally iron. Paisley Museum

400 Iron and brass crimping machine. Gustav Holst's Birthplace Museum, Cheltenham

crimping machine of the second half of the nineteenth century. This resembled a miniature mangle, but its brass rollers were corrugated in order to crimp the material. The rollers were hollow and were heated in the same way as the tally iron by the insertion of red hot cylindrical irons which produced instantaneous crimping of the material passed through the rollers. Various sizes of crimping rollers were made to take fabric of different widths (400).

After centuries of heating up box and sad irons by use of the open fire and the stove, experiments into the idea of a self-heating iron began to be successful by the mid-nineteenth century. Gas-heated irons were the first to be satisfactorily operated, but between the 1850s and the early twentieth century a number of other substances were also experimented with to fuel an iron which heated itself: oil, paraffin, naphtha, methylated spirits, carbide acetylene, petrol. These met with a varying degree of success, but some models were notably dangerous to use.

Box irons fuelled by coal gas were in use in the USA from the 1850s as, for example, the one patented by David Lithgow of Philadelphia in 1858. English gas irons followed, later designed with a flexible tube to connect to the gas supply (402, 406). These were still being made in the 1930s and models designed for use with bottled gas were in production in the late 1960s.

Colza oil burning irons were developed from the designs of lamps using the same fuel, but these were distinctly unsafe to use so did not become very popular. Paraffin-heated irons developed in the 1890s were only a little more reassuring. In America experiments were made with the use of naphtha, but there is only doubtful evidence of the production of this dangerous type of self-heating iron.

The spirit iron, made in considerable numbers from the 1850s onwards, was a great deal more satisfactory. Heated by methylated spirits, these were much safer and many models survive. The spirit iron resembled a charcoal-burning iron in appearance; it was deep and had a row or rows of holes along the sides to permit air to enter. At the back was a fuel tank for the liquid spirit; a pipe led from this to the burner and the flow was controlled by a valve. The spirit iron was primarily developed from the 1890s when it was widely available in the USA and Europe (401).

The spirit iron had long been popular as a travelling instrument. This became even more so when solidified cubes impregnated with the spirit became available which were safer and easier to transport than containers of the liquid.

In the early years of the twentieth century two different forms of fuel were added to the possible means of self-heating irons: carbide-acetylene and petroleum. The former was, in this respect, of limited development, but petrol, despite the difficulties of adapting it for use in these circumstances, was widely used in self-heating irons. In Britain Tilley, known for its petrol- and paraffin-burning lamps, developed a satisfactory model which was manufactured until the Second World War and of which a considerable number survive (408).

All of these various means of fuelling a self-heating iron became obsolete when the electric iron became widely available, but this was seriously delayed in Britain by slowness in introducing electric supply into homes. In the USA the electric iron first appeared in the 1880s, a patent being issued in 1883. This model was not, however, connected to the electric supply but needed to be heated frequently on a special stand. In Europe by 1890 an iron was being developed which was connected by a flexible cord to the electric supply. Also, a French iron was designed to be heated by an electric arc between two carbon rods in a similar manner to the arc lamps of a few years earlier (page 100). None of these types of iron was very safe or shockproof (405, 409).

In Britain Crompton's (page 102) were producing electric irons from 1891 and their 1900 catalogue lists six different designs which, like the early electric kettles and vacuum cleaners were suitable for plugging into electric light sockets (pages 42, 135). The electric iron made little progress until the late 1920s, mainly because so few homes were wired for electric current. Once this was done, sales forged ahead. The irons of this date were still clumsy in comparison with the modern streamlined iron. They were very heavy (about eight or nine pounds in weight) because, due to fluctuation and unreliability in the power supply, the iron needed to be able to store heat to allow for when it was forced to cut out. There was as yet no thermostatic control (this followed just before the outbreak of the Second World War) so the temperature of the iron still had to be judged in the same way as it had been for centuries (page 105) and the iron switched off or on when it became too hot or cool (403).

The steam-or-dry iron appeared in the 1950s. This was designed to iron dry fabrics which were still

401 Spirit iron. Steel with wood handle. Lynn Museum, King's Lynn

402 Gas iron, c. 1910. Steel with wood handle. Christchurch Mansion Museum, Ipswich

403 Electric iron, 1935. Enamelled and polished steel, wood handle

404 Gas iron. Steel with wood handle. Elizabethan House Museum, Great Yarmouth

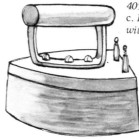

405 Electric iron, c. 1885. Iron with wood handle

406 Gas iron, 1920–30. Steel with wood handle. North of England Open Air Museum, Beamish Hall

407 Morphy-Richards electric iron, c. 1965. (Author). Enamelled and polished steel, plastic handle

408 Tilley iron, 1940–50. Enamelled and polished steel, plastic handle. North of England Open Air Museum, Beamish Hall

409 Electric iron, 1900. Iron with wood handle

damp, but to emit jets of steam to dampen those which had become too dry. The modern iron (407) has become slenderer, lighter in weight and much easier to handle. The temperature is fully thermostatically controlled as is the moisture emission. The iron is fitted with a non-stick, stainproof sole plate.

CHAPTER EIGHT

The Making of Fire and Light

Fire-making

It is extremely difficult, even for the most imaginative of us, in the last quarter of the twentieth century, to conceive of the problems over hundreds of years, at least until the middle of the nineteenth century, of creating a flame and so being able to make a fire to warm oneself or to cook and to make a light and push back the darkness. Because of the difficulties, especially in a cool, damp climate such as ours in Britain, for centuries people kept the kitchen fire alight night and day, or alternatively, a perpetually-burning lamp. For this reason they damped down the fire at night, covered it with a couvre-feu and blew life into it in the morning with the aid of a pair of bellows (see page 59).

For thousands of years from the days of primitive man until the advent of the exciting and dangerous inventions developed in the late eighteenth century to make fire with the aid of such substances as vitriol, gunpowder and phosphorus, two chief means have been employed: the flint, steel and tinder method and that of wood friction. For the latter a dry climate is essential so, in Britain, the tinder box has been the normal method since before Roman times. Any sharp-edged, hard stone may be used as a flint and this is used to strike a piece of iron pyrites which is a compound of iron and sulphur. In striking the flint needs to pare off a minute fragment of the metal which becomes very hot in the process. This is encouraged to fall upon some dry flammable material (tinder) so that it ignites it and may be blown into flame. Many materials are suitable for tinder. In later times charred silk, cotton or linen was used, in more primitive days,

dried fungi or moss, down feathers or fluffy plant down such as dandelion or thistle clocks.

By the seventeenth and eighteenth centuries the process had become a little more sophisticated but was basically unchanged. The flint (now called a strike-a-light) was sharpened, the steel was shaped to fit the hand and be easier to manipulate (410, 411) and the tinder of cotton or linen rags was prepared in the kitchen so that it was thoroughly dry. This was all kept ready for use in a wood or metal tinder box which was often fitted with a candle holder and snuffer (413, 414). Home-produced sulphur matches made it easier to obtain a light from the smouldering tinder. These had been available since Roman times but were dangerous to handle. They were made by melting sulphur over a fire in a special container and dipping lengths of wood, cardboard or straw into it and then leaving them to cool (415).

The journal *Tinder Box* (1832) describes how at that time beggars used to sell sulphur matches on the streets, having first begged off-cuts from the local carpenter and then cut them up into slivers. The same publication also tells of the difficulty in winter in getting a spark from one's tinder box and of how one had to work for several minutes (three on average) on a cold dark morning, often striking one's knuckles instead of the steel, before a flame could be coaxed.

A particularly vivid account of the frustration and even fear that could be instilled into an intelligent person as late as the eighteenth century by the lack of a flame was given by James Boswell in his *London Journal* (1763). He had decided to sit up late one night to write, but at 2 am he accidentally snuffed out his

164

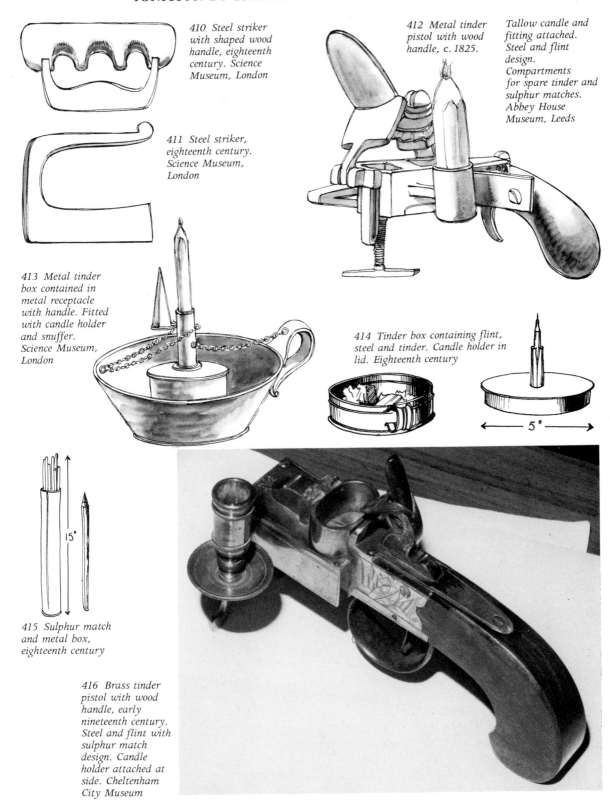

410 Steel striker with shaped wood handle, eighteenth century. Science Museum, London

411 Steel striker, eighteenth century. Science Museum, London

412 Metal tinder pistol with wood handle, c. 1825.

Tallow candle and fitting attached. Steel and flint design. Compartments for spare tinder and sulphur matches. Abbey House Museum, Leeds

413 Metal tinder box contained in metal receptacle with handle. Fitted with candle holder and snuffer. Science Museum, London

414 Tinder box containing flint, steel and tinder. Candle holder in lid. Eighteenth century

5"

415 Sulphur match and metal box, eighteenth century

15"

416 Brass tinder pistol with wood handle, early nineteenth century. Steel and flint with sulphur match design. Candle holder attached at side. Cheltenham City Museum

candle. His fire had died and he was left in darkness. He crept down to the kitchen to search for the tinder box but could not find it. He says:

> But this tinder box I could not see, nor knew where to find. I was now filled with gloomy ideas of the terrors of the night. I was also apprehensive that my landlord, who always keeps a pair of loaded pistols by him, might fire at me as a thief. I went up to my room, sat quietly until I heard the watchman calling ''past three o'clock''. I then called to him to knock on the door.

Happily Boswell then got his 'candle re-lumed without danger'.

Tinder pistols were developed in the seventeenth century from the flint-lock pistol. Early designs contained tinder (usually amadou prepared from fungi) inside the split barrel. When triggered a spark ignited a charge of gunpowder, the flame from which lit the tinder. By the eighteenth century a more common design incorporated a flint and steel to make the spark which then fell upon the tinder. Sulphur matches were used to produce a flame from the glowing tinder. More sophisticated tinder pistols of the early nineteenth century contained special compartments for sulphur matches and extra tinder and were fitted with candle holders (412, 416). Some designs were incorporated into a combination tinder pistol and alarm clock, others a desk inkwell.

Although the tinder box continued to be the staple means of producing a flame for most people until matches became reasonably cheap in the second half of the nineteenth century, varied means of ignition were more or less successfully experimented with from about 1775–80 onwards. For about 40–50 years these were based on the interaction of one chemical upon another and, since the chemicals were highly inflammable substances, using the devices was a hazardous proceeding. Fortunately these 'instantaneous lights', as they were called, were expensive so were not in widespread use.

The development of the phosphorus and chlorate matches (instantaneous lights) made considerable advances in the eighteenth century due to the increasing ability to manufacture sulphuric acid. In 1775 Carl Wilhelm Scheele (the Swedish chemist, 1742–86) succeeded in preparing phosphorus from bone-ash by treatment with sulphuric acid and subsequent reduction by charcoal. This led to the phosphoric taper, the first instant flame device, in 1780. It consisted of a wax taper sealed in a glass tube with a little phosphorus. To produce a flame the tube had to be heated to melt the phosphorus on to the tip of the taper. The sealed end of the tube was then broken (at a specially weakened place), the taper was withdrawn and it would ignite immediately upon contact with air. Such devices could be carried on the person, but this was very dangerous as the fragile glass tubes were easily broken so instantaneously igniting the contents.

The phosphorus box followed in 1786. This was first made in Paris (though soon afterward in Britain), where it was called *le briquet phosphorique*. In the box was a supply of sulphur matches, a bottle coated internally with phosphorus and a cork. The sulphur-tipped matches were inserted into the bottle to attract a little phosphorus and were then rubbed on the cork so that the heat generated by this friction would ignite the match (419).

These various forms of phosphorus matches were not very successful or safe, but more dangerous still was the chemical or chlorate match (also called an acid-dip match) introduced in the early years of the nineteenth century. The heads of these matches were tipped with a mixture of chlorate of potash, sugar and gum arabic. For ignition they had to be dipped in vitriol (sulphuric acid). Provision for this type of ignition was generally contained in a small box known as an instantaneous light box. Inside would be a supply of tipped matches, a small bottle of vitriol and some candles and a holder (417).

It goes without saying that waking up in bed in darkness and fumbling on the bedside table to make a light from a device which included a bottle of vitriol was a dangerous proceeding, so Henry Berry's partly-mechanised instantaneous light box of 1824 was a great advance. The box was made of metal. As long as the lid was closed the stopper on the acid bottle was held firmly in place. When it was opened a string on a pulley lifted the stopper on the end of which was one drop of vitriol. The matches were held on a turntable which brought the chlorate-tipped match past the stopper, ignited it and moved it on to light a spirit lamp which was also provided in the box.

A number of new patents were taken out in the decade 1825–35. Samuel Jones of the Strand in London brought out the Promethean match in 1828 (418). This provided a series of single lights in an instantaneous light box. Inside a single drop of vitriol

417 *Instantaneous light box, early nineteenth century. Made by Berry of London. Lignum vitae case containing bottle of vitriol and chlorate matches. Science Museum, London*

418 *Promethean match box, c. 1828. Science Museum, London*

420 *John Walker's friction lights, 1827, placed upon his sale day book for that year. Science Museum, London*

419 *Phosphorus box, 1795–1805. Made by Jarvis of London, Science Museum, London*

was sealed in each of the tiny glass vesicles supplied. Each vesicle (only 3/16 inch long) was then wrapped in a rolled spill of paper which had been treated with a mixture of chlorate of potash, sugar and gum arabic. When a light was needed the vesicle was crushed by a small pair of pliers supplied in the box and the released vitriol reacted on the treated paper to give a flame.

John Walker was a pharmacist in Stockton-on-Tees. In 1827 he began selling a new product he had made, which he called friction lights, in tins at one shilling (5p) per 100 and so made them available to many people. They were thin, flat sticks of wood the heads of which had been dipped in a paste mixed from chlorate of potash, sulphide of antimony, gum arabic and water. This head had to be nipped in a fold of

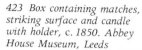

421 *Metal match box, c. 1850. Relief design of portrait heads of Queen Victoria and Prince Albert with the Royal Arms between. Paisley Museum*

422 *Metal match container and lighter, c. 1840. Matches are inserted in one end but pulled out at the other, the friction igniting them. Cheltenham City Museum*

423 *Box containing matches, striking surface and candle with holder, c. 1850. Abbey House Museum, Leeds*

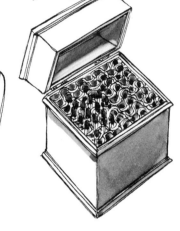

424 *Pellet secured in holder to be struck on surface of box, c. 1900. Abbey House Museum, Leeds*

425 Top left *Bell's lucifers with sandpaper for ignition, 1833.* Top right *Congreves, 1835 (German)*   Bottom left *Lucifers, 1832 (Dutch)* Bottom right *Jones' lucifers, 1831. Science Museum, London*

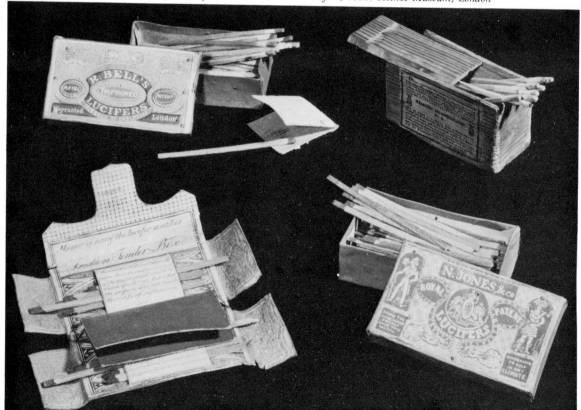

sandpaper, pulled smartly and mostly it ignited, accompanied by a shower of sparks and an offensive odour.

Walker's friction lights opened up a new chapter in ignition, but he had not patented his invention so others moved in on the idea. Samuel Jones (inventor of the Promethean match) copied it and called it a lucifer (1831). Richard Bell of Wandsworth followed (1832) and in 1829 Isaac Holden added sulphur to the paste to improve ignition. Watts, a chemist in the Strand, added camphor to his lucifer match heads (420, 425).

The next advance in these strike-anywhere matches[1] was to substitute yellow phosphorus for the sulphide of antimony, as in Congreves for example. These ignited much more readily, in fact too readily, causing numerous accidents. They also took an appalling toll in the health of match factory workers, who succumbed to 'Phossy Jaw'. This terrible complaint, which killed and maimed many workers, was caused by the phosphorus entering the body via defective teeth. Many children also died from sucking the match heads.[2]

It was Professor Anton von Schrotter's discovery of amorphous, red phosphorus in 1845 which led to the development of the safety match, credited to Johan Lundstrom of Sweden in 1855. In this he divided the chemical constituents between the match head and the striking surface on the match box so markedly reducing the chances of spontaneous combustion. He used amorphous (red) phosphorus with sulphide of antimony on the box and potassium nitrate and biochromate with red lead and sulphide of antimony on the match heads.

Some of the types of matches made in the nineteenth century were designed for special purposes or made in a particular way. The stem of the Vesta match (named after the Roman goddess of the hearth symbolised by an eternal flame) was made of cotton threads coated in wax. The term was given to friction matches of this type in the 1830s and they continued to be made for many years[3]; in some countries, notably Italy and Spain, this type of stem is still in use.[4]

Many especially large-headed matches were designed in the nineteenth century to be used to light cigars and pipes out-of-doors. Samuel Jones introduced fusees in the 1830s. These were composed of a piece of thick card which had been saturated in saltpetre and potassium biochromate. The card was partially cut through into strips which were still attached at the base but could be separated at will. The heads were dipped in a phosphorus compound (426). After this came a number of matches with extra-large heads which had been made by dipping them repeatedly in a compound of saltpetre, charcoal and gum. The igniting compound was then added to the tip of the head. These matches burned so long that it was necessary for their stems to be of a strong, lasting material such as braided cotton or ceramic. They were marketed under various names: Vesuvians, Flaming Fusees, Flamers, Braided cigar lights (427).

Nineteenth-century matches were contained in strong boxes, often of metal, for protection against accidental combustion. Boxes for strike-anywhere matches were provided with an abrasive panel for striking; boxes for safety matches were left open at one side to expose the phosphorus striking surface. Some boxes were fitted with candle-holders (421, 422, 423).

Light-making in the home

One of the oldest forms of domestic lighting prepared at home was the rushlight or rush-candle. It was an inexpensive form of lighting made by repeatedly dipping a dried, peeled rush into fat which had been melted in a greasepan. The fat was usually tallow which had been derived from animal fat; the best was from bacon or mutton. A greasepan was a cast-iron oval vessel with a long handle standing by the hearth on short stubby legs (431, 432). Rushlights were used in Britain from Roman times onwards. They did not burn for as long as a candle but were very economical. It was an advantage that the rush was totally consumed in the flame and needed no snuffing or trimming.

A detailed, explicit account of the country craft of gathering and preparing rushlights is given by Gilbert White in his letter of 1775[5]. He says:

The proper species of rush for this purpose seems to be the *juncus conglomeratus* or common soft rush, which is to be found in most moist pastures, by the sides of streams, and under hedges. These rushes are in best condition at the height of summer; but may be gathered, so as to serve the purpose well, quite on to autumn. It would be needless to add that the largest and longest are best. Decayed labourers, women and children, make it their business to procure and prepare them. As soon as they are cut

426 Bell's fusees with flat iron pocket container, c. 1850.
Science Museum, London

427 Bryant and May's Royal Hunt matches. Cheltenham
City Museum

428, 429 and 430 *Iron rushlight holders, two with wood block bases*

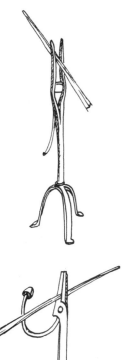

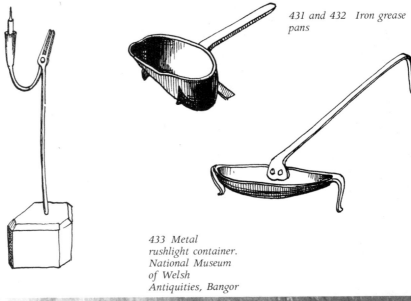

431 and 432 *Iron grease pans*

433 *Metal rushlight container. National Museum of Welsh Antiquities, Bangor*

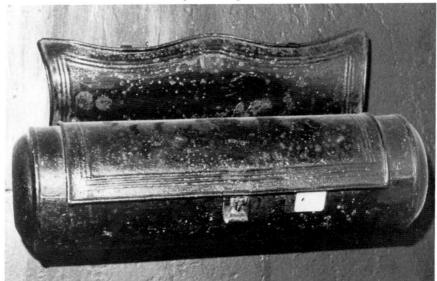

they must be flung into water, and kept there; for otherwise they will dry and shrink, and the peel will not run. At first a person would find it no easy matter to divest a rush of its peel or rind, so as to leave one regular, narrow, even rib from top to bottom that may support the pith: but this, like other feats, soon becomes familiar even to children; and we have seen an old woman, stone-blind, performing this business with great despatch, and seldom failing to strip them with the nicest regularity. When these *junci* are thus far prepared, they must lie out on the grass to be bleached, and take the dew for some nights, and afterwards be dried in the sun.

Some address is required in dipping these rushes in the scalding fat or grease; but this knack also is to be attained by practice. The careful wife of an industrious Hampshire labourer obtains all her fat for nothing; for she saves the scummings of her bacon pot for this use;[6] and, if the grease abounds with salt to precipitate to the bottom, by setting the scummings in a warm oven. Where hogs are not much in use, and especially by the sea-side, the coarser animal oils will come very cheap. A pound of common grease will dip a pound of rushes; and one pound of rushes may be bought for one shilling (5p): so that a pound of rushes, medicated and ready for use, will cost three shillings (15p). If men that keep bees will mix a little wax with the grease, it will give a consistency, and render it more cleanly, and make the rushes burn longer: mutton suet would have the same effect.

A good rush, which measured in length two feet four inches and a half, being minuted, burnt only three minutes short of an hour: and a rush still of greater length has been known to burn one hour and a quarter. These rushes give a good clear light.

In a pound of dry rushes, avoirdupois, which I caused to be weighed and numbered, we found upwards of one thousand six hundred individuals.

Now suppose each of these burns, one with another, only half an hour, then a poor man will purchase eight hundred hours of light, a time exceeding thirty-three entire days, for thee shillings. According to this account each rush, before dipping, costs 1/33 of a farthing, and 1/11 afterwards. Thus a poor family will enjoy $5\frac{1}{2}$ hours of comfortable light for a farthing (approximately 1/10 of 1p.). An experienced old housekeeper assures me that one pound and a half of rushes completely supplies his family the year round, since working people burn no candle in the long days, because they rise and go to bed by daylight.

Burning rushlights had to be gripped firmly by metal clips called rush-nips or rush- (rushlight)

434 Tallow candle moulds and rushlight holder. Castle Museum, York

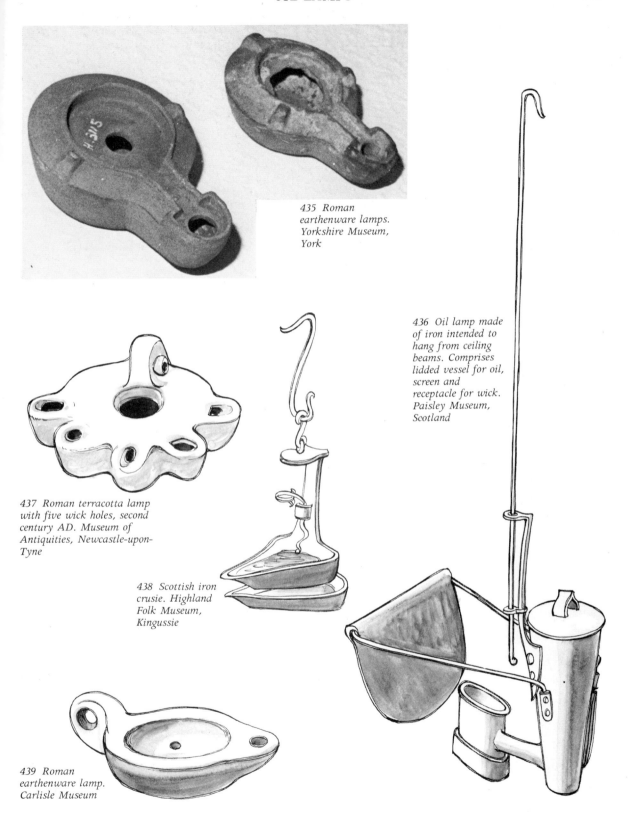

435 *Roman earthenware lamps. Yorkshire Museum, York*

436 *Oil lamp made of iron intended to hang from ceiling beams. Comprises lidded vessel for oil, screen and receptacle for wick. Paisley Museum, Scotland*

437 *Roman terracotta lamp with five wick holes, second century AD. Museum of Antiquities, Newcastle-upon-Tyne*

438 *Scottish iron crusie. Highland Folk Museum, Kingussie*

439 *Roman earthenware lamp. Carlisle Museum*

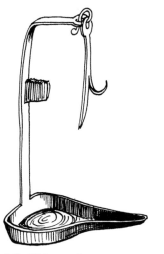

440 Oil lamp of
iron, eighteenth
century

441 Medieval
lantern of copper
alloy with horn
panel

442 Late Medieval
lantern of copper
alloy with glass
door panel

443 Scottish iron
crusie. Weaver's
Cottage,
Kilbarchan,
Scotland

holders. There were many designs of these, but it was essential that the lighted rush be held at its centre by a metal jaw-clip which was part of a stand (428, 429, 430). As the rush burnt down its position could be adjusted in the clip. If more light were needed the rush was lit at both ends.[7]

In moorland and low-lying areas where conifers grew abundantly, as in the mountain and lake districts of Britain, fir-candles were similarly used for lighting, being held in a clip on a stand. These were splinters cut from resinous fir and pine wood, especially from the roots growing in the peat and moss. The splinters were dried thoroughly by the fire, then were lit, but they burnt for only a short while.

Candles have also been in use for at least 2000 years. These could be made at home or purchased. The majority were home-made from tallow melted down from the kitchen cooking fats. The candles were made in metal moulds which could be single but were more often multiple (434). The wicks were inserted first, then the mould was dipped into a pan of hot melted fat until the tubes were filled. After cooling the hardened candles were hung up in bunches by their wicks to store. Those intended for immediate use were kept in candle-boxes hung on the wall (433).

Tallow candles needed constant trimming while burning as the wicks burned more slowly than the fat. They dripped, smoked and gave off noxious odours.

Beeswax was used for the best candles, but these were expensive and in short supply: they were also more heavily taxed. Wax candles burned brighter and needed less attention, also they did not smell so unpleasant. During the nineteenth century paraffin wax superseded other materials and was a great improvement, giving a clear flame accompanied by little smoke (441, 442).

The simple oil lamp was also in use from very early times. At first these were earthenware saucers or simply shells which contained oil or grease and a fibrous floating wick. The Roman lamp was designed to burn olive oil; it was usually circular or oval in shape. The common earthenware ones were produced in large numbers, moulded in two halves then joined together. The lamp was shallow; it had a handle at one side and a spout at the other from which protruded a wick made from twisted flax. The flat top of the lamp was enclosed (to keep the oil clean) except for a hole in the centre through which the oil could be poured in (435, 439). This flat top was decoratively patterned in better quality lamps. More costly ones could be made in bronze. Such single-wick lamps would burn for about 45 hours for a pint of oil. They gave a fair light but might be odorous and the wick needed frequent trimming. In larger homes some lamps were designed with several apertures through which a number of wicks burned simultaneously (437).

Lamps continued to be used in Britain for centuries after the departure of the Romans (436, 440). The Medieval cresset lamp was one type which was usually made of iron and was most commonly hung from the roof or was mounted on a post or pole.

The Scottish crusie (cruisie) was a traditional lamp in use for centuries. It was made of iron and intended to burn fish oil (in coastal and island districts) and tallow elsewhere. The crusie was a metal version of the Roman lamp, but it was fitted with a tray beneath to catch the drips of oil. It was characteristically shaped with a markedly pointed spout at the front to take the wick which was made from a peeled rush or twisted textile strands. Most crusies were made to hang, above the fireplace or from a beam, or on the wall (438, 443).

All these lamps had been made locally and were fuelled with fat or oil which was home-produced. With the developments in design of oil lamp in the eighteenth and nineteenth centuries inspired by such inventors as Argand and Carcel, and the availability of colza and whale oil and later paraffin, oil lamps no longer represented home-produced lighting. Before long they were followed by illumination from gas and electricity (see pages 93, 100).

The working conditions and function of a housewife are still changing and the appliances of one generation quickly become 'museum pieces' to the next. An important reason for the interest aroused by local museums displaying domestic equipment is that older people enjoy reminiscing with nostalgia and a feeling of relief that they no longer have to use the appliances common in their youth, while children are intrigued by what that strange-looking article might have been used for. The speed of change is vividly illustrated by a question put to Barbara Fairweather, Secretary of the Glencoe and North Lorn Museum: a child had asked her 'What is ink?'

Notes

Chapter One: The Kitchen p. 11

1 A list, arranged in counties, is given of a selection of these (see page 181).

2 *Beeton's Book of Household Management*, published S.O. Beeton, 1861. This remarkable work presents a comprehensive and illuminating picture of housewifery in mid-Victorian Britain. It was written by Isabella Beeton and appeared first as a series of articles in threepenny, monthly supplements to her husband's publication of 1859–61, the *Englishwoman's Domestic Magazine*. It became so popular that Sam Beeton satisfied demand by publishing a bound edition of the whole work on 1 October 1861 at a price of 7s 6d. The work has remained in successively revised editions the housewife's mentor ever since.

It is remarkable not only for its size and comprehensiveness, covering as it does all aspects of domestic management from a description of the ideal kitchen and the duties of mistress, housekeeper, cook and servants to first aid and medicine, child-bearing and the management of children, the natural history of all animals, birds and vegetables from which food is obtained and providing a wealth of information about utensils, their care, fuel, cooking and recipes, but also because its author was so young. Isabella Beeton began her ambitious work at the age of 21 after the death of her first child. It took her four years to write. Not surprisingly she begins her preface with the words 'I must frankly own, that if I had known, beforehand, that this book would have cost me the labour which it has, I should never have been courageous enough to commence it'. In 1865, at the age of 29, she died from a fever after the birth of her fourth child.

3 Anticipation, perhaps, of the organisation and method approach to kitchen planning in the twentieth century (page 30).

4 Croft is an Old English word for an enclosed field and came to refer, as for example in the Highlands of Scotland, to a small agricultural holding worked by a peasant tenant.

5 Before the advent of refrigerators a kitchen and larder were generally designed to face north or east in order to keep the food as cool as possible.

The idea, current in the 1920s and 1930s, that the working day would be at the time when the sun is in the east or south pre-dates the post-war working wife who does much of her kitchen work in the evenings.

Chapter Two: The Preparation of Food p. 35

1 The name derives from the Old French word *ewe* meaning water. In Anglo-French it was *eweire*.

2 A Scottish term derived from the Gaelic *cuach*. The quaich is a shallow bowl-shaped drinking vessel, often standing on a rim, and having ears at the sides. The quaich was mostly made of turned or staved wood but could be of pewter or silver (27).

3 In feathering the sides of the staves are cut finely to fit into one another and so make a watertight joining.

4 Unfermented grape juice.

5 In cold weather it was customary to heat or mull wine and spirits in the fire (page 53 and figs 134, 135). The word toddy refers to a drink made from whisky or often spirituous liquor mixed with hot water and sugar.

6 A type of gelatin derived from some freshwater fish, notably sturgeon. A corruption of the Dutch word *huisenblas* meaning 'sturgeon's bladder'.

7 Believed to be a corruption of *catty*, derived from the Malay *kati* = weight of $1\frac{1}{3}$ lb.

8 These are articles more in use in the dining or drawing room and so beyond the scope of this book. Many examples survive and can be seen in museums or studied in books on ceramics and metalware.

9 Hence the phrase 'a pretty kettle of fish'.

10 The American born Benjamin Thompson, renowned for his work in the eighteenth century on heat conservation in kitchen range design (see chapter 4, page 84).

11 A hard, nearly waterproof wood was preferred, such as alder or sycamore.

12 A staved tub with one handle standing up at the side. They were called cog since one meaning of the word is 'a projection or tenon on a beam or wall.'

13 From the Scots word lug = ear.

14 A preparation made from dried, salted maws, that is, the stomach membrane of a suckling calf mixed with lemon juice. Before the nineteenth century, when rennet could be purchased from the grocer, the preparation was made at home.

Chapter Three: The Cooking of Food 1/The Open Hearth: Roman Times to *c.* 1800 p. 54

1 Andirons were also known as fire-dogs because the horizontal bar and foot resembled the hind leg of a dog.

2 The word derives from the French *couvre-feu*. In the Middle Ages, according to law, a bell had to be rung at a fixed hour each evening to tell everyone that it was time to cover their fires. The word curfew has survived to indicate a time at which certain municipal or military regulations come into force.

3 From the eighteenth century only dead wood was permitted to be burnt as fuel by the country labourer, who was allowed to collect it from the hedgerows with the aid of his weeding hook or shepherd's crook. It has been suggested that this gave rise to the phrase 'by hook or by crook', but evidence is lacking to support the contention.

4 So many people found coal fires difficult to light that in many towns the men who delivered the fuel offered a fire-lighting service also.

5 Kilp was a term used to describe the detachable handle of such cauldrons.

6 Famous Roman epicure, *temp.* Tiberius.

7 *Beeton's Book of Household Management*, 1859–61.

8 Referred to by Apicius. The vessel is believed to have acquired its name because of the gentleness of this method of warming the food. It could also be used for slow cooking.

9 These were generally made of iron and had a heart-shaped blade.

10 A wooden board scored with criss-cross lines which were retained on the oatcakes after baking.

11 Apparently the reason for using a ridged rolling pin was that this enabled a current of air to pass beneath the oatcakes and so make them lighter.

12 The word jack is applied to mechanisms or contrivances which take the place of a boy or man and so save human labour.

13 See chapter 4 page 84.

14 Enclosure sides of fire-box area.

15 So-called from its resemblance to the shape of a bottle.

16 Sometimes mis-named as a Dutch oven (see page 83).

17 Roman bricks were hard and large but only about one inch thick; they resembled tiles.

18 These ovens were known as scuffle ovens because the ashes were raked or scuffled out on to the floor.

Chapter Four: The Cooking of Food 2/The Range, Stove and Cooker: 1780s to the Present Day p. 84

1 In 1791, in gratitude for his services, the Elector made him a Count of the Holy Roman Empire. Thompson chose his title of Rumford from the name of the American town where his wife's family resided. Earlier, in England, George III bestowed a knighthood upon him.

2 He disagreed with the currently-held view that heat was a material substance and believed it to be a form of motion. He presented his paper entitled 'Enquiry concerning the Source of Heat which is excited by Friction' to the Royal Society, London, in 1798. He is the Rumford whose pioneer contributions to the conversion of energy from the mechanical form into the form of heat are studied by the pupil at school doing elementary science.

3 Unfortunately it has not proved possible to trace the present whereabouts of this equipment.

4 *Beeton's Book of Household Management.*

5 *The Kitchen in History*, by Molly Harrison, Osprey 1972.

6 Dr Dalen used *kieselguhr* as insulating material.

This is a diatomaceous earth which has been used for more than a century as an absorbent for nitroglycerine in making dynamite. The earth is suitable because it is particularly porous. It is permeated with holes made by diatoms, which are microscopic unicellular algae found especially at the bottom of the sea.

7 This was, of course, the old penny (1d.), in value at decimalisation in 1971 of slightly less than one half-penny ($\frac{1}{2}$p).

8 It is ironic that this improvement should have taken so long. It was as far back as 1884 that John Wright and Company purchased the patent rights of what they termed 'a beautiful grey enamel' which only needed to be washed with water. It seems that it was not until the middle-class housewife had to work in her own kitchen did she demand and obtain such a labour-saving finish to her basic equipment.

9 Richmond Gas Stove Co. Ltd., Fletcher Russell and Co. Ltd., Wilsons and Mathiesons Ltd., John Wright and Co., Arden Hill and Co. and Davis Gas Stove Co.

10 In America Thomas Alva Edison (1847–1931) independently produced a carbon filament lamp in the years 1878–80.

11 In modern aluminium cookware at about 550°C.

12 Commonly termed 18:8.

Chapter Five: The Storage and Preservation of Food p. 111

1 Cupboards from which 'liveries' or rations of food were served out to servants and retainers.

2 A term used from the Middle Ages onwards for a cupboard, press, pantry or storehouse for containing necessary articles, especially victuals.

3 Jack leather was coated with tar or pitch to make it hard and waterproof. It was widely used in the seventeenth century for boots as well as jugs.

4 Canister was soon abbreviated to can and canneries were set up to make tin cans. The modern can is made of 98.5% sheet steel thinly coated with tin.

5 Some of these tins were later brought back to England and eventually opened in 1911. The food was discovered to be edible still.

6 Work in 1895 at the University of Wisconsin demonstrated how much higher temperatures were required to destroy fully all bacteria and,

two years later at the Massachusetts Institute of Technology, certain of the bacteria were identified and, by experiment, it was shown which foods needed a longer and higher heating process.

7 The name derived from Domestic Electric Refrigerator.

8 A.B. Lux was founded in Sweden in 1901. The word 'Electro' was added as a prefix in 1919.

9 In the 1890s housewives could purchase a tinned prepared mixture called 'Inexhaustible Freezing Crystals'.

Chapter Six: Cleaning in the Home p. 124

1 From *The Natural History of Selbourne* a letter written by Gilbert White on 1 November 1775 to the Hon. Daines Barrington.

2 *Beeton's Book of Household Management* published by S.O. Beeton, 1861.

3 Graphite (a crystalline form of carbon). The name dates back to days before the real composition of the substance was known. It was mixed into a paste with turpentine and was applied to the grate with a cloth or brush, then polished up with another brush and, finally, with a soft cloth.

4 During the nineteenth century this was necessary because of the heavy deposits of soot on all surfaces, partly from the outer atmosphere polluted by extensive coal-burning and partly from the use of coal fires for heating and oil and gas for lighting.

5 From the Latin *tergere* (*detergere*)= to wipe or cleanse. Detergent is a general term for a whole group of cleansing substances which includes soap but, in the modern sense, refers more specifically to synthetic or soapless detergents.

6 One of these was at the Royal Mint. After a successful demonstration the van was stopped by police when it was returning to the company and escorted back to the Mint: the dustbag of the cleaner had inadvertently sucked up a quantity of gold dust.

7 Hand-operated suction cleaners continued to be sold for quite some time after the appearance of the Hoover because they were so much cheaper. The first Hoover machine in 1908 marketed at 75 dollars.

8 Models can be purchased but are widely hired for specific cleaning purposes.

Chapter Seven: Laundering of Personal and Household Linen p. 141

1 So-called because it was originally made from copper.

2 The word laundering is a contraction of the original lavendering.

3 *Beeton's Book of Household Management*, published by S.O. Beeton, 1861.

4 Blue was most commonly made from the indigo plant; fig-blue is Mrs Beeton's expression.

5 In the Middle Ages a tenter was a wooden frame on which cloth was stretched after being milled so that it might dry evenly. Tenter-hooks were set in a row along the upper and lower bars of the tenter frame to hold the cloth. In a nineteenth-century laundry room tenterhooks were fixed to a similar frame to hold the woollen articles in shape while they dried.

6 There was no steam power here. This refers only to the steam which rose from the hot water in the tank.

7 Centrifugal force comes into play, in effect, when a body revolving around a centre tends to fly away outwards from that centre. The simple example is that of a stone attached to the end of a string being whirled around by hand; when the other end of the string, in the hand, is released, the stone flies away.

8 The later box mangle certainly resembled such a military weapon (page 154).

9 Some designs had metal-lined boxes which could be filled with water instead.

10 This painting is a copy of an earlier silk one painted by Chang Haiian in the eighth century but which, unfortunately, has not survived.

11 Mrs Potts is also renowned for her original design of sad iron which was pointed at back and front (393).

12 This is perpetuated in the well-known verse of the popular pub song of the time:

> *Up and down the City Road*
> *In and out the Eagle*
> *That's the way the money goes*
> *Pop goes the weasel.*

The Eagle public house was situated on the corner of the City Road.

13 The term goffering iron is, to a certain extent, a mis-nomer in that its function was to smooth and set rather than to flute or goffer.

Chapter Eight: The Making of Fire and Light p. 164

1 The friction match was popularly so-called because all the ingredients for ignition were contained in the head and any abrasive surface would serve for striking. This was in distinction from the safety match (page 169).

2 Eventually, from 1898, the non-toxic sesquisulphide of phosphorus replaced other forms of the chemical in match production.

3 Bryant and May's Swan Vesta match is not a true Vesta because the match stems are of wood.

4 This type of match is known in Italy as a *cerino* from *cera* = wax.

5 A letter written on 1 November 1775 to the Hon. Daines Barrington. *The Natural History of Selbourne*, republished 1965 by The Folio Society.

6 This was common practice.

7 Giving rise to the expression, 'to burn the candle at both ends'.

Appendix

Museums which possess on display especially interesting collections relevant to this book

AVON
Bristol – The Georgian House Museum
          – Blaise Castle House Museum

BERKSHIRE
Reading – The Museum of English Rural Life

BUCKINGHAMSHIRE
Aylesbury – Buckinghamshire County Museum

CAMBRIDGESHIRE
Cambridge – Cambridge and County Folk Museum

CHESHIRE
Chester – Grosvenor Museum

CORNWALL
Helston – Helston Folk Museum

CUMBRIA
Carlisle – Carlisle Museum and Art Gallery
Kendal – Museum of Lakeland Life and Industry
Millom – Millom Folk Museum Society

DEVONSHIRE
Dawlish – Dawlish Museum Society
Exeter – St Nicholas Priory
        – Rougemont House Museum
Plymouth – City Museum and Art Gallery
           – The Elizabethan House
Tiverton – Tiverton Museum
Torquay – Torquay Museum
Totnes – Totnes Museum Society

DORSET
Shaftesbury – Shaftesbury and District Historical
               Society Museum

DURHAM (Co.)
Beamish, Stanley – North of England Open Air
          Museum, Beamish Hall
Barnard Castle – The Bowes Museum

ESSEX
Colchester – Colchester and Essex Museum

GLOUCESTERSHIRE
Cheltenham – Central Museum and Art Gallery
             – Gustav Holst Birthplace Museum
Cirencester – Corinium Museum
Gloucester – Bishop Hooper's Lodging

HEREFORDSHIRE
Hereford – Churchill Gardens Museum
          – City Museum
          – The Old House

HERTFORDSHIRE
St Albans – City Museum
            – Verulamium Museum

KENT
Hollingbourne – Eyhorne Manor

LANCASHIRE
Salford – Art Gallery and Museum
          – Ordsall Hall Museum
          – Lark Hill Place

LINCOLNSHIRE
Alford – Manor House Folk Museum

Grantham – Grantham Museum
Lincoln – Museum of Lincolnshire Life

LONDON
The British Museum
The Geffrye Museum
The Museum of London
The Science Museum
The Victoria and Albert Museum

NORFOLK
Dereham – Norfolk Rural Life Museum
Great Yarmouth – Elizabethan House Museum
King's Lynn – The Lynn Museum
          – The Museum of Social History
Norwich – Stranger's Hall Museum of Domestic Life
Thetford – Ancient House Museum

NORTHAMPTONSHIRE
Northampton – Abington Museum

OXFORDSHIRE
Banbury – Banbury Museum
Cogges – Manor Farm Museum
Oxford – Museum of Oxford
Woodstock – Oxfordshire County Museum

SHROPSHIRE
Aston Munslow – The White House Museum of
   Buildings and Country Life
Ironbridge, Telford – Ironbridge Gorge Museum
   Trust

STAFFORDSHIRE
Shugborough – Staffordshire County Museum

SUFFOLK
Stowmarket – Museum of East Anglian Life

SUSSEX
Lewes – Barbican House
      – Anne of Cleves House

TYNE AND WEAR
Newcastle-upon-Tyne – Museum of Antiquities
   Department of Archaeology, The University

WILTSHIRE
Malmesbury – The Athelstan Museum

Salisbury – Salisbury Museum

WORCESTERSHIRE
Worcester – Tudor House Museum

YORKSHIRE
Halifax – Shibden Hall Folk Museum
Hutton-le-Hole – Ryedale Folk Museum
Leeds – City Museum
      – Abbey House Museum, Kirkstall
Wakefield – Wakefield Museum
York – The Castle Museum
     – Yorkshire Museum

SCOTLAND
Brechin – Glenesk Trust Museum
Dunfermline – Dunfermline Museum
Glencoe – Glencoe and North Lorn Folk Museum
Fort William – The West Highland Museum
Kingussie – Highland Folk Museum

WALES
Abergavenny – Abergavenny Museum
Bangor – Museum of Welsh Antiquities, University
   College of North Wales
Cardiff – Welsh Folk Museum, St Fagans
Chepstow – Chepstow Museum
Monmouth – Monmouth Museum

*Some of the houses, castles and abbeys which contain
kitchen or laundry premises and equipment*

Buckland Abbey, Devonshire
Charlecote Park, Warwickshire
Compton Castle, Devonshire
Cotehele House, Cornwall
Durham Castle
Erdigg House, Clywd
Glastonbury Abbey, Somerset
Hampton Court Palace, Greater London
Hardwick Hall, Derbyshire
Lanhydrock House, Cornwall
Raby Castle, Durham
Royal Pavilion, Brighton, Sussex
Saltram House, Devonshire
Shibden Hall, Halifax, Yorkshire
Snowshill Manor, Gloucestershire
Upark, Sussex
Weaver's Cottage, Kilbarchan, Scotland

Bibliography

Books recommended for further reading

ADAMSON, G., *Machines at Home*, Lutterworth Press, 1969

BAYNE-POWELL, R., *Housekeeping in the 18th Century*, John Murray, 1956

BEETON, S.O., *Beeton's Book of Household Management*, facsimile edition Jonathan Cape, 1977

BIRLEY, A., *Life in Roman Britain*, Batsford, 1976

BROOKE, S., *Hearth and Home*, Mills and Boon, 1973

BURKE, J., *Life in the Villa in Roman Britain*, Batsford, 1978

BURTON, E., *The Georgians at Home*, Longman, 1967; *The Jacobeans at Home*, Secker and Warburg, 1962

CALDER, J., *The Victorian Home*, Batsford, 1977

CARCOPINO, J., *Daily Life in Ancient Rome*, Routledge and Kegan Paul, 1973

CARTER, E.F., (Ed.), *Dictionary of Inventions and Discoveries*, Muller, 1974

CLAIR, C., *Kitchen and Table*, Abelard-Schuman, 1964

COLLINGWOOD, R.G., and RICHMOND, I., *The Archaeology of Roman Britain*, Methuen, 1969

CONRAN, T., and C., *Kitchens Past and Present*, Hygena Ltd., 1976

COWELL, F.R., *Everyday Life in Ancient Rome*, Batsford, 1973

ENCYCLOPAEDIA AMERICANA

ENCYCLOPAEDIA BRITANNICA

FEARN, J., *Domestic Bygones*, Shire Publications, 1977

GLISSMAN, A.H., *The Evolution of the Sad Iron*, Carlsbad, California, 1970

GRANT, I.F., *Highland Folk Ways*, Routledge and Kegan Paul, 1977

HAAN, D. de, *Antique Household Gadgets and Appliances c. 1860–1930*, Blandford Press, 1977

HARRISON, M., *The Kitchen in History*, Osprey Publishing, 1972

HODGE, P., *The Roman House*, Longman, 1975

HOLE, C., *English Home Life 1500–1800*, Batsford, 1949; *The English Housewife in the 17th Century*, Chatto and Windus, 1953

HOWARD, A.V., *Dictionary of Scientists*, Chambers, 1951

JEWELL, B., *Smoothing Irons*, Midas Books, 1977

JOICE, D., and J., *Talking about Bygones*, The Boydell Press, 1976

LABARGE, M.W., *A Baronial Household of the 13th Century*, Eyre and Spottiswoode, 1965

LINDSAY, J.S., *Iron and Brass Implements of the English Home*, Tiranti, 1964

LIVERSIDGE, J., *Britain in the Roman Empire*, Routledge and Kegan Paul, 1968

MARSHALL, J., *Kitchenware*, Pitman, 1976

McROBERT, R., *Ironing Today and Yesterday*, Forbes Publications, 1970

MEGSON, B., *English Homes and Housekeeping 1700–1960*, Routledge and Kegan Paul, 1973

NORWAK, M., *Kitchen Antiques*, Ward Lock, 1975

QUENNELL, M., and C.H.B., *A History of Everyday Things in England* (4 vols.) *1066–1914*, Batsford, 1961; (5th vol.) *1914–68* by Ellacott, S.E., Batsford, 1968

RUMFORD, *The Complete Works of Count Rumford* (4 vols.), American Academy of Arts and Sciences, Boston, 1870

SCOTT, A. and C., *Collecting Bygones*, Max Parrish, 1964

SINGER, C., HOLMYARD, E.J., HALL, A.R., and WILLIAMS, T.I., (Editors) *A History of Technology*, Oxford Clarendon Press, 1958 (5 vols.)

SWAN, V.G. *Pottery in Roman Britain*, Shire Archaeology, 1975

WRIGHT, L., *Home Fires Burning*, Routledge and Kegan Paul, 1964

YARWOOD, D., *The English Home*, Batsford, 1979

Museum publications

Bangor, National Museum of Welsh Antiquities
Beamish, North of England Open Air Museum
Bristol, The Georgian House Museum
Carlisle Museum
Cirencester, Corinium Museum
Colchester and Essex Museum
Fort William, The West Highland Museum
Glencoe and North Lorn Museum
Kendal, Museum of Lakeland Life and Industry
Kilbarchan, Weaver's Cottage
Leeds, Abbey House Museum, Kirkstall
London, British Museum
  Greek and Roman Pottery Lamps
  Science Museum
  Making Fire
  R.E.B. Crompton, Pioneer Electrical Engineer
Norwich, Stranger's Hall Museum
St Albans, The Roman City of Verulamium
Tiverton Museum
Worcester, Tudor House Museum
York, The Castle Museum

Index

Illustration references are printed in **bold** type